JOSEPH SCHUMPETER

JOSEPH SCHUMPETER

Scholar, Teacher and Politician

EDUARD MÄRZ

YALE UNIVERSITY PRESS
NEW HAVEN AND LONDON · 1991

First published as *Joseph Alois Schumpeter –*
Forscher, Lehrer und Politiker
copyright © 1983 Verlag für Geschichte und Politik Wien

Set in Baskerville by SX Composing Ltd, Essex, England
Printed and bound in Great Britain by St. Edmundsbury Press

Library of Congress Cataloging-in-Publication Data

März. Eduard.
    (Joseph Alois Schumpeter. English)
    Joseph Schumpeter: scholar, teacher, and politician / Eduard
März.
        p.   cm.
    Translation of: Joseph Alois Schumpeter.
    Includes bibliographical references (p. 194) and index.
    ISBN 0-300-03876-3
    1. Schumpeter, Joseph Alois, 1883-50.   2. Economists–United
States–Biography.   3. Economists–Austria–Biography.   I. Title.
HB119.S35M3713   1992
330′.092–dc20
    [B]   91-25049
                                                              CIP
    TP

Contents

v

Publisher's Note

An earlier version of this volume was published in German in 1983, under the title *Joseph Alois Schumpeter – Forscher, Lehrer und Politiker* (Verlag für Geschichte und Politik Wien). Before his death in July 1987, the author had completed a first draft of a substantially revised version, including two additional essays, intended for publication in English. For the current edition stylistic improvements have been made to Dr Eduard März's English text, and an appendix of personal letters from Schumpeter, included in the German edition, has been omitted. In all significant respects however the edition remains faithful to the author's own text. The provenance of the essays is indicated in footnotes to individual chapters.

Foreword
by James Tobin[*]
(Sterling Professor Emeritus of Economics, Yale University)

Like the author of this book, I had the good fortune to know Joseph Schumpeter at Harvard. I knew him when I was an advanced undergraduate 1937-9, a graduate student 1946-7, and a post-doctoral Junior Fellow 1947-8. I took all the courses he offered, and he was my dissertation adviser. Like most of my American contemporaries, I knew little of Schumpeter's pre-Harvard history in Austria and Germany, beyond his alleged and admired youthful boast that he would be the 'greatest horseman in Vienna, the greatest lover in Austria, and the greatest economist in the world'.

All but two of the ten essays gathered here first appeared in book form in German in 1983. I have read the essays only in Eduard März's English translation, which he had completed with preliminary revisions, though not alas with final polishing, before his death in 1987. The essays illuminate for us who knew Schumpeter in America the intellectual and personal background of this fascinating immigrant. And not just for us, of course. World events and intellectual developments over the past two decades have heightened interest in Schumpeter, not only among economists but also among other social scientists and political philosophers. Indeed people of all ages and from all walks of life have discovered Schumpeter and think that his ideas can help them understand the world they live in.

* I am grateful to Professor Wolfgang F. Stolper of the University of Michigan for commenting on a draft of this Foreword and saving me from some errors of fact and of interpretation. Professor Stolper, like Schumpeter an immigrant from Austria, was a Harvard graduate student in the 1930s. He is a leading authority on Schumpeter. I alone am responsible for any remaining errors.

We Harvard students of the late 1930s told each other that the two greatest living economists in the world were Schumpeter and Keynes. The one was in our midst, aweing us by his Austrian accent, his command of our native tongue, his amazing erudition, his mischievous wit, and his evident self-confidence. The other had just published a heretical book causing ferment and excitement throughout our profession. They were the same age. We imagined, rightly or wrongly, that Schumpeter too regarded Keynes as his main rival and resented the lift the *General Theory* gave Keynes.

In the American economics profession, it has been Schumpeter's fate to have multitudes of admirers but few disciples. Schumpeter himself invited that fate in several ways.

At Harvard, Schumpeter as teacher promoted neo-classical orthodoxy rather than his own heresies. He developed close personal ties with many of the best students and young faculty, especially those adept in formal theory and mathematical methods. I think of Paul Samuelson, Lloyd Metzler and Richard Goodwin. I remember an advanced theory course of Schumpeter's in which these three, plus R.G.D. Allen, visiting from England fresh from his work with J.R. Hicks in formal consumer theory, dominated the presentations. A boom in mathematical economics was beginning, and Schumpeter was anxious to be one of the boys. He and Professor W.L. Crum published a primer of mathematics for economists.

Yet Schumpeter as economic historian and social theorist regarded neo-classical theory as mostly irrelevant to the understanding of capitalism. For example, his famous 'circular flow' can, I think, be regarded as a *reductio ad absurdum* of the logic of the neo-classical stationary state. Schumpeter's point was that no phenomena worth studying – not profits, not interest, not growth – can arise in that sterile, stagnant and repetitive environment. How could anyone take seriously an economy with infinitely long-lived ageless consumers and with constant tastes and technologies? How could Böhm-Bawerk have thought he was *refuting* Schumpeter by citing, as in the passages März quotes in Chapter 8, the many ways in which real world economic variables take on values other than those implied by the 'circular flow'?

Schumpeter's young Harvard friends admired his theory of development as a *tour de force* of historical interpretation, but none of them were doing Schumpeterian economic research and writing. Most of them were Keynesians and neo-classicals at the same time. As my dissertation adviser, Schumpeter was friendly and helpful, although clearly my Keynesian subject, the consumption function, did not excite him. Some others, like Goodwin, Sidney Alexander and Paul Sweezy, used Keynesian and neo-classical tools and were also Marxists. Sweezy's strong Marxist convictions and Marxist scholarship helped to make him and Schumpeter great friends, though their public intellectual combat was a memorable event.

I did not personally find Schumpeter and Keynes seriously contradictory. Keynes stressed the essential unpredictability of business investment, and Schumpeter gave important reasons why this should be so. While Schumpeter regarded bank credit and forced saving as the necessary sources of finance for investment booms, this was because he assumed his circular flow, with full employment, to be the starting point. Once the process was under way, a Schumpeterian investment boom starting from conditions of unemployment and excess capacity could generate its own saving via Keynesian multiplier mechanisms. Both Schumpeter and Keynes expected nominal prices to move procyclically. The unconvincing part of Schumpeter's model, it seemed to me, was his assertion that production and consumption increased in recessions, which he described as inevitable adjustments and benignly therapeutic. Keynes's proposition that the downswings of business cycles were mostly deadweight loss made much more sense, especially in the 1930s. Perhaps the difference was one of degree, because Schumpeter did recognize extreme downswings, depressions and severe monetary deflations, as inessential and unconstructive.[*]

As März points out, Schumpeter himself almost never taught, discussed or assigned his own substantive work. Most students read his writings, at least those available in English, but in my experience he did not gratify our hopes of hearing the master himself expound his ideas. He wrote *Business Cycles* pretty much on his own. He didn't recruit students to help him; he didn't suggest topics arising in his own research to students for papers or dissertations; he didn't try out the ideas or findings of his draft chapters in seminars. That so enormous an achievement was the product of lonely research tells what a great scholar Schumpeter was.[†]

Schumpeter did share with students his great work on the history of economic thought, published posthumously. His course rarely got much further than Adam Smith, but as he reviewed Smith's many predecessors he was led to comment on the nineteenth- and twentieth-

---

[*] I am indebted to Professor Stolper for pointing this out to me.
[†] Professor Stolper recalls one seminar Schumpeter gave on *Business Cycles* shortly after its publication, where young Harvard economists attacked him unmercifully, to his considerable annoyance.

century economists they anticipated. From those comments we could infer many of Schumpeter's views on the modern economists of interest to us, from Ricardo to Walras to Marshall to Keynes. But he gave us no hints as to where Joseph Schumpeter fitted in to the history.

Why did Schumpeter feel so much more comfortable teaching and discussing the ideas of other economists? It is hard to believe it was modesty, for we knew from evidence in this book and elsewhere that Schumpeter was really quite egotistical. Was he afraid some of his ideas and empirical findings would be shot down by his bright young friends?

However, even if Schumpeter himself had made more effort to spread his word among students, his theories of development and business cycles were difficult to incorporate into the style and method that came to dominate economics, especially American economics, over the past fifty years. Formal model-building was quickly coming into vogue in the 1930s and 1940s. Schumpeterian theory does not lend itself easily to model-building, either statics or dynamics. Both in theory and in application, economists have been looking for comparative static or comparative dynamic results. These are often conclusions about policy effects – what happens if governments increase income taxes or central banks buy bonds with money in the open markets.

One could believe Schumpeter's general proposition, that innovations are responsible both for capitalism's progress and for its instabilities, and one could learn from Schumpeterian versions of past history. But the innovations themselves seem unpredictable and uncontrollable. Schumpeter doesn't attempt to tell us how to speed them up or slow them down, or how to channel them in one direction or another. He does suggest some diffuse cultural and institutional conditions that are favourable to innovations, and others that are unfavourable. These suggestions might carry diffuse ideological morals of a conservative or 'supply-side' cast, but they say little about how to prevent recessions and inflation or how to speed up the growth of productivity in particular countries.

In contrast, Keynesian economics was tailor-made for the analysis of policy effects. Keynes told us students in the 1930s what to do about the major problem that confronted us, the Great Depression. He gave us the fun of playing with a new set of analytical tools, combined with the confidence that their application to practical policy could save the world. Schumpeter had written a surprisingly orthodox chapter in a 1934 Harvard book taking to task the New Deal recovery program.[*] But in our years he participated very little in the exciting current debates about fiscal and monetary policy, except to sneer from the sidelines at the 'future champions of bureaucratic self-interest', presumably the graduate students whom Professor Alvin Hansen, the leading American apostle of Keynesianism, was sending to jobs in Washington.

While Schumpeter was writing *Business Cycles*, Ragnar Frisch, Jan Tinbergen and others were trying to bring mathematical rigour to cycle theory. According to their new methodology, a theory that cycles are endemic to capitalist economics should display mathematically mechanisms that generate regularly repetitive cycles. Proper cycles were to be distinguished from fluctuations that simply mirror random exogenous shocks and could not be expected to be regular or periodic. At Harvard Samuelson, Metzler and Goodwin were practicing the new methodology.

Schumpeter's theory, credible as it was as historical interpretation, is not cycle theory in Frisch's sense. At least Schumpeter's presentation of it is not such theory. Rather it is an account of fluctuations resulting from irregular exogenous shocks, Schumpeter's innovations. It is not clear what endogenous mechanism transforms those shocks into cyclical alternations of prosperity and recession, even less clear how the Schumpeterian process results in superimposed Kitchins, Juglars and Kondratieffs.

Frisch himself suggested a mechanical analogue of Schumpeter's theory; he said it could be formulated mathematically, but he did not do so. The analogue model assumes a fairly steady flow of water into a reservoir, meant to represent the stream of potential innovations. When the reservoir is high enough, water flows down a pendulum pipe. As the water escapes through a valve on one side of the pendu-

---

[*] Douglass V. Brown *et al.*, *The Economics of the Recovery Program* (New York, 1934). Schumpeter explained that depressions have happened before, that they perform necessary economic functions, that they are structural not monetary, and that recoveries occur on their own and will probably do so again in the absence of unwise political interference. He did concede that the 1930s Depression had been aggravated by non-economic forces, and he acknowledged the existence of 'widespread suffering and needless waste' and saw some role for temporary '[public] expenditure to blot out the worst things without injury to the economic organism'. Schumpeter was also a member of a Columbia University commission which produced a report, *Economic Reconstruction* (New York, 1934). In a personal addendum, Schumpeter foreshadowed some postwar Keynesians: '. . . [T]axation itself may be made a useful instrument of remedial policy if taxes which are in any way proportional to business success are systematically lowered in depression and increased in prosperity, in which case they would operate in a way similar to that of the variations of the rate of interest.' The quotation occurs in Herbert Stein, *The Fiscal Revolution in America* (Chicago, 1969), 88.

lum, it makes the pendulum swing, but the opening of the valve is contrived to contract when it swings in the direction of the valve. When the valve contracts, the reservoir fills up again and is ready to flow down the pendulum once more when it swings back to its vertical position and the valve reopens. Although Frisch reports 'long conversations and correspondence with Professor Schumpeter', it is not clear that Schumpeter found the model helpful. I doubt that he did. Presumably the swings of the pendulum represent business cycles, and the actions of the valve represent the receptivity of the economy to the innovations. The analogy is strained.[*]

What is beyond doubt is that Schumpeter had the highest opinion of all these pioneers and the highest hopes for their new methods. Schumpeter was an optimist about economics and observed with pride and admiration its professional and scientific advances. The last pages of his posthumous *History of Economic Analysis* celebrate 'macrodynamics', Schumpeter's term for formal business cycle modelling, as the wave of the future. His ultimate judgement of Keynes's *analytical* contribution is that Keynes, himself a static theorist, 'unintentionally . . . gave a mighty impulse' to macrodynamics (p.1184).

The reader of *Business Cycles* finds its historical and empirical chapters wise and informative accounts. But he or she may wonder what, aside from the style and scope of the author, is distinctively Schumpeterian about them. They are only loosely related to his general thesis. Moreover, these empirical and statistical narratives eschewed econometric methods – another example of Schumpeter's deviation from methodologies that were starting to become orthodox in the 1930s and 1940s, beginning with Tinbergen's statistical model of the interwar USA economy.[†]

It is for these reasons that Schumpeter has been greatly admired but not imitated or elaborated by the main-line economics profession, especially in his adopted country. However, this situation may be changing. The stochastic models of fluctuations and growth currently engaging able theorists and econometricians look more compatible with Schumpeter's ideas than the models of the past. Perhaps his theory can now be rigorously mathematically formulated and tested, without sacrificing its distinctive content.

Economists may have neglected Schumpeter, but he successfully

[*] R. Frisch, 'Propagation Problems and Impulse Problems in Dynamic Economics', in *Economic Essays in Honour of Gustav Cassel* (London, 1933), 1-35. The Schumpeter model occurs at the end of this famous essay.
[†] Jan Tinbergen, *Business Cycles in the U.S.*, (Geneva: League of Nations, 1932).

played to a larger audience, thanks largely to *Capitalism, Socialism and Democracy*. He has made a bigger splash than Keynes or other mainstream economists with economic historians, general historians, political scientists and political philosophers. In this respect he rivals Marx.

I have always thought that Schumpeter's ambition was to develop a theory of history of the same sweep and scope as Marx's, while at the same time turning Marxism upside-down. I have inferred this from what Schumpeter did and wrote; I cannot know his subjective intentions and aspirations. März seems to confirm the hypothesis that Marx was both Schumpeter's idol and his target. His account of economic development follows, like Marx's, a dialectic. In Schumpeter, as in Marx, capitalism undermines itself and gives way to socialism. In Schumpeter, it is capitalism's economic success that does it in; in Marx it is capitalism's failure. Schumpeter provides theories of the state, of social classes and of imperialism, all with explanations contrary to those of Marx. Like Marx, Schumpeter pretended to scientific objectivity, telling us history and the immutable future, not telling us his own hopes and preferences.

We students used to speculate about Schumpeter's politics. Much of his economic message seemed to be conservative – capitalism will do fine if left alone – but he also seemed to be put off by the culture of capitalism. Although he stressed 'supply-side' incentives – he thought even estate taxes would discourage saving and enterprise – the crude anti-government *laissez-faire* doctrines of Reaganomics would certainly have offended him. He assured his readers that socialism will work and will even have certain virtues. He sounded resigned to the necessity of taking medicine he didn't like. Our favourite hypothesis was that he was nostalgic for feudalism, perhaps for the Austro-Hungarian Monarchy – not that he viewed restoration of such regimes as at all possible. That hypothesis gained some credence from his expressed admiration for the Japan he visited before the war. One of the few passionate opinions I ever heard Schumpeter express was his condemnation of the American bombing of Hiroshima.

Capitalism, Socialism and Democracy in some ways looked better twenty years ago than it does now. Schumpeter's uniquely optimistic forecast of the growth of US GNP to 1964, which had looked unrealistically rosy in 1940, had been over-fulfilled. And in 1970 his scenario for the death of capitalism did not look far-fetched. The children of the bourgeoisie were turning against the democratic-capitalist system that had given them the luxury of choice and the freedom to revolt, the system that had nourished the anti-capitalist intellectuals who taught them. I used to teach an undergraduate course on economic growth theory, which wound up in the spring with a lecture on Schumpeter. In both 1969 and 1970 I was in the midst of Schumpeter's reasons for the inevitable march into socialism when outside our classroom other Yale students were engaged upon a loud march into administrative office buildings. But today the defection of the bourgeois kids looks to have been only transient. Radical students of 1970 became yuppies of the 1980s.

More important, the dramatic collapse of communist governments and centrally planned economies in 1989 and 1990 suggest that Schumpeter overestimated the viability of socialism and understated the survivability of capitalism – or more precisely, of the Western combinations of capitalism and social democracy of the past 45 years. Of course, communism was not Schumpeter's idea of socialism, and despite recent conservative trends in capitalist democracies, it is possible that the march into a humane form of socialism will eventually be resumed.

Schumpeter would not be disappointed, or disheartened, by the evidence that capitalism may have at least one more Kondratieff upswing ahead of it.

New Haven
October 1990

Author's Preface

Joseph Alois Schumpeter, the centenary of whose birth was celebrated in February 1983, is one of the few social scientists to have left behind him an intellectual legacy that continues to attract new generations of students, teachers, scholars and politicians. Not only are there numerous new editions of his best-known books, but also an increasing number of essays, monographs, and collective volumes are being devoted to his work, many of which will be mentioned in the following pages.

It may be asked, therefore, why this volume is being offered to the public, especially as it contains a number of essays published some years ago in specialist journals and elsewhere, as well as in the German volume that forms the basis for the present collection, along with two others hitherto uncollected. Certain considerations were decisive in persuading me to present a 'new' Schumpeter exegesis to my readers.

Schumpeter never tired of pointing out to his students and readers the importance of economic history as a branch of learning which he thought indispensable for academic economists – and not only for them. In his conviction that economics is essentially historical in character he was of course following in the footsteps of Karl Marx and his followers. Therefore I thought it logical and also interesting to present Schumpeter's ideas against a background of contemporary, and especially intellectual, history. All the essays included here were composed with this intention.

Clearly, many digressions into the recent economic history of Austria were inevitable, for that history provided Schumpeter with his most important theoretical categories, among them the exceptional phenomenon of the creative entrepreneur. The reader will find a comprehensive and concise description of the period 1848-1914 in section ii of Chapter 3 of this volume ('On the Genesis of Schumpeter's Theory of Economic Development'). To sum up my views on the much-discussed problem of dividing Austrian economic history into periods, I include, in Chapter 7, comparative and quantitative findings (prepared in collaboration with Hans Kernbauer) on the growth of the German and Austrian economies.

The Schumpeterian system cannot be seen simply as the product of experience, and of thorough study which sharpened his eye for the development of economic processes; it stems above all from a heroic struggle on the part of a great scholar with the competing theories of his time, which in part he rejected, but which he also, to a considerable degree, integrated into his own work. His theory of economic development is an impressive and highly original synthesis of ideas as divergent as those of the school of marginal utility, sociological theories of the élite, and, last but not least, Marxism. For Schumpeter, as did no other bourgeois social scientist of his time, saw and came to terms with the exceptional phenomenon of the theorizing revolutionary and the revolutionary theorist à la Trier. It may not be an exaggeration to say that in trying to take this huge statue down from its pedestal, he had to realize the limits of his own strength.

Thus no special explanation or justification is required for showing, from various angles in the following chapters (especially Chapters 1 and 3), the close relationship between the teachings of Marx and Schumpeter. Schumpeter's ambivalent attitude towards Austro-Marxism and its ideological and practical aspects is the subject of a brief analysis (Chapter 6). Chapter 4 deals with the modern theory of imperialism inspired by Marx, towards which Schumpeter took a pointed, well-documented but, to my mind, not very convincing antagonistic position.

Chapter 2 is devoted to the central concept of Schumpeterian theory: the entrepreneur. This concept defines the ideological outlook of the Harvard economist better than any other of his intellectual categories. Schumpeter's affinities with Pareto, Mosca, Gabriel Tarde and the other élite theorists of his time become patently obvious here. Thus his antithetical attitude towards the Marxian system and towards the neo-classical school as well, becomes the crucial point of his theory of development. Ragnar Nurske's opinion, that 'Schumpeter's theory offers the mould which all of us have to use even though changing the ingredients a little', will be shared only by those prepared to adopt this central dogma of the Schumpeterian system (cf. R. Nurske, *Problems of Capital Formation in Underdeveloped Countries* [1953], 12).

The subject of Part Three, chapters 9 and 10, is Schumpeter the teacher and Schumpeter the politician. During his lectures Schumpeter used to stress the fact that he was completely lacking in pedagogical ability and that his only reason for being a teacher was to earn his living. Sometimes his students concurred with this view, for often enough his lectures lacked a clear structure and he gave an impression of extemporizing and of insufficient preparation. There can be no doubt that Schumpeter was not a conventional teacher, but his enthusiasm for economics, his attention to each tiny historical detail of economic theory, and his brilliant mastery of the subject with regard to its theoretical and its historical interconnections, communicated themselves to his students and made them feel as if they were witnessing a ritualistic act. In fact Schumpeter was something of a high priest in his chosen science.

While Schumpeter the scholar and teacher was famous all over the world, his success as a politician was ephemeral. After only six months he had to hand over his portfolio as Austrian Minister of Finance to a colourless and much less well-qualified successor. Chapter 9 shows that Schumpeter's failure as a politician stemmed from two factors: the unfavourable circumstances – 1919 was one of the most critical years in the brief and tragic history of Austria between the wars – and his highly individual way of handling matters, completely eschewing political tactics. In thwarting the socialization plans of the Austrian Social Democrats he was taking a fateful step, the consequences of which he could hardly have foreseen in that first year of the Austrian Republic.

Some of Schumpeter's personal letters from a later period, his years at the University of Bonn (1925-32), reveal not a coolly arguing scholar and teacher but a man passionately struggling against his – sometimes rather adverse – fate.[*] The years in Bonn were perhaps the most difficult of Schumpeter's life. In 1925 he had resigned his position as president of the reputable Biedermann bank, which went into liquidation a year later, and accepted an offer from Bonn University.

Schumpeter had left a mountain of debts behind him in Vienna: unpaid loans from his bank, private debts, and large tax arrears. His liabilities to the bank alone amounted to about 120,000 Austrian

---

[*] A group of these letters, kindly made available to me by Professor Gottfried Haberler, was published in the German edition (1983) of the present collection.

schillings (the equivalent of some 5,000,000 schillings in today's [1983] currency). Richard von Mises, the mathematician and philosopher, whom I met in Cambridge (Massachusetts), told me that when he was dean at Humboldt University in Berlin he had to deal with Schumpeter's candidature for the chair of theoretical economics there. Mises was chairman of the commission which turned down Schumpeter's application because of the circumstances leading to his high personal debts. This humiliating result seems greatly to have influenced Schumpeter's ultimate decision to emigrate to the New World.

In Bonn, Schumpeter tried hard to pay off his debts as quickly as possible, especially the sums lent him by some of his friends, but he had only a modest income as a professor and his only other source of funds was from occasional lectures and essays. Meanwhile he had been divorced and remarried, and fate struck him hardest when, shortly after the move to Bonn, he lost his young second wife and their newborn child. He seems to have been almost completely paralysed for a time, and lack of concentration robbed him of the pleasure he took in writing and theorizing. In addition, he may have found it difficult to adjust himself intellectually to the academic environment.

The forced return to life in the ivory tower probably caused the former Minister of Finance and bank president many hours of bitterness and resignation. However, the recognition he soon won among experts reconciled him to the role of observing and theorizing social scientist, which he was to fill from that time on until the end of his life.

Vienna, 1987   E. M.

Joseph Alois Schumpeter (1883-1950)

A CHRONOLOGY

1883   b. 8 February, Triesch, Moravia (now Czechoslovakia), s. of Joseph Alois Schumpeter, a textile manufacturer, and Joan Marguerite (Grüner) Schumpeter, d. of a physician

1887   Death of father; mother remarried (1893) Lt. Gen. Sigismund von Kéler, military commander Imperial Forces, Vienna

1901   B.A., Theresianum Gymnasium, Vienna

1906-7   Doctorate in Law, University of Vienna, 1906; m. (1) Gladys Ricarde Seaver, d. of a Church of England dignitary, 1907 (marriage dissolved, 1920); began private practice in law, Cairo, Egypt

1908   Publication of first book, *Das Wesen und der Hauptinhalt der Theoretischer Nationalökonomie*

1909-11   Lecturer, University of Vienna; Professor of Economics, University of Czernowitz (Cernauti, then in Romania); publication of *The Theory of Economic Development* (1911/12; tr. 1934)

1911-14   Professor of Economics, University of Graz; 1913-14, exchange professor, Columbia University, New York City; Ph. D., Columbia University, 1913

1919-20   Austrian Minister of Finance in government of Karl
          Renner

1924   Failure of Biedermannbank, Vienna, of which he was
          president; loss of his personal fortune

1925-32   Professor of Economics (chair of public finance),
          University of Bonn, Germany; m. (2) Annie Resinger,
          d. of apartment-house caretaker, 1925; her death in
          childbirth, 1926; visiting professor, Harvard
          University, 1927

1932-50   Professor of Economics, Harvard University; m. (3)
          Elizabeth (Boody) Firuski, economic historian, 1937;
          publication of *Business Cycles* (2 vols., 1939); co-founder
          and first president, Econometrics Society; 1939-41;
          publication of *Capitalism, Socialism and Democracy* (1942);
          elected president, American Economic Association,
          1948; elected first president, International Economic
          Association, 1950

1950   d. 8 January, Taconic, Connecticut

1954   Posthumous publication of his *History of Economic Analysis*,
          edited and completed by his widow E.B. Schumpeter

PART ONE

Schumpeter the Economist

Chapter 1

Schumpeter's Theory in Its Relationship to Marxism[*]

The writings of the Austro-American Joseph A. Schumpeter have a special place in the economic literature of the recent past, for his work – like that of two other great economists of this century, Eugen von Böhm-Bawerk and John Maynard Keynes – is characterized by a notable internal consistency. It must also be emphasized that 'Schumpeterian economics' contains elements of sociology, history and political science, as does that of his two German contemporaries Max Weber and Werner Sombart, and of the American Thorstein Veblen. But Schumpeter differs from these authors in being a first-rate economic theorist. In fact, one has to go back to the classics and to Karl Marx to find a theory of a similarly universal character in which 'pure economics' ('*reine Ökonomie*') remains in the foreground. Therefore it is only logical in an evaluation of Schumpeter's thought to consider his affinity with Marx.

Here I want to discuss Schumpeter's work as a whole, dealing only with the most fully developed and most mature stage of his theories, attained in his late works *Business Cycles* (1939) and *Capitalism, Socialism and Democracy* (1942). But even if Schumpeter had never written those books, he would still rank among the most original authors of this century, because his *Theory of Economic Development* (1934), published in German before he was thirty, largely anticipates his mature life-work. In this he presents another striking parallel to Karl Marx, because Marx too sketched out the rough contours of his economic and sociological theories in his late twenties.

* First published in *Wirtschaft und Gesellschaft* (Vienna), vol. VI, no. 3 (1980).

Like Marx, Schumpeter tries to trace the basic law of social development. And he arrives at the hypothesis, again like Marx, that this law, or rather this group of laws, is located above all in the economic sphere. The ultimate cause of social development is to be found in the sporadic changes brought about by creative individuals in the 'productive combinations' or, in Marx's terms, in the 'productive forces'.[1] Sooner or later these lead to institutional adjustments giving rise to a qualitatively new social structure.

The main emphasis in Schumpeter's theory of development is on the sporadic emergence in history of the innovator. Thus he distinguishes with perfect logic between only two great social formations: capitalist and socialist societies. In his brilliant essay 'Capitalism', published in the 1946 edition of the *Encyclopaedia Britannica*, he maintains that antiquity and the Middle Ages are to be regarded as primitive stages on the way to modern capitalism.[2] It is only when the creative producer or entrepreneur is replaced by a team of managerial specialists, working in accordance with modern business-management methods, that a new social formation, clearly distinguishable from capitalism, comes into being.

If we exclude the most recent stage of development of industrial society, we find the *individual* propensity for innovation, according to Schumpeter, at every level of social development.[3] He thinks that innovation and the claim to social leadership arising from it are an inherent feature of economic life. Marx and the school of historical materialism founded by him believe, on the other hand, that this 'characteristic' is not a general but a historical category. It is of course true that in all social formations man is confronted with the task of harnessing the forces of nature. But throughout the historical periods preceding the capitalist era fulfilling this task did not give rise to a claim to social leadership. In the era of feudalism or in the more recent age of the 'enlightened' principalities, the claim had to be pressed home by methods of a completely different kind.

What does Schumpeter regard as the principal differences between the primitive stages of capitalism and the fully developed form of that system? He sees the *differentia specifica* in the modern credit system. It is only with the introduction of institutions engaged in the 'production' of finance on a commercial basis that the transition to a more advanced stage of capitalism takes place; its most important feature is the perpetual, though discontinuous, transformation of the productive forces.[4]

In accordance with the tradition of classical economics, Schumpeter begins with an analysis of the stationary economy. Looked at superficially, his definition of the circular flow of the economy appears to be identical with that of the neo-classical or Marxian schools. The value of the factors of production is merely another way of expressing the income of those classes which take part in one way or another in the process of production. And this income is equivalent to the prices paid for the consumer goods which are the final result of the process. In this way the markets can be completely cleared, and through the earnings flowing back from circulation into production the circular flow can enter a new phase.

In a stationary economy neither the quantities nor the prices put on consumer goods change. The needs of the consumers and the quality of the goods offered do not alter in any way. This model completely disregards what seems to be the quintessence of the capitalistic system, namely the drive towards innovation in the field of production. It must be remembered, of course, that Marx – and representatives of the neo classical school along with him – was working with a scheme of reproduction based on the same simplified assumptions. Schumpeter's break with nineteenth-century tradition is to be seen elsewhere.

According to Schumpeter the only compensation the circular-flow producer (*Kreislaufwirt*) receives for his efforts is the 'wages of management'. All other revenue resulting from the process of production accrues to the original factors of production – to land and labour. Or, to put it in a different way: in a stationary economy the prerequisites for the formation of entrepreneurial profits do not exist. And thus savings, capital, interest and productive credit are all incompatible with a stationary economy. In his model Schumpeter abstracts much more from reality than does the neo-classical school, or Marx.

For Schumpeter the entrepreneurial profit is a purely dynamic category. It is earned only by those producers who try to overcome the condition of the economy by introducing new combinations of production. By taking over this role, which dynamizes the circular flow, the producer becomes an entrepreneur, whose most important function is defined by Schumpeter in the graphic term 'creative destruction' ('*schöpferische Zerstörung*'). The qualitative leap from the stationary to the dynamic economy is brought about by the appearance of the entrepreneur and the innovations initiated by him in the areas of technology, product differentiation, marketing etc.[5]

How, in Schumpeter's view, does the phenomenon of profit come about? With the help of innovation, the entrepreneur manages to gain a – usually temporary – cost advantage over the greater number of traditionally oriented circular-flow producers. As long as his unit cost remains *below* the market price, he reaps a surplus from his entrepreneurial activity. But this advantage, which accrues to him from an innovative use of the factors of production, is sooner or later eroded in one of two ways: first, very soon imitators appear, causing pressure on the market price; and secondly, the cost of producing the new goods will rise sooner or later because of the increased demand for the factors of production.

Schumpeter's theory of profit and interest is, as we shall see later, not at all new. The only aspect that is new is the claim to exclusiveness established *vis-à-vis* all other traditional theories of interest. Neither the Marxian explanation of the 'exploitation' of human labour nor the neo-classical theory, which attributes a value premium to present purchasing power over that of the future, meets with his approval.[6] The stability of the phenomenon of interest, in view of the admittedly sporadic innovations, is attributed by Schumpeter to the appearance of new combinations 'in clusters' during an upswing in the business cycle. The periods of more or less intensive innovative entrepreneurial activity are reflected most noticeably in the fluctuations of the rate of profit and the rate of interest.

Schumpeter's concept of entrepreneurial profit is linked, of course, with a specific concept of capital and interest on capital. According to him, capital is only a fund of purchasing power enabling the entrepreneur to withdraw factors of production from their previous uses in order to employ them in a more profitable way. A certain sum of money thus makes it possible for its lucky owner to acquire temporary dominance over men and material.[7]

Since the phenomenon of savings is lacking in a stationary economy – all the *dramatis personae* use their entire income for the acquisition of consumer goods – the question arises as to where an additional fund of purchasing power, making it possible to pursue new courses of production, is to come from. Schumpeter's answer is that the commercial banks create investment credit out of *thin air*.[8] Thus he polemicizes against Fullarton and other representatives of a narrowly conceived 'banking theory'. The concept of credit creation is a focal point in Schumpeter's theory of economic development. We have already seen that he assigns a central place in the genesis of modern capitalism to the emergence of an efficient credit system.

In this way the banks help the entrepreneur to come into possession of additional financial resources, to which there is no corresponding supply of additional goods. The result is an inflationary process in which the purchasing power of the circulating monetary units is compressed and the entrepreneur thus enabled to enter into the process of production. The concept of voluntary saving, which has no logical place in Schumpeter's system, is here put in opposition to the concept of 'forced saving', which relates to the process of 'expropriation' of the circular-flow producers set in motion by means of credit creation.

It is now evident by what means the entrepreneur is able to repay the borrowed capital along with an adequate rate of interest to his credit institution. Once the new combination of factors of production has proved successful, the entrepreneur, having completed the process of marketing or realizing on the new product, re-acquires the capital advanced together with a surplus, however high or low. The bank's interest is thus the result of a division of part of the surplus derived from circulation.

We saw earlier that, according to Schumpeter's model, innovations appear in 'clusters'. Schumpeter attributes this peculiar phenomenon essentially to two factors: first, the great number of imitators who follow hard on the heels of a successful entrepreneur; and secondly, the growing readiness of the public to accept innovations after the first great pioneering moves have succeeded. The jerky changes in a previously stationary situation lead to cyclical upswings which, after some time has elapsed, are superseded by a distinct downswing in the economy. The economic development under capitalistic premises thus proceeds in the form of cyclical fluctuations.

Schumpeter always referred to the business cycle as the 'Juglar cycle', in honour of the French author who, he believed, first described this phenomenon. It must be noted, however, that it would be more appropriate to call the business cycle the 'Marx cycle', as the latter recognized very early on the cyclical nature of the capitalist process of production. The following passage is from the *Communist Manifesto*:

> For many a decade past the history of industry and commerce is but the history of the revolt of modern productive forces against modern conditions of production, against the property relations that are the conditions for the existence of the bourgeoisie and of its rule. It is enough to mention the commercial crises that by their

periodical return put on trial, each time more threateningly, the
existence of the entire bourgeois society.[9]

What, according to Schumpeter, is the cause of the cyclical ups and
downs? As already noted, the abrupt onset of a wave of innovations is
accompanied by a rise in prices. In the course of the cyclical upswings
initiated by primary innovations, the well-known signs of a boom can
be observed.

The phase of prosperity contains, however, the seeds of its own destruction. We have seen that the rise in prices is caused by the disturbance of the equilibrium, primarily in those markets where the increased demand for the means of production is not matched by a
corresponding supply. As the new productive combinations become
effective, the supply of goods increases. Shortages now increasingly
give way to a partial over-saturation of the markets. As a result prices
begin to fall. According to Schumpeter, the pattern of inflation succeeded by deflation is an element in the process of development.
Moreover, as the two phases fulfil the logical conditions of his model,
Schumpeter regards them as the empirical proof of his theoretical proposition. The transition from prosperity to recession is explained
chiefly by two facts: the exhaustion of innovative activity and the increasing imbalance between the different spheres of the economy
during the phase of prosperity. Looked at from this angle, the phase of
recession can be seen as a natural purging process, to which many of
the less viable businesses founded during prosperity fall victim. In
this, Schumpeter is adopting a position contrary to that of Marx and
Keynes, both of whom regard the phase of recession as an expression
of the chronic illness of our economic order.

One would hardly do Schumpeter an injustice by classifying his
theory of business cycles as a variant on the theory of disproportional-
ity, which was fashionable at the beginning of this century. Its most
important representative was the Russian Tugan-Baranowsky, who
published in 1901 his *History of the Commercial Crises in England*, in which
he elevates a notion discussed by Marx in *Capital* to the rank of a fully-
fledged theory. Tugan influenced not only Schumpeter but also Hilferding, Otto Bauer and many other socialist thinkers in their views of
the business cycle.

The Juglar cycle comprises a period of seven to ten years. But
Schumpeter also takes into consideration the longer-term Kondratieff
cycle and, beyond that, the economic development of an entire social
epoch. Thus we come to a question which is of very great interest to

the present generation, namely the mechanism by which a society moves from a capitalist to a socialist economy, discussed at great length in what is perhaps Schumpeter's most famous book, *Capitalism, Socialism and Democracy*. But before entering an area involving economic, sociological and historical distinctions, we shall take a brief critical look at the *oeconomia pura* of Schumpeter's model.

As we have seen, the entry of the entrepreneur into the static circular flow is, according to Schumpeter, the ultimate cause of economic development. It must be stressed that the important factor here is not the myriad continuous changes in the production process, but the sudden qualitative shift in the method of production, e.g., from stage coach to railway, or from conventional electrical energy to atomic energy. The motive for entrepreneurial activity is the entrepreneur's potential profit, which as we already know originates in the difference between the prevailing price under equilibrium and the individual unit cost of the innovating factor.

The systematic profit-oriented activity of the entrepreneur is not, however, as Schumpeter believes, a prevailing human pattern, but a social phenomenon confined to a relatively brief historical period. It appears only late in history, in the cities of western and central Europe towards the end of the age of feudalism, and will probably vanish some time during the next century. But this point, touched upon earlier, is only a kind of 'Open Sesame!' to Schumpeter's economic theory.

From the point of view of 'pure' theory, the linchpin of Schumpeter's system is the dynamic theory of interest. This is where it really differs from neo-classical or Marxist theory. According to Schumpeter, in the static circular flow there is no entrepreneurial profit. Here the businessman must be satisfied with 'wages of management', while the remaining income is divided among the original factors of production, i.e. land and labour. In his famous polemic with Böhm-Bawerk, Schumpeter dealt, or so we believe, a fatal blow to the premium, or 'agio' theory of interest, which deduces the phenomenon of interest from the fact that present goods are assigned a higher value than future goods. Schumpeter reverses the causal connection and explains the agio phenomenon by the existence of interest on capital. Thinking to cut the ground from under Karl Marx's theory of exploitation by attacking its basis, the labour theory of value, Schumpeter in so doing adopts the most important arguments of the school of marginal utility. (Schumpeter's ambivalent attitude towards the Böhm-Bawerkian agio theory of interest is dealt with at greater length elsewhere in this book.)

In his *Business Cycles* Schumpeter tried to demonstrate the main empirical core of his theory of interest. As we have seen, according to Schumpeter the essence of the entrepreneurial innovation is to be found in the sporadic occurrence of qualitative change in the method of production of the stage coach/railway type. The routine handling of the tasks which are part of simple reproduction – that is, the constant tiresome routine that characterizes the working environment of the average businessman – is assigned by him to the circular-flow producer, whose efforts are compensated by management wages.

The German-American Fritz Redlich has argued that in his theory Schumpeter does not properly take account of the achievements of the great number of imitators who contribute scarcely less to disseminating new modes of production than the pioneer and the innovator.[10] One has to go a step further, and attribute to those doing the continuous spade-work involved in inventing, improving and marketing the great number of products used in daily life, the really decisive role in the production process. A good example is the chemical industry, where it is hardly possible even for specialists to keep track of developments in a wide range of products. Revolutionary innovations may be important for the longer-term Kondratieff cycle, as witness the invention of the railway in the nineteenth century and the introduction of electrical energy and the motor car in the first half of the present century, but they do not explain the more prosaic events during those periods in which the great innovations do not play a dominant role.

The great merit of Marx's theory of exploitation and interest lies in the fact that it can explain both minor continuous changes and the great discontinuous changes. The theory of exploitation provides a rational explanation for the existence of interest on capital in a stationary economy not shaken by radical innovations. But the thrusting forward of innovators and pioneers also fits in logically with Marx's system. Schumpeter's basic idea, that capitalism has an inherent tendency towards innovation and that the innovator gains a temporary monopoly, which becomes a source of (temporary) profits, was repeatedly and very clearly expressed by Marx, as in this passage from *Capital*, volume I:

Hence, the capitalist who applies the improved method of production, appropriates to surplus-labour a greater portion of the working-day, than the other capitalists in the same trade. He does individually, what the whole body of capitalists engaged in producing relative surplus-value do collectively. On the other hand, however, this extra surplus-value vanishes, so soon as the new method of production has become general, and has consequently caused the difference between the individual value of the cheapened commodity and its social value to vanish. . . .[11]

A footnote added to this passage by Marx, to be found in the earlier editions of *Capital* in the original English version, shows that Schumpeter's theory already existed *in nuce* at the beginning of capitalism. The anonymous pamphlet *The Advantages of the East India Trade* (London, 1720) contains the following passage:

> If my neighbour by doing much with little labour can sell cheap, I must contrive to sell as cheap as he. So that every art, trade, or engine, doing work with labour or fewer hands, and consequently cheaper, begets in others a kind of necessity and emulation, either of using the same art, trade, or engine or of inventing something like it, that every man may be upon the square, that no man may be able to undersell his neighbour.

It may be argued that Marx's concept of innovation refers to only *one* types of innovation, namely improvements in the methods of production leading to cost reductions, while Schumpeter distinguishes between different kinds of innovation, including those aimed at opening up new markets. However, we must not deduce Marx's concept of what he repeatedly called the 'revolutionary' consequences of the capitalist mode of production solely on the basis of the passage cited above. In reality Marx was very well aware, even more so than Adam Smith and Ricardo, that the influence of entrepreneurial activity penetrates all the spheres of social life. In the *Communist Manifesto* there is a passage which contains implicitly the greater part of the types of innovation mentioned by Schumpeter:

> The bourgeoisie, during its rule of scarce one hundred years, has created more and more colossal productive forces than have all preceding generations together. Subjection of Nature's forces to man, machinery, application of chemistry to industry and agriculture, steam navigation, railways, electric telegraphs, clearing of whole continents for cultivation, canalisation of rivers, whole populations conjured out of the ground – what earlier century had even a presentiment that such productive forces slumbered in the lap of social labour?[12]

Marx's theory of exploitation stands and falls on the validity of his labour theory of value. The events of the past few decades suggest a modification of this theory already hinted at by Marx. Marx's version of the labour theory of value centres on labour as a commodity, the value of which – like that of any other commodity – is determined by the value of the amount of consumer goods necessary for its reproduction. It must be added, of course, that this refers not to a physiological subsistence minimum, but to a quantity of goods reflecting the *historically* evolved claim of the working class to a certain standard of living.

How are wage claims kept within limits beneficial to the realization requirements of capital? This is ensured by the so-called industrial reserve army, that is, a relatively surplus population which expands and grows smaller again in the course of the process of accumulation.[13] This mechanism described by Marx was certainly still effective in the first half of this century. But its significance has become controversial in the era of monopoly capital, which has seen the greatly increased bargaining power of the trade unions, as compared with the pre-war era; the policy of full employment; and the dwindling of labour reserves in the rural and small business sectors of the economy.

During the 1950s and '60s the place of the industrial reserve army was increasingly taken by two new mechanisms, the 'incomes policy' and the policy of 'mark-up pricing' which makes for the commonly observed wage–price spiral. It is thus no exaggeration to say that the labour market has lost its 'golden balance' of previous times, because the situation of 'bilateral monopoly' does not allow a determinate solution. By the way, Marx describes the situation of bilateral monopoly in his early essay *Value, Price and Profit* as follows:

> The maximum of profit is . . . limited by the physical minimum of wages and the physical maximum of the working day. It is evident that between the two limits of this *maximum rate of profit* an immense scale of variations is possible. The fixation of its actual degree is only settled by the continuous struggle between capital and labour, the capitalist constantly tending to reduce wages to their physical minimum, and to extend the working day to its physical maximum, while the working man constantly presses in the opposite direction. The matter resolves itself into a question of the respective powers of the combatants.[14]

During the 1970s, when inflationary pressures rose to a level far higher than during the previous two decades, economic policy in the leading capitalist countries once again made use of the 'classical' instrument of the industrial reserve army – under the influence, not least, of Milton Friedman and his school. It is no longer rare for the rate of unemployment to reach a level varying between 5 and 8 per cent. Economists have coped with this unpleasant fact by declaring that unemployment rates of this order are compatible with a state of full or nearly full employment. In this way both sides of the wage bargain seem at ease: the trade-union leaders, who demand full employment, and the businessmen, who are looking for the lost golden balance of the labour market.

Before leaving the area of so-called *oeconomia pura*, which even in its own sphere, the theory of prices and wages, cannot be completely detached from social aspects, we will glance at Schumpeter's theory of capital, credit and accumulation. Schumpeter defines capital as a 'fund of purchasing power', which the banks make temporarily available to the entrepreneur. Two years before Schumpeter, Hilferding had described finance capital as capital which 'is at the banks' disposal and used by industry'.[15] Both authors were obviously influenced in their ideas by the powerful position held at that time in the economies of central Europe by the investment banks.

The capital fund, which the bank temporarily makes available to the entrepreneur, enables him to gain control over commodities and human beings so as to give them a new productive orientation. Thus bank credit is only a means of initiating new relations of production. Here Schumpeter makes a radical break with the materialist concept of capital, which can be traced back to the era of classical economics. But the similarity of Schumpeter's concept of capital to that of Marx is, to my mind, purely verbal. While it is true that the control over human beings and commodities obtained by means of bank credit leads to the phenomenon of surplus value, this surplus does not originate in the sphere of production, as Marx has it, but in the sphere of circulation.

As noted above, the investment banks played a decisive role in the genesis of capitalism during the last decades before World War I. Hilferding regards the dominance of finance capital as characteristic only of a certain phase of historical development; Schumpeter, on the other hand, sees it as a general social category. For him, bank credit created out of thin air is the demiurge of economic progress. But he thereby neglects the much more important phenomenon of savings in the business sector, which is characteristic of the growth mechanism of early capitalist enterprises as well as of modern industrial trusts.

The process of accumulation is accomplished, according to Schumpeter, by means of bank credit; according to Marx, and to certain more recent authors, accumulation comes about through entrepreneurial profit or, to put it in the terms usually employed today, by means of the company's internal capital resources. But this is not the only difference, and, we believe, not the most important one, between Schumpeter's and Marx's view of the expanded reproduction of capital. That difference lies above all in the fact that Schumpeter interprets the process as a psychological phenomenon, while Marx views it as a sociological one.

The immanent tendency of capitalism to innovation is ascribed by Schumpeter, as is well known, to certain personal motives, such as the will to succeed, the desire to found a dynasty, etc. Marx, we believe, would not have denied the significance (and maybe also the virulence) of these motives, because he saw the process of accumulation as a mechanism typical of the capitalistic social order, through which social prestige and power can be achieved. 'Accumulation', Marx says in *Capital*, 'is the conquest of the world of social wealth. It is the extension of the area of exploited human material and, at the same time, the extension of the direct and indirect sway of the capitalist.' (I. 739-40) But Marx, we think, would have added that only in capitalism does the *auri sacra fames* – the 'inextinguishable passion for profit' – take the shape of the accumulation process. The capitalist differs from the medieval hoarder of treasure above all in putting his capital again and again into circulation instead of withdrawing it. This 'restless movement of profit' (as Marx puts it) is not a product of the mental make-up of the individual capitalist, but of the economic conditions in which capital exists. For the competition on the commodity market *forces* every capitalist to enlarge his plant, to improve the technical equipment of his workers, to introduce new and more productive forms of organization and so on, because otherwise he is in danger of losing his place in the sun.

'It must not be forgotten', Marx writes, 'that the production of surplus-value – and the reconversion of a portion of it into capital, or accumulation, forms an indispensable part of this production of surplus-value – is the immediate purpose and the compelling motive of capitalist production' (*Capital*, III. 285). Yet Schumpeter realizes in his early book *The Theory of Economic Development* that in the latter stages of capitalism changes begin to occur which amount to a 'collectivization' of the accumulation process. In his later essays Schumpeter repeatedly returned to this theme, and in his book *Capitalism, Socialism*

and Democracy he made it the starting-point of a large-scale analysis of
the transition from capitalism to socialism.

* * *

Innovations and bank credit are, according to Schumpeter, the economic mechanisms which define a large part of the history of mankind
down to the present day. But in recent times the introduction of new
productive combinations becomes more and more a routine business,
no longer carried out by the individual entrepreneur, but by a team of
managerial specialists. Progress becomes, in a way, automatic and
depersonalized.

The notion of what Karl Renner calls the 'productive' function of
capital becoming detached from its 'distributive' function at a certain
stage in the development of capitalism, goes back to Karl Marx. Werner Sombart has also treated this phenomenon in his book *Der Moderne
Kapitalismus (Modern Capitalism)* and refers to the 'tendency of entrepreneurship to break away from the possession of capital'.[16] Hilferding had, moreover, described the collectivization of the entrepreneurial function rather vividly two years before Schumpeter's *Theory of
Economic Development* appeared: 'The expansion of the capitalistic
enterprise which has become a stock corporation, free from the fetters
of individual property, can now be pursued purely in conformity with
the demands of technology. The introduction of new machines, the
adoption of related branches of production, the utilization of patents
is strictly guided by the aspect of technical and economic adequacy.'[17]

The climax of this process has, of course, been reached only in the
era of giant industrial corporations and 'multinational' business concentration. Eventually, Schumpeter states in *Capitalism, Socialism and
Democracy*: 'The perfectly bureaucratized giant industrial unit not only
ousts the small or medium-sized firm and "expropriates" its owners,
but in the end it also ousts the entrepreneur and expropriates the
bourgeoisie as a class which in the process stands to lose not only its
income but also what is infinitely more important, its function'.[18]

The depersonalization or collectivization of the entrepreneurial
function is, according to Schumpeter, the ultimate cause of the gradual withering away of the capitalist mode of production. Like the
feudal lord in the era of gunpowder, letter-press printing and manufactories, the owner of capital now loses his function, and he increasingly lacks the will to defend his position, which from society's
point of view has become superfluous.

In addition to the entrepreneurial function being taken over by a
collective of managers, there are other aspects favouring the process of

transformation towards socialism. Schumpeter specifies four such factors:

Firstly, the process of concentration leads to the destruction of the commercial existence of the small proprietors. Schumpeter adds: 'The very foundation of private property and free contracting wears away in a nation in which its most vital, most concrete, most meaningful types disappear from the moral horizon of the people' (*Capitalism*, 140-1).

Secondly, while late capitalism does lead to a steady improvement in the standard of living of the masses, the repeated changes of profession and location characteristic of any industrial society increase the insecurity of the individual. 'Secular improvement that is taken for granted and coupled with individual insecurity', Schumpeter points out, '. . . is of course the best recipe for breeding social unrest' (ibid., 145).

Thirdly, the large family unit, formerly the most important adhesive element in bourgeois order, is becoming more and more an exception, and with it perhaps the most important motivation for entrepreneurial activity vanishes.

Fourthly, the rationalist criticism formerly directed against feudalism is now turned increasingly against private property and the values of the bourgeoisie. This criticism is advanced by the intellectuals, whom Schumpeter sees as the real cause of ferment in bourgeois society. He thinks that the growing social and political importance of the intelligentsia are connected with the spread of education and the tendency to proletarianism within this social stratum. From this class the intellectual cadres of the labour movement are recruited.[19]

Schumpeter ascribes such an explosive effect to the four factors mentioned above that he not only thinks of the replacement of the capitalist economic order by a socialist one as inevitable, but also as a process whose final stage can be clearly discerned.

Of course, some of the aspects mentioned by Schumpeter which prefigure the coming transformation of our mode of production coincide with Marx's arguments. This applies to the social consequences of the concentration process, to the splitting off of the entrepreneurial function from that of the ownership of capital, and finally to the dissolution of the bourgeois family, dealt with especially by Friedrich Engels.

Schumpeter's statement that under late capitalism the standard of living of the masses would rise substantially is, it is clear, diametrically opposed to Marx's 'theory of impoverishment'. But it must be remembered that Schumpeter had the opportunity of studying the economic implications of the so-called 'Keynesian revolution' over more than a decade. And he also knew, through direct observation of the economic consequences of two world wars, that full employment can easily be achieved by means of public spending. However, if Schumpeter were able to join us today, he might be rather surprised to learn that one-fifth of the population of the world's richest country, the USA, still live below the poverty line.

Schumpeter's analytical gifts are perhaps seen at their best when he is analysing the role of the intellectuals in late capitalism. First of all he predicted with amazing accuracy the enormous expansion of the educational system. And his close contact with the younger generation at American universities made him realize very early that it is the intellectuals who feel most keenly the drawbacks of a too formalistically designed democratic system. From this observation it was only a step to his realization that the quantitative growth of an intellectual proletariat must give rise to dangerous social ferment

Professor Haberler once compared Schumpeter to Cassandra, whose prediction that a new era is approaching is to be interpreted both as a warning and the expression of an inner dissociation. It must remain an open question whether such an interpretation of Schumpeter's position is correct, because unlike Max Weber, for example, he attributed a higher degree of rationality to a socialist economy than to a capitalist one. He gave four reasons for this:

Firstly, under oligopoly, prices and output are undetermined. In a socialist economy, on the other hand, these data are clearly determined and thus permit a rational and optimal solution to the production problem. 'Unless the resources thus saved are completely wasted', Schumpeter adds, 'efficiency ... must necessarily increase' (*Capitalism*, 194).

Secondly, oligopoly favours the development of large excess capacities, which are necessary above all to support monopolistic positions.

Thirdly, in capitalism the cyclical fluctuations can only be restrained, while a planned economy leads to the complete elimination of the business cycle. Schumpeter summarizes these ideas in the following passage: 'Socialist management may conceivably prove as superior to big-business capitalism as big-business capitalism has proved to be to the kind of competitive capitalism of which the English industry of a hundred years ago was the prototype' (ibid., 196).

Fourthly, capitalism is characterized by a constant struggle between public administration and private business. Many of the best brains of a country are engaged in this conflict: highly qualified bureaucrats on the one side, and brilliant lawyers as well as managerial specialists on the other side. Thus many of these best brains are withheld from the productive tasks of society.

Marx would probably have added one very essential factor to this list of advantages of a socialist system. Socialism, he might have said, paves the way for overcoming that ancient disease, alienation, by putting an end to the separation of the worker from the object of work. In Marx's system democracy means deliberately regulating the process of production at *all* levels at which important socio-political decisions are taken.

But it is not by chance that this point was not taken up by Schumpeter, because in the final analysis it goes against his basic sociological concept. To Schumpeter the essence of democracy is identical, not with the process of democratic policy-making, but with the periodic process of democratic voting, which results in policy-making on the part of those who are 'called' to lead. So Schumpeter could await with equanimity the arrival of a socialist society. For he agreed with Pareto, Nietzsche and other élite philosophers of his time that the phenomenon of class was based ultimately on 'individual differences in aptitude' and that any social formation was divided into two social groups – the 'élite', that is the class of superior individuals, and the 'rest of the population', that is the group of individuals of, to cite Pareto, inferior qualification.[20]

Thus Schumpeter's socialism displays the characteristics of Plato's state rather than those of the community of the future as visualized by Sir Thomas More, Robert Owen or Karl Marx. A society in which – to echo a famous *mot* – every cook is potentially qualified to conduct the affairs of state was not only alien to Schumpeter; he also thought it Utopian and unfeasible.

1980/1983

Chapter 2

The Schumpeterian Entrepreneur

At the centre of Joseph A. Schumpeter's work on economics and sociology is the concept of the entrepreneur. He is the demiurge of economic progress, the *dramatis personae* of socio-economic development, the agent of social change in general. The Schumpeterian entrepreneur is not to be identified with the bourgeois of the nineteenth century, although he bears many of the same traits. The entrepreneur emerges, Schumpeter believes, at the lowest level of human civilization, where the role of a leader falls to him because of his ability to decide, to direct, to push matters through and to lead the way. And, Schumpeter adds in his essay on 'Social Classes in an Ethnically Homogeneous Environment', that social leadership can only assert itself in individual social situations that are constantly new and that would not occur if the lives of individual members of society and of the people in general always evolved in the same way and along the same paths.[1]

Social leadership, if we limit it to the above-mentioned qualities of deciding, directing, pushing matters through and leading the way, is a timeless category and can be applied to every upper class in society, no matter what its actual historical character. Under capitalism another quality comes to the fore which gives to the leader what one is tempted to call its Schumpeterian character. To the qualities of directing and pushing matters through, required for the purely routine handling of social tasks, must now be added a very special quality, namely the ability to introduce new productive methods or combinations. But Schumpeter believes that modern capitalism, and with it the above-mentioned qualities of leadership, had already appeared in rudimentary form in antiquity and in the Middle Ages.

One has the impression that he views the original forms of barter and trade as initial stages in a profit-oriented economy characterized by the division of labour.

Be that as it may, Schumpeter thinks that enclaves of the capitalist mode of production can be recognized very distinctly in western Europe as early as the tenth century. Let us emphasize, once again, that according to Schumpeter the entrepreneurial function is not necessarily restricted to capitalist society; it can also exist in primitive phases or the preliminary stages of this mode of production.[2] This view is perhaps most forcefully and elegantly presented in his short essay on 'Capitalism' published in the *Encyclopaedia Britannica* (1946).

Assuming that the Western European type of capitalism sprang from obscure origins in the dawn of history and gradually developed and advanced, Schumpeter argues against the Weber-Sombart thesis, viz., that the emergence of the capitalist mode of production can be explained by a new attitude which 'some time between 1400 and 1600 induced people to adopt a novel way of thinking and acting'. In this connection Schumpeter refers to the competition between handicrafts and the 'cottage system' (or 'putting-out system'), the latter of which he considers an early example of a basic innovation. It is not necessary, in Schumpeter's opinion, for a 'new social, cultural, spiritual world . . . to emerge in order to make . . . possible' this new approach (*Business Cycles*, I.228-9).

According to Schumpeter a more mature stage of capitalism is reached only when the entrepreneur is able, in his innovative activity, to rely on a sufficient amount of credit being provided by the banking system. Thus Schumpeter defines capitalism as 'that form of private-property economy in which innovations are carried out by means of borrowed money, which in general, though not out of logical necessity, implies credit creation'. From this it follows that he dates *modern* capitalism from the moment when credit creation began to be carried on as routine commercial activity. The frictionless interplay of industry and banks Schumpeter sees as an essential prerequisite for undisturbed capitalist production. Thus he arrives at the following resigned statement, 'that the failure of the banking community to function in the way required by the structure of the capitalist machine accounts for most of the events which the majority of observers would call "catastrophes"' (ibid., I.117).

The Schumpeterian entrepreneur differs from his colleague who produces in a routine manner, especially in applying new methods of production, in placing new products on the market, in opening up new markets, etc. In this way he accumulates a surplus – which is eroded, however, as imitators appear who increasingly use the same or similar methods. The profits and interest derived from a temporary monopoly on the part of the entrepreneur are thus conceived as purely dynamic phenomena.

The Schumpeterian entrepreneur – as has been shown in some detail in Chapter 1 – is doubtless a close relative of the entrepreneur described by Marx. The prevailing laws of capitalist production make themselves felt as coercive laws of competition, and lead the individual capitalist to improve the methods of production so as to have a greater portion of the working day to himself than is possible for other capitalists in the same line of business. Marx says the capitalist does as an individual 'what capital itself taken as a whole does when engaged in producing relative surplus value'.[3] But Marx, as opposed to Schumpeter, treats profit as both a static and a dynamic category.

Marx does not attempt to analyse in great detail the psychology of the individual entrepreneur, but alleges that the entire capitalist class is subject to the coercive laws of competition. Of course he cannot have overlooked the fact that in the process of accumulation the more efficient entrepreneur prevails over his less efficient colleague. However, Marx bases his analysis of the production process on the assumption of an average type of entrepreneur, very much in the same way as he proceeds, in his study of labour productivity, from a worker of average intelligence and efficiency. Not so Schumpeter: again and again he refers to individual differences of aptitude within the capitalist class and the working class. 'The captured surplus-value', Schumpeter writes,

> obviously does not invest itself but must be invested, and this means first of all that the capitalist must not use it in a consumptive way and furthermore that it is important how it will be invested. But both lead us away from the objective automatism and to the behaviour of the individual capitalist, i.e. to his motives, and consequently from the social force to the individual – the physical individual or the family – and from the objective to the subjective.[4]

Then Schumpeter tries in what one is almost tempted to call his permanent dialogue with Marx to define his position still further. Again I quote from the essay 'Die sozialen Klassen im ethnischhomogenen Milieu':

> If someone argues that social logic forces the individual to invest the profit and that individual motivation is only a contingent tran-

sitional stage, the rejoinder must be that this is, in so far as it is correct, accepted by every sensible human being – of course the individual psyche is only the result, offshoot, reflex and conductor of the inner necessities of any given situation –; but that the social logic or the objective situation, if one omits to take into account the aptitude of the individual, do not determine clearly how much profit there will be, and how it is going to be invested. If this is done, however, it is no longer the inner logic of the apparatus as such, basically separable from the personality of the industrialist [which determines the final decision – E.M.]. In fact in this case as well – as quite generally – Marx implies an exception to the average behaviour, in which again lies an entire, though very imperfect, economic psychology.   ('Die sozialen Klassen', 163)

It must be noted in this context that, while repeatedly stressing the rather different endowments of the individual entrepreneur who has innovative abilities, Schumpeter says nothing concrete about the actual dispersion and distribution of this kind of talent over the whole class of capitalists. Moreover, Marx attaches far less importance to the ability of the individual capitalist to conduct his business, namely to amass capital in the course of the process of accumulation, than does Schumpeter. In contrast to the latter, Marx stresses the difference in the financial endowment of individual capitalists, from which he deduces that large amounts of capital generally grow far faster in the course of accumulation than do small amounts. In this way a relatively smaller number of enterprises get control over an increasing amount of social capital. Another factor, especially in times of economic recession and crisis, is the transformation of many small capital sums into a small number of large sums. In this analysis, then, Marx attaches relatively little significance to differences in aptitude within the capitalist class.

To return now to the development of Schumpeter's system. It is obvious that the individual entrepreneur (or the entrepreneurial family) will try to exceed his temporal and personal limitations. But this reaching out ('Weitergreifen', as Schumpeter calls it) is not possible for everyone who is able to save money and to do his routine work promptly. For an endeavour of this kind requires getting off the beaten track. Then on what does the typical career of a successful industrial family depend? Schumpeter's answer is: 'What is decisive is neither saving nor the prompt handling of business as such, but being equal to the task' (ibid., 166).

Schumpeter views the ability to achieve entrepreneurial innovation as the sole qualification for admission to, and permanent membership of, the managerial class in bourgeois society. By the same token, he believes that the social rise of working-class families in the capitalist system is dependent exclusively upon entrepreneurial ability. The essential criterion for an individual's (or a family's) membership in a social class is thus its possession of certain characteristics which, so Schumpeter believes, are required for the performance of socially essential functions. According to this definition, a social class is composed of individuals of rather similar characteristics, and thus of rather similar social position. Schumpeter thinks that the reinforcement of such a social grouping and the continued existence of what has been reinforced is 'a special problem requiring a special explanation, basically the very specific class problem'. (Ibid., 178, 205)

Here I would note the striking similarity between Schumpeter's theory of class and that of Vilfredo Pareto. Schumpeter himself, in a brilliant article on the main features of Pareto's theories, described the quintessence of the sociological system of this great social scientist as follows: 'The morphological schema [of Vilfredo Pareto] centres in the proposition that all societies consist of heterogeneous masses of members – individuals or families – and are structured according to the aptitudes of these members for the relevant social function.' The differences in aptitude result in the emergence of social classes which develop a certain persistence, because the higher-ranking classes possess the will and the means to defend their privileged position. In this way social tensions arise which lead finally to the replacement of the ruling élite by a new élite. In paraphrasing the main thesis of the *Communist Manifesto*, Pareto says that history is nothing but a succession of aristocratic élites competing for dominance. Schumpeter lists among Pareto's intellectual forerunners Charles Darwin and the Frenchmen Gabriel Tarde, Durkheim and Lévy-Bruhl. But he adds that Pareto's system is also strongly influenced by ideologies that may be called anti-intellectual, anti-utilitarian and anti-egalitarian. It must be said that such anti-egalitarian currents also had an influence on Schumpeter's theory of class, which displays an unmistakable affinity with that of Pareto.[5]

In contrast to Pareto, Schumpeter deduces the persistence of élites not primarily from the fact that they possess the will and the means to defend themselves, but from a biological law – the handing down of intellectual qualities from one generation to the next. In a characteristic passage in his essay 'Die sozialen Klassen', Schumpeter says:

'If aptitudes were not hereditary and in each case distributed according to the law of probability, the position of the classes and the families belonging to them would obviously be much less stable than it actually is.' And in another passage he states again, perhaps more peremptorily, that the supra-individual loyalty to family and class is possible *only* because the qualities of leadership are hereditary. ('Die sozialen Klassen', 209, 211 [italics mine – E.M.]) Pareto's influence, which Schumpeter does not acknowledge explicitly in his analysis of the social classes, is less dominant here than the influence of Sir Francis Galton and Karl Pearson, both very prominent authors frequently cited in Schumpeter's day. Karl Pearson coined a phrase which was often and approvingly quoted by Schumpeter: 'Ability runs in stocks'.[6]

Thus it is evident that in judging human qualities Schumpeter attaches much more importance to heredity than to the influence of environment and education. It would be wrong to accept the conclusion that has sometimes been drawn, that Schumpeter's views on the racial theories of Gobineau or Gumplowicz were ambivalent. It must be said, however, that he was not completely without guilt in this matter as can be seen in, amongst other things, his digression on Gobineau in his *History of Economic Analysis*. There he offers (791n.) 'a piece of advice that unfortunately imposes itself often in sociological and economic matters: read the enemies of the racial theory in order to see its strong points; read the exponents of the racial theory in order to see its weak ones'.

In the feudal period, the lord of the manor performed military, administrative and judicial functions all at one time. From the fifteenth century onwards he was increasingly replaced by the capitalist, whose main task is seen by Marx and Schumpeter as the continuous revolutionizing of the forces of production. But there are basic differences between the two authors in their view of the motivation of the capitalist entrepreneur. To Marx 'accumulation is the conquest of the world of social wealth. It is the extension of the area of exploited human material and, at the same time, the extension of the direct and indirect sway of the capitalist.' (*Capital*, I. 739) Schumpeter too would I think hardly have denied that the process of accumulation is the ladder to social power and social prestige; but he thought that the very mainspring of the exercise of the entrepreneurial function is the powerful will to assert economic leadership. The joy in carrying through innovations is the primary motive, the acquisition of social power a subsidiary to it.

Without doubt, Schumpeter felt a certain nostalgia for the individual capitalist and the economic and social order he represented.
Bureaucratized capitalism, personified by the so-called 'Organization
Man', seemed to him only a preliminary stage leading to a totally col-
lectivized and socialized economy. His attitude towards these two
systems – a bureaucratized capitalism and a fully socialized economy
– was not disapproving. In striking contrast to Mises, Hayek and the
new Austrian school, Schumpeter ascribed to those systems an even
higher degree of rationality than to the free entrepreneurial economy
he himself idealized and glorified. Yet he could not help preferring a
social order whose exponents were not anonymous and faceless
bureaucrats but courageous, imaginative, and in some instances also
socially callous, champions of their own interests.

As is well known, Schumpeter distinguished between the innovator
and the mere imitator. The innovator (not to be confused with the
original inventor) provides the decisive impulse for the transformation
of the economic environment. He is responsible, according to
Schumpeter, for the great spontaneous but discontinuous changes in
the economy. Only when one of the new combinations has succeeded
does the inert mass of imitators begin to stir. The conceptual contrast
of entrepreneur with imitator corresponds to the antithesis of innovation and routine.

Schumpeter's Romantic concept of the spontaneity of the entrepreneurial achievement has been criticized, in particular by A.P. Usher
and Fritz Redlich. They argue that important inventions are usually
the result of processes incubating over centuries, in which generations
of inventors, businessmen and sometimes even adventurers take an
active part. In this connection one recalls Victor Hugo's famous
words: 'On explique comment François II succède à Henri III,
Charles IX à François II et Henri III à Charles IX, mais personne
n'enseigne comment Watt succède à Papin et Fulton à Watt.'

If it is true that innovations and the act of pushing them through
commercially are, as a rule, carried out not by individuals but by a
generation, then the contrast between the leader and the imitator
appears irrelevant. This has been best expressed, perhaps, by Fritz
Redlich:

[it is] impossible to contrast innovator with follower, with the dis-
paraging implication that certain outstanding qualities are necessary to innovate but only lesser ones to follow the trail thus marked
out. Reality is not so simple. The transfer of any primary innova-

tion in the Schumpeterian sense to another geographical area or to another industry . . . demands in many, if not in all cases, capacities as great as primary innovation.[7]

Just as the strict contrast between leader and imitator may be misleading, the belittling of all achievements that are not financially successful must also be seen as a grave defect in the Schumpeterian model of development. Again it is worth quoting Redlich on this point:

> What, then, about those who have tried but have not succeeded? Were they actually unimportant for economic development? Were they necessarily men of minor capacities? Surely these questions must be answered in the negative. The dead hand of Schumpeter's prestige should not keep us from recognizing that which his model veils, namely the great importance of failure in economic development.[8]

Redlich's criticism of the Schumpeterian concept of the entrepreneur leads logically to the rejection of the theory of development inseparably bound up with this concept. Redlich does not go that far, but some of his conclusions, such as the following, show that he was on the verge of doing so:

> . . . once a dynamic economic life has come into existence, what the followers do determines the course of economic development just as much as the actions of the primary innovators; and the speed with which they come in and imitate, if that is the right word, determines the speed of economic development as much as the frequency of primary innovation.[9]

The conclusion Redlich shrank back from drawing was reached by other writers at about the same time (the mid-1950s). As we have seen, Schumpeter believed that the origins of the capitalist mode of production can be traced to the early history of mankind. Markets, the exploitation of human labour and the pursuit of profit can be demonstrated to have existed in almost every historical period. But the market economy that evolved in Western Europe in the course of the fifteenth and sixteenth centuries, and which spread all over Europe in subsequent centuries and to other parts of the world later on, has certain structural features which quite clearly set it apart from earlier economic periods. Unlike Schumpeter (and also his mentors Böhm-Bawerk and Wieser), I believe that to distinguish it in this way makes our analytical task not more difficult, but easier.

It cannot be denied, of course, that in every social structure there are individuals set apart from their fellows by their will to succeed, their joy in creative activity, their urge to found a dynasty and by certain other lofty ambitions persuasively described by Schumpeter. But one must ask what objective can best satisfy these ambitions under varying social conditions. Even in the nineteenth century, when the Schumpeterian entrepreneur scored his greatest triumphs, in certain societies economic man was assigned a relatively low rank in the social hierarchy. Thus Carlin rightly says:

> The only difficulty with the Schumpeterian analysis of the entrepreneur's motivation is that while the type is postulated as contributing to endogenous, capitalistic, economic change the motives for action offered were applicable to any system. . . . The charismatic leadership gains specificity under certain systems of social organization and becomes the entrepreneur type. . . . In other words the conditions associated with capitalism have, at most, channelled the characteristics of charisma in a peculiar way.[10]

Schumpeter's hypothesis, that capitalism has an inherent tendency to innovation, is doubtless more useful than that of his neo-classical contemporaries, who regard technical progress and other Schumpeterian 'combinations' as 'given data'. But Schumpeter fails to see that there were long periods in the history of mankind when such a built-in tendency to innovation was completely lacking. As Yale Brozen puts it: 'In a society with no need or desire for change, entrepreneurs or other men who might institute New Combinations are unnecessary.' And Felix Rexhausen, who quotes this passage, adds that not every economy aims at development and progress.[11]

Schumpeter's historical approach gives him a special position among the exponents of modern economics. But his view of history suffers from his overvaluing the entrepreneurial concept, which he sees as an essential feature of the periodization of social change. He divides world history into three consecutive periods:

the pre-capitalist period – characterized by the sporadic and relatively rare appearance of entrepreneurial individuals;

the capitalist period – characterized by the new entrepreneurial class dedicated to its innovative activity;

the socialist period – characterized by the collectivization of the entrepreneurial function.

But today even Schumpeter's most devoted followers have to concede that the most recent monopoloid phase of capitalism, epitomized by the managerial teams of big corporations, does not yet signal a fundamental change in the system. The heroic, self-reliant entrepreneur who symbolized an earlier stage in the development of capitalism may in fact be a dying species, while the institutions of property, a market economy and profit-oriented enterprise have proved durable enough to ensure that the capitalist mode of production will continue in the foreseeable future. In so far as the system is threatened with a crisis, it will certainly not be caused by the 'collectivization' of the entrepreneurial function.

In economic folklore, the concept of the entrepreneur has undergone strange transformations. Adam Smith does not disapprove of the capitalist entrepreneur, the *homo novus* of his epoch, but he remains unmistakably sceptical and reserved. The 'masters', as he calls the entrepreneurs of the early period of capitalism, tend to form a conspiratorial community opposed to consumers and workers, the anti-social tendency of which is largely neutralized through the harmonizing function of the market. Smith speaks in his *Wealth of Nations* of 'the mean rapacity, the monopolizing spirit of merchants and manufacturers'.

As does Smith, Marx begins with the power differential in the relationship between entrepreneur and worker. He sees the capitalist mode of production primarily as an enormous machinery to extract the surplus value from a working class able to defend itself to only a limited extent through the pressure of the industrial reserve army. Even the trade unions cannot bring about any substantial change in this position of weakness, inherent in the system, except in periods of boom. In the Preface to volume I of *Capital*, Marx argues that the callousness and consistency with which the capitalist class as a whole carries out its impersonal mission, of accumulating more and more surplus value, have no bearing on a judgement of the character of the individual capitalist. Marx's conception of the entrepreneur has, none the less, a basic similarity to that of Adam Smith, in that both impute to the entrepreneur the unscrupulous pursuit of his class-specific interests.

The adversary position of the neo-classical school was perhaps best summarized by Alfred Marshall, towards the end of the last century. In deliberate contrast to Smith and Marx, Marshall stresses the co-operative relationship between capital and labour, based on the principle of partnership. The entrepreneur obtains his dominant position in the production process because of his superior managerial abilities: from this point of view the possession of capital is a function of his special entrepreneurial aptitude. It follows that the capitalist entrepreneur has a higher income mainly because his contribution to the national product is greater than the average. The harmony of the whole system is ensured by the high degree of social mobility that allows able members of the lower classes to acquire a place in the sun.

Obviously, Schumpeter annexed certain features of the Marshallian entrepreneur for his own concept. He too holds that command of the means of production and of people is not a prerequisite for, but results from, special entrepreneurial competence. Again, he believes that the mobility which makes possible a continuous process of regeneration within the entrepreneurial class is a particularly important factor in the stability of the system. But, unlike Marshall, Schumpeter thinks that any tendency of the social structure towards a basic transformation bears the stamp of the bourgeois ruling class. On the one hand, the big corporation with its novel institution (that is, collective management) increasingly deprives the old-fashioned single entrepreneur of his field of action. On the other hand, the bourgeoisie, as representative of a certain mentality and of a waning moral and political authority, visibly loses its prestige and respectability. It becomes the target of criticism from a rationally arguing intelligentsia which is clearly subject to proletarianizing tendencies as the spread of education widens. And thus the halo which Alfred Marshall and some other representatives of neo-classical economics confer on the entrepreneur and on the economic system represented by him, slowly vanishes.

It may be argued that the Schumpeterian entrepreneur was largely anticipated by the work of J.B. Say and Leon Walras. Walras, in particular, is generally assumed to have had great influence on the young Schumpeter. In the Walrasian system, however, there is no place for real decision-makers: the entrepreneur is rather the instrument of the market. Moreover, there remains some doubt that Schumpeter was in fact influenced in his formative years to any great extent by Walras. I would argue that it was Friedrich von Wieser, rather than Walras, who acted as midwife to the Schumpeterian entrepreneur.

The American economist E.S. Mason, who in the late 1950s tried to legitimate the dominant managerial class and the hierarchical order upheld by it, arrived at the following resigned conclusion:

> As everyone recognizes, classical economics provided not only a system of analysis, or analytical 'model', intended to be useful to

the explanation of economic behaviour, but also a defense – and a carefully reasoned defense – of the proposition that the economic behaviour promoted and constrained by the institutions of a free-enterprise system is, in the main, in the public interest. . . . It cannot be too strongly emphasized that the growth of nineteenth-century capitalism depended largely on the general acceptance of a reasoned justification of the system on moral as well as on political and economic grounds. . . . It seems doubtful whether, to date, the managerial literature has provided an equally satisfying apologetic for big business.[12]

1983

Chapter 3

On the Genesis of Schumpeter's Theory of Economic Development[*]

1 The Schumpeterian system

When in 1912 the young Joseph Schumpeter published his work *The Theory of Economic Development*, economics was under the spell of the micro-economic approach. Among the leading bourgeois scholars of the time, it was mainly Alfred Marshall who was dealing with problems of economic development; but he too did so only cursorily and unsystematically, and followed on the whole the beaten track of classical economics. An exception was the American J.B. Clark, to whom Schumpeter owed his concept of dynamics and to whose work he paid tribute in two of his early essays.[1]

It might appear that Schumpeter's work, to which relatively little attention was paid at the time, was a bolt from the blue; but I think this would be wrong. Three factors were decisive for the original achievement of the young theorist: (a) the state of the Austrian economy, which was clearly lagging behind the development of the Western countries, a situation that did not go unnoticed in the economic debate of the period; (b) the fashionably élitist theories which reflected the need of the *haute bourgeoisie* to surround its chief representatives with an aura of heroism; and (c) the general discussion of 'collapse, imperialism and war' over which tempers ran high, especially

* This chapter is a modified and expanded version of a contribution to the *festschrift* for Oskar Lange, *On Political Economy and Econometrics* (Warsaw, 1964).

among the younger Marxists (Hilferding, Luxemburg, Bauer, Gross-mann and Lenin).

Schumpeter dealt at length with the theory of economic development in two later works, *Business Cycles* (1939) and *Capitalism, Socialism and Democracy* (1942), as well as in many earlier and shorter essays, the best-known being his pioneering study of 1912, *The Theory of Economic Development*, and in his article 'Capitalism' for the *Encyclopaedia Britannica* (1946).

Much has been written elsewhere about Schumpeter's theory of development,[2] of which the reader needs to be reminded here of only the most important elements, i.e.: (1) of the fact that economic development is an endogenous process (i.e., inherent in the economy); (2) of the central significance of entrepreneurial activity in the Schumpeterian system; (3) of the disturbance of equilibrium caused by entrepreneurial innovation, which constitutes the very essence of development; and (4) of the particular role of the banks, which by creating money provide the entrepreneur with the means to withdraw production forces from their old uses and to divert them to new employments.

The Schumpeterian 'entrepreneur', who may be the chief of a savage tribe, the leader of a socialist state or a prosaic capitalist profiteer,[3] is the demiurge of economic development and progress. He differs from the 'static producer', who represents a purely traditionalist mental attitude, in continuously looking for new methods of production, new products, new markets, new sources of raw materials and new forms of organization.[4]

Schumpeter repeatedly refers to the entrepreneur's motivation for his creative, but at the same time destructive, behaviour. The will to succeed, the joy in being creative, the urge to found a dynasty, etc. are the forces which give rise to the introduction of new, productive 'combinations'.[5] The success of such an undertaking is rewarded with entrepreneurial profit, which Schumpeter sees as a purely dynamic phenomenon. The successful innovator can maintain his profits only as long as 'the equivalence of costs with proceeds, which holds good under free competition as a result of the law of costs, does not immediately assert itself'.[6] Thus the profit results from the temporary monopoly position of the innovator.

As the Schumpeterian entrepreneur can be found in every society, albeit with varying degrees of frequency, we are dealing with a theory which tries to explain the process of economic development pure and simple. Schumpeter thinks that the capitalist form of profit-oriented management existed at least in rudimentary form in very early periods of the history of mankind.[7] But it is only the combination of entrepreneurship with the modern manifestations of the credit system that, in his opinion, produces the patterns of social behaviour and the institutions characteristic of the capitalism of the past few centuries.[8]

Thus the creative entrepreneur – or just plain entrepreneur, because the adjective 'creative' is only applied to the entrepreneur who is prepared to blaze new trails – is the *primum agens* in the Schumpeterian system. Once the historical connection between the entrepreneur and the modern credit system has been established, the parvenu class of entrepreneurs revolutionizes the forms of production and the organization of the economy, and through these the whole superstructure of society. As a result of its growing bureaucratization and rationalization, the entrepreneurial function succeeds – at a later stage of development – in making itself superfluous.[9] Like Marx, Schumpeter believes that socialism is unavoidable, yet – unlike him – not because the expropriators will be expropriated but because the expropriators will quit the stage, as it were, of their own free will.

As will be seen, this is a socio-economic theory which encompasses virtually the entire history of mankind – up to that stage of development at which the entrepreneur is replaced by a collective group of specialists. While the neo-classical school – to which Schumpeter, by his own testimony, felt very closely related[10] – detaches economics from its social context, Schumpeter takes the opposite course from the very beginning. A series of interesting studies bears witness to this truly catholic attitude.

The similarity between the Marxian and the Schumpeterian systems is obvious.[11] It may therefore come as a surprise that Schumpeter himself recognized the affinity between the two systems relatively late. Only in the second German edition of his *Theory of Economic Development*, which appeared in 1926, did he write on this topic:

> But the other two (changes in technique and in productive organization) require special analysis and evoke something different again from disturbances in the theoretical sense. The non-recognition of this is the most important single reason for what appears unsatisfactory to us in economic theory. From this insignificant-looking source flows, as we shall see, a new conception of the economic process, which overcomes a series of fundamental difficulties and thus justifies the new statement of the problem in the text. This statement of the problem is more nearly parallel to that of Marx.

For according to him there is an *internal* economic development and
no mere adaptation of economic life to changing data.

(*Theory*, 60n.)

In his preface to the Japanese edition of *The Theory of Economic Development* Schumpeter also refers to the affinity of his system with that
of Marx. He thinks that the reader will immediately recognize what
was not at all clear to him at the beginning, namely that the intention
to construct a theory of economic development which relates to forces
inherent in the economy is also the basis for the Marxian system.[12]

2 The process of industrialization in 'Imperial Austria'[*]

At the beginning of this chapter I mentioned certain historical circumstances, in particular the fact that the Austrian economy had
lagged behind the development of the West, which may have influenced the thinking of the young Schumpeter.

The factory system in imperial Austria had a comparatively late
start. It is true that industrialization made substantial progress before
1848 in certain parts of the Monarchy, especially in Bohemia,[13] but for
a number of reasons its tempo markedly increased after the revolution. Still, taking the nineteenth century as a whole, Austria must be
considered a laggard compared to most of the countries of Western
Europe.

Long before quantitative analyses were carried out, it had become
obvious, even to observers without economic training, that the Danubian Monarchy presented a typical example of slow industrialization.[14] Although the era of proto-industrialization had opened in Austria in the second half of the seventeenth century (that is, at a
comparatively early date), the frequent involvement in wars, the
counter-Reformation and the resulting expulsion of a great part of the
urban population, and, not least, the shift of the European trade
routes to the west proved heavy fetters on the further development of
an economy based on manufacturing and the putting-out system.
Even the large-scale reforms of Maria Theresa and Joseph II could
moderate but not overcome the state of economic backwardness that
had arisen.[15]

In England, where the feudal monarchy had made its exit by the
middle of the seventeenth century, there had been no basic conflict of

* By 'imperial Austria' we understand the Cisleithanian half of the Monarchy, which after the
so-called '*Ausgleich*' of 1867 bore the rather clumsy official name 'the Kingdoms and Lands Represented in the Reichsrat'.

interest between trading capital and industrial capital. Both classes of the bourgeoisie aimed at a rapid improvement of the infrastructure of the country; both recognized the necessity of developing the fleet on a large scale in order to be able to sell domestic and foreign products, and also slaves, in overseas markets with as little foreign competition as possible. This twofold purpose was supported by the landed aristocracy, in whose hands the governmental power was largely concentrated, because a century-long process had brought about a kind of symbiosis between it and the merchant class. In terms of historical materialism, in England production relations had developed which favoured the rapid development of the productive forces.[16]

Not so in Austria. Towards the end of the eighteenth century a number of antagonisms had arisen there: between the crown and the higher nobility allied to it, on the one side, and the bourgeoisie – or rather certain sections of the bourgeoisie – on the other. For the bourgeoisie was not at all a homogeneous social class, but formed a hodgepodge of social forces, a small minority within which – the financial bourgeoisie – supported the status quo, while the majority indulged in more or less Jacobin ambitions. The progressive sectors of the bourgeoisie often found allies among the senior bureaucracy, where traditions from the era of Joseph II were preserved well into the prerevolutionary period.[17] Thus none of the acute problems in the areas of politics and economic policy could be tackled: the liberation of the peasants which had begun under Joseph II, came to a halt; the customs machinery with which Austria had surrounded itself to prohibit the entry of foreign products remained in force; the customs barrier against Hungary was maintained; the guild system continued to limp along, unable to carry on or to die. Finally even Metternich felt obliged to protest – of course without success – against the Austrian state of mind which observed Germany's rapid economic advance with indifference and incomprehension.[18]

Thus it is hardly surprising that in Austria the transition to a factory system progressed at a rather slow pace. In any case, the starting position must be described as extremely unfavourable. With the exception of Vienna, which at the beginning of the nineteenth century had a population of about 200,000, there were no major urban centres. Also, consumption must have been very limited in the imperial capital, where a tiny number of aristocrats, upstart bankers and factory owners were confronted by a grey anonymous mass of small craftsmen, badly paid journeymen and *lumpen* proletarians who had come in from the countryside. Class antagonisms in the city, which was marked by the absence of a large, well-to-do middle class, are very aptly described in many of the plays of Johann Nepomuk Nestroy, especially in the farce *Zur ebenen Erde und im ersten Stock (At Street Level and on the First Floor)*, the very title of which expresses the harsh contrast between poor and rich. The radicalism of the Viennese population which suddenly surfaced in 1848, and which deeply impressed Marx and Engels, is rooted in this antagonistic class situation.[19]

During the entire pre-revolutionary period, industry and the crafts in Vienna were working mainly to satisfy the needs of a small but moneyed upper class. This was true of the approximately 500 silk manufactories, where machines were without exception operated by hand, and which on average employed but a handful of people – rarely, and then only temporarily, numbering more than 100. Velvet, damask, brocade, ribbons, silk shawls and other luxury textiles were mostly produced in other, even smaller workshops or manufactories. Only porcelain, furniture and fine metal products came, to some extent, from larger establishments. The products associated with a comfortable way of life also determined the taste of the lower classes, for whom so-called 'luxury goods' of cheaper quality were marketed. Subcultures thus emerged, during the Baroque and Biedermeier periods; they should not, however, be seen as an expression of protest, but rather as an adjustment to and an imitation of the way of life of people 'on the first floor'.[20]

Modern manufacturing methods, in the form of factories in which machines were operated by a source of energy other than that of beasts, were introduced in Austria about the end of the eighteenth century. The first factories, the great majority of which were cotton mills, were established in the valleys of Lower Austria and of the Sudeten countries (i.e., parts of Silesia, Bohemia and Moravia), which abounded in water power. The first steam engine in Austria was put into operation about 1815, but it remained an isolated and much-admired phenomenon until well into the 1830s. As late as the mid-nineteenth century there were only 50 stationary steam engines installed in factories in Austria, while Prussia had 260 such engines at that time.[21]

Techniques of modern metallurgy, too, were adopted only very hesitantly in Austria. The iron works of Wittkowitz, which had come into the possession of the Rothschild family at the beginning of the 1820s, introduced the puddling system in 1829. In the mid-1830s the same concern tried out the first coke-fired blast furnace. Similar efforts were initiated a few years later in Stará Hut in Bohemia, by an English

master mechanic, Edward Thomas, who combined smelting, puddling, and rolling works in one large metallurgical complex.[22] But it
was to take almost another fifty years for the coke-fired blast furnace
to gain a dominant position.[23] The situation during the 1880s was
described by Matis and Bachinger as follows:

> During the '80s conditions in heavy industry began to consolidate.
> By 1881 pig-iron production surpassed the level of output of 1873,
> thus overcoming a period of stagnation which had lasted for more
> than seven years. Thus the Austrian iron industry had remained
> relatively stagnant for almost a decade while its foreign competitors
> continued to expand in spite of the crisis.[24]

It is hardly an exaggeration to say that in the 1880s Austrian metallurgy was still almost a century behind its much-admired English
rival.

The markedly slow advance of the new iron technology was
ascribed to the fact that Austrian forest resources abounded. It is evident that coal remained a relatively expensive source of energy as long
as Austria lacked an efficient system of communication. Although the
Austrian government turned its attention to railway construction in
the 1840s, progress in this area was slow and unsatisfactory because of
a chronic dearth of public finance. When the Railway Licensing Act
was passed in 1854, guaranteeing interest payments to private enterprise and – in the event of a deficit – costs subsidies as well, a brief
period of intensive railway construction began. This was thanks primarily to the substantial financial backing of the Creditanstalt, the
first commercial banking house in Austria, founded by the Rothschild
interests in 1855. But it was only in the so-called 'Gründerzeit' (1867-73)
that a more or less integrated Austrian railway system was finally
established.[25]

Progress in the way of railway construction, the exploitation of new
coal deposits, the rapid spread in the use of the steam engine, and the
resulting large-scale shift from manual to mechanical methods of production are developments that give rise to, complement and reinforce
each other. Their close interconnection can be observed in earlier
decades in England, Belgium, and also, to some extent, in Germany
and in the Czech territory of Austria. In Austria at large this complex
development had come into play only in the 1850s. Unlike some
authors, I would therefore date the full flowering of the industrial age
in Austria as no earlier than the 1850s.[26]

But the faster growth of productive forces had become possible only because in 1848 the *ancien régime* ceased to exist in its offensive Metternichian backwardness. It is true that the crown, the higher nobility, the army and the bureaucracy remained the politically decisive forces even after the revolution, but they recognized at long last that the bourgeoisie had to be granted certain opportunities for development if the Monarchy was to be prepared for a new era, marked by a more rapid advance in the capitalist mode of production.

Liberal historiography presents the neo-absolutist regime as a variation on the old order, with only slight changes. In fact, the Crown and its counsellors tried to maintain Austria's position as a great European power with all the means available – a policy which not only inflicted humiliating defeats upon the Monarchy and finally made its collapse inevitable, but also imposed on the economy an almost intolerable financial burden. Moreover, efforts were made to administer the empire as a centralized state, although in the year of the revolution its heterogeneous national character had manifested itself more strongly than ever before. But this quixotic undertaking was bound to fail sooner or later, because the Hungarians, who could only be defeated with the armed assistance of Russia, opposed almost unanimously any administrative interference and direction from Vienna. The policy of external megalomania and undisguised internal repression naturally met with the sharpest criticism and was rejected by bourgeois chroniclers. For example, Waentig wrote: 'Much as people talked, in that period of fruitless experimenting, about a "political" system by which the country should be ruled, there was a complete lack of any such system, based on a thorough analysis of the actual conditions, which might have offered a prospect of lasting success.'[27]

But liberal historians have underestimated the reforming zeal of men like Bach, Bruck, Stadion, Toggenburg and others, and the systematic character of some of their reforms. In the autumn of 1848 the Austrian Reichstag, product of the first general elections, abolished the centuries-old feudal system of serfdom and thus integrated the peasants, who still at that time made up three-quarters of the population, into the nexus of the capitalist market economy. In 1850 the customs frontier between Austria and Hungary was abolished. Two years later Austria switched from the virtually closed economy established by Joseph II to a protectionist system. In 1853 a trade agreement was signed with the German customs union, the Zollverein, which Austria hoped would be the first step towards a customs union between the two countries. In the following year came the new

Railway Licensing Act, and in 1855 the founding of the Österrei-chische Creditanstalt für Handel und Gewerbe, closely modelled on the French Crédit Mobilier, which was intended mainly to finance the construction of an Austrian railway system and to foster large-scale industry. Toggenburg's trade regulations, the outlines of which were completed as early as 1856 but which became law only in 1859, may be considered the liberal reform law *kat exochen*: while on the one hand they decreed almost unlimited freedom of trade, on the other hand they made it a punishable act for workers to enter into agreements for the purpose of achieving better wages and working conditions.

After the defeat at Solferino, in 1859, the political climate deterio-rated and the era of great economic reforms came to an abrupt end. But the decade following the revolution had left such deep marks on Austria that the eminent Austrian statistician and economist Czoer-nig was to exclaim: 'Anyone who tries to judge the present situation of Austria by the standards of 1847 would be committing an enormous anachronism; such a judgement would be closer to the year 1758 than to that of 1858.'[28]

Before dealing with Austria's economic history in the second half of the nineteenth century, I want here to mention briefly the role of the entrepreneur in the genesis of Austrian capitalism.

Because in Austria capitalism took root at such a late stage, it was necessary to fill up the thin ranks of local entrepreneurs, and Maria Theresa and Joseph II encouraged the immigration into Austria of German industrialists, English master mechanics and Jewish finan-ciers and wholesalers. Joseph II's Edict of Tolerance, the secular-ization of the monasteries, the improvement in the legal position of Austrian Jews, the taking over of a number of large-scale manufacto-ries by the state and certain other mercantilist measures are to be seen primarily as steps to promote capitalism and the emergence of a national middle class. Although the capitalist mode of production was dominant by the middle of the nineteenth century, the proportion of foreigners among the Austrian entrepreneurs remained remarkably high. The career of a businessman seemed questionable, according to prevailing attitudes (largely determined by feudal values), despite the prospect of profits and material wealth. Certainly Austria did not lack entrepreneurial personalities, but these did not seem to be as numerous as in the older industrial countries. It could be said that in Austria entrepreneurs were so important because there were so re-markably few of them.

Those who agree with Professor Rudolph in finding no historical evidence of Austria's economic development being affected by the scarcity of entrepreneurial personalities, should bear in mind that almost every European country was hampered to some degree in the development of its productive forces by its feudal past. Even England, where capitalism had become established much earlier than in Austria, suffered until very recently by its feudal past. As Professor Habakkuk shows:

> There is a general argument . . . that the English social structure and English public opinion were less favourable than the American to the entrepreneurship, less favourable both to the recruitment of ability and to full exertion of ability once recruited. . . . In England, as, of course, in other countries of Western Europe, . . . there existed a strongly entrenched social system which limited social mobility, a social system inherited from pre-industrial times when landowners were the ruling group. Moreover, there were sources of power and prestige besides business. Landownership, bureaucracy, the army and the professions were all powerful competitors of business for the services of the able men. There was therefore a haemorrhage of capital and ability from industry and trade into land-ownership and politics.[29]

In a similar vein Professor Klima describes the situation in the most advanced industrial provinces, Bohemia and Moravia, in the first half of the nineteenth century:

> By far the greater proportion of the entrepreneurs in the machine-building industry in Bohemia and Moravia were foreigners, especially Germans and Englishmen. Their factories employed hundreds of workers, and formed the basis of an industry which was subsequently to expand greatly. In the textile industry, . . the great Bohemian and Moravian entrepreneurs of the first half of the nineteenth century were exclusively of German or Jewish background. Technical progress meant that the organizers of the textile and machine-building industries had to be found among a new breed of men. They needed to be liberated from the attitudes of the feudal period and to disregard the privileges which the owners of the great manufactories had once used. This was why the aristocratic owners of early manufactories were rarely able to effect the transition to mechanized and modern production.[30]

In the middle of the nineteenth century Austria's lag *vis-à-vis* France and Germany was not yet serious. Austria's per-capita consumption of iron was hardly less than that of the German customs union. Its cotton industry was definitely equal, if not superior, to that of Prussia or even of the German customs union. By about 1913, more than half a century later, the average income of employed persons in Germany was about 38 per cent higher than in the Austrian part of the Monarchy. But within Cisleithania there were considerable regional differences. In some of the industrial centres the average income may not have differed much from the German level, but on the whole, it can be said that after fifty years of capitalist development Austria had fallen considerably behind its western and northern neighbours.[31]

The data given here show clearly that Austria's industrial development proceeded relatively slowly in the second half of the nineteenth century. According to Kondratieff, Schumpeter and Hans Rosenberg, three long cyclical waves can be distinguished during that period, which manifested themselves more or less distinctly in all the larger Western and Central European countries. (This should not be seen, however, as an attempt to defend Kondratieff's broader theory of the general validity of long business cycles in the era of industrial capitalism.) A rather distinct long wave extends from the beginning of the 1850s to the fatal year of 1873. It is clearly marked by intensive railway construction and thus is sustained by very strong buoyant forces.

But in Austria those buoyant forces were not as effective as in the other industrial countries. This had several causes: first, financing the railways proved to be difficult in spite of the new Railway Licensing Act and the founding of the Creditanstalt. It is true that during the second half of the 1850s some important railway lines were built, especially to establish the urgently required connections with the western and eastern parts of the Monarchy. But towards the end of the decade railway construction came to a standstill because the new lines were not profitable, and had to claim government subsidies in order to maintain their guaranteed return on investment. The government, once again finding itself in an acute financial crisis, especially after Solferino, was unable to compensate by means of public projects for the loss of private initiative.[32]

The stagnation in railway construction at the beginning of the 1860s of course had unfavourable effects on mining and iron production. At that time metallurgy was said to be in acute crisis in Austria. Crises in two further sectors soon darkened the economic climate, namely in silk and cotton, caused by the loss of Lombardy and by the American Civil War and the resulting shortage of cotton. These recessionary influences were aggravated by the policies of the Minister of Finance, Ignaz von Plener, who tried to stabilize the currency situation by systematically curbing the circulation of banknotes.[33]

In the fateful year of 1866, the nadir was reached. The defeat at Königgrätz showed at long last that the government's absolutist and centralist policies were bound to produce only one result – the moral and physical bankruptcy of the empire.[34] The new and complex constitutional structure of 'dualism', patched up, literally, in great haste and behind closed doors by the crown, its closest counsellors and the representatives of the Hungarian higher nobility, came into effect as early as December 1867. As its realization hinged on the return to a constitutional system in Austria, its inauguration seemed to usher in an era of order and peace. The German Austrian bourgeoisie and the Hungarian nobility, the two main beneficiaries under the new order, thought they had found a sound basis for the continued existence of the Monarchy.[35]

This is not the place to examine the dual structure in detail.[36] In fact it produced two independent states, related to each other through several joint institutions – the crown, the army, the administration of foreign affairs and the currency. According to the Hungarian interpretation of 'dualism', economic policy was not among the affairs managed jointly, and therefore a customs and trade agreement had to be signed by representatives of the two states every ten years. It was quite natural for these periodically recurring negotiations to be marked by a growing militancy – especially on the part of the Hungarians, who acted with greater unity than the Austrians. As the very existence of the Monarchy was consequently under discussion at the end of each ten-year period, a witticism referring to the Monarchy as 'subject to notice' soon became current.[37]

The dual structure was not only the reason for growing tensions between Austria and Hungary; it barred the way to any solution that would have ensured a certain amount of political autonomy for the Slav population, which constituted the vast majority of the polyglot empire. It is no exaggeration to say that dualism led to the petrifaction of the political structure of Austria-Hungary. As Robert A. Kann, perhaps the greatest expert on the nationality problems of the Danubian Monarchy, has written: 'It can safely be said that the modest chance of a non-revolutionary solution to the vexed problem of integrating the peoples of the Monarchy was further reduced after Dualism had been put into effect.'[38]

But in 1867 the dire long-term consequences of dualism could hardly have been foreseen. The return to constitutionalism, the establishment of a purely bourgeois cabinet – the so-called '*Bürgerministerium*' – in the Austrian part of the Monarchy and the onset of a more favourable economic cycle paved the way for a boom the almost explosive vehemence of which had never before been observed in Austria. The material basis of the '*Gründerzeit*' (the period during which a particularly large number of business enterprises were founded), which lasted for a scant seven years, was railway construction, carried on with growing intensity at that time. Within the brief period 1867-73 the railways were extended to more than one and a half times their previous span, and the basic network completed.[39]

The sudden revival of railway construction, which had been stagnant until 1867, had an all but electrifying effect on the other branches of the economy. Coal-mining, iron production and mechanical engineering made particularly rapid progress during that period. At a later stage most sectors of the consumer-goods industry were caught up in the momentum of the upswing. At Vitkovice a technically advanced ironworks was built, on the basis of the Bessemer method, which was followed by similar plants in Graz, Kladno, Teplitz, Zeltweg and especially at Ternitz. The well-known metallurgist Tunner and his disciples Kupelwieser, Kerpely and Gängl gave decisive impetus to technological improvements in the coal, iron and steel industries in those years. But smelting using coke was generally adopted only at the end of the 1870s, after the introduction of the Thomas-Gilchrist process. As a consequence, the centre of the Austrian iron industry was shifted from the Alps to the Sudeten region, where deposits of both iron and coal were near at hand.[40]

The most intensive founding of businesses was in the field of banking. Until 1867, investment banking was limited to a few banks, among which the Creditanstalt held a dominant position. The bourgeois government, which professed with almost religious fervour to a liberal economic philosophy, unhesitatingly licensed new investment banks which tried to organize industrial activity in whatever field, in the form of joint stock companies. Very soon brokerage firms and stock exchange counters were initiated whose function was to encourage as many people as possible to gamble on the stock exchange. A part of the press which had close financial relations with the new banks kindled the flame of speculation with extravagant reports of the profits that would accrue to even the modest venture on the exchange. This was the first big wave of speculation to which the Austrian people succumbed and it brought unspeakable misery to its many victims after the crash of 9 May 1873. Most of the roughly 130 banks which had been established during the '*Gründerzeit*' vanished without trace in the muddy waters churned up by the crash.[41]

The political, economic and moral consequences of the 1873 collapse of the stock market were still being felt in the recent past. The ideas of liberalism had received a blow from which they have never fully recovered, at least in Austria. In 1867 a new millennnium had been foreseen, based on the inviolability of property, personal freedom and the free play of market forces. Seven years later the 'millennium' collapsed spectacularly. The anti-liberal Prague newspaper *Politik* seems to have recognized this very clearly on the day after 'black Friday':

> Our political antagonists have been favoured long enough by almost unprecedented good luck, but now it seems the time has come for them to pluck thorns rather than roses. . . . we have so far always been very strongly opposed in the field of economics by our political-national antagonists, the more so as they have viewed this field as their undisputed domain. . . . It is well known how great their sins were in that field and how they cultivated with special partiality and brashness the dangerous and poisonous plant of swindle. . . .[42]

The political currents which filled the intellectual vacuum caused by the demise of liberalism were all influenced to some degree by the trauma of 1873 and by the following years of depression. All displayed a militant anti-capitalist mentality. Only in the case of the social democrats, who had overcome their political teething troubles in the early 1870s, did the criticism of capitalism lead to clear social objectives.[43] The mass movements of small farmers and of the petty bourgeoisie combined anti-capitalist resentments with demands which amounted to a preservation of the status quo. It must be added that their agitation met with some success – reflected, for example, in the trade regulations of 1883 and 1885.[44]

In the course of time the pan-German movement too was caught up in the wake of an emotionally charged anti-capitalism, in which the terms 'capitalism' and 'Jewry' took on a monstrous identity, which was to bear horrible fruit only half a century later.

The year 1873 ushered in a new phase of economic development which came to an end only at the beginning of the 1890s. This new wave was guided by relatively weak innovative forces. The depression that ensued in 1873 caused serious setbacks in almost all areas. It was only towards the end of the decade that an upswing set in which continued at a rather leisurely pace into the 1880s. Although there were important innovations during that time – e.g., the new methods in the iron industry and in mechanical engineering, the beginnings of the electrical industry and the oil industry, and the rapid expansion of the sugar and textile industries – none of these could match the way the railway system had revolutionized the economy both technologically and commercially. Only in the 1890s did the Austrian economy enter once again upon a phase of rapid expansion that was to last until the eve of World War I.

The 1870s and 1880s brought a turning point in the policy that would govern economic events in Austria-Hungary until the outbreak of World War I. Towards the end of the Great Depression, following the example of Bismarck's Germany, the big landowners of Austria-Hungary entered into an alliance with heavy industry. This new constellation soon put an end to the brief episode of a liberal foreign trade policy, which had lasted for scarcely two decades.[45] At first the switch to protectionism had little effect on the agrarian price structure, because the Monarchy had a grain surplus until about the end of the century; consequently it had to sell its surplus on foreign markets at world market prices. It was only when it became necessary at the beginning of the twentieth century to import grain from abroad that the protective tariff had the effect intended by the big landowners. During the last years before the outbreak of World War I, when the grain deficit assumed considerable proportions, there was a serious increase in the cost of living and a dramatic deterioration in the balance of payments. This was a bad omen for a time of armed conflict with the Great Powers, who were provided with enormous supplies of foodstuffs or had easy access to them.[46]

High food prices had, of course, an unfavourable impact on the cost structure in industry and trade. In addition, the prohibitive tariffs in heavy industry, which came into effect in the 1880s, tended to set off a chain reaction, affecting Austrian industry as a whole. Expensive iron raised the production costs of machines, and expensive machines influenced unfavourably the price level in the consumer-goods industry. Such a policy was very likely further to intensify the traditional 'introversion' of the Austrian economy. The customs tariff of 1906 reached a level reminiscent of the bad old days of super-protectionism under early Austrian capitalism. It is hardly surprising that at the beginning of the twentieth century the Monarchy had the lowest ratio of foreign trade per capita of the population of any of the great powers of Europe, followed only at some distance by Tsarist Russia.

To make full use of the customs protection, the individual branches of industry organized themselves into cartels. The first of these was the railway cartel, formed in 1878 by the industrialist Carl Wittgenstein. A few years later the iron cartel was formed, comprising all the important branches of the iron industry.[47] The wave of associations reached a climax during the decade before the outbreak of World War I. At that time the initiative for streamlining the organization of Austria's large-scale industry came from the great commercial banks, which tried to safeguard their considerable industrial holdings by 'pacifying' the markets. In 1910 there were at least 120 cartels in Cisleithania; many of them extended over the entire territory of the Monarchy. There was then hardly another Western or Central European country in which cartels held such a dominant position in the economy as in Austria-Hungary.[48] Germany under Kaiser Wilhelm does not seem to have accomplished a comparable degree of concentration.

The high protective tariff, under whose umbrella the cartels prospered, found many defenders, among them such powerful popular leaders as Karl Lueger. In more recent times the Austrian historian Heinrich Benedikt has called the cartels a 'blessing' for the Austrian economy and attributes the economic upswing of the past decades mainly to the activities of these institutions.[49] I am inclined, however, to believe that the favourable economic situation at that time was the result not of protective tariffs and cartels, but developed in spite of them – in response to certain powerful upward forces that were worldwide.

Protective tariffs and cartels were not the only factors hampering progress. During the Great Depression the number of industrial associations increased, and small-scale producers also tried to avert the consequences of the crisis, wherever possible, by forming co-operative societies and other trade associations. In the brief period between 1873 and 1877 the number of registered co-operative societies and associations of co-operative societies rose from 169 to 1,114.[50] The movement of the 'little men' – as the petty bourgeoisie and the small farmers who were beginning to organize themselves into a political force came to be called – assisted by the German clerical and Feudal-Conservative parties, very soon began to assault the political and economic bastions of liberalism. In 1879 the liberal government was brought down. Its place was taken by the 'Iron Ring', a coalition government consisting of Polish landowners, Old-Czechs and Feudal-Conservatives, which led to a complete shift of power within the Austrian Reichsrat.

The new political constellation intensified the curious political twilight which seemed to prevail in the Monarchy during its last years of existence. The trade regulations of the 1880s encroached upon many of the liberal achievements and put handicrafts on a legally privileged, though not necessarily profitable, basis. The new protective labour legislation, designed on the model of Bismarck's Germany, was limited to factories and displayed an unmistakably anti-capitalist character. Finally, towards the end of the century a reform of the tax system was carried out which put the joint-stock companies at a great disadvantage compared with private companies or partnerships, and this impeded the formation of effective means of enterprise. But the counter-offensive of the anti-liberal forces could score only a partial success. The spread of the capitalist system could be hindered or even checked for some time, but it was never seriously jeopardized. The German scholar Waentig, in his book *Gewerbliche Mittelstandspolitik*, passes the following judgement on the attempts of the conservative latter-day Luddites:

> The result of half-hearted attempts and inconsistencies was that nobody was satisfied: not the government, because it had to pay for the achievement of its long-planned protective labour legislation with a number of not quite negligible concessions; nor the clerical conservative party because its feudalizing plans had been thwarted by the vigilance of the central power in spite of all apparent successes; nor the bourgeoisie because notwithstanding its success in removing any obligation on the part of large-scale industry to organize in the form of co-operatives, the new trade regulations were anything but a realization of the principle of economic freedom; nor the petty bourgeoisie because many of its programmatic demands had remained unfulfilled; and finally not the workers because they viewed what they had achieved as scant partial payment for years-long demands. . . . But a legal status which was not accepted as appropriate by any of the parties concerned, and furthermore was in contradiction to the general trends of economic development, could not possibly be the promised land which the process of industrial reform had aimed at throughout all those years.[51]

My analysis of the various factors hampering progress would hardly be complete without a mention of the conflict of the nationalities. We have already seen that the dualist solution was felt by the rising Slavs to be a straitjacket, because it barred the way to a comprehensive federalist reform of the constitution. To the foreign observer it may have seemed that the noisy conflict between German Austrians and Magyars over the periodic renewal of the customs and trade agreement threatened the continued existence of the Monarchy, but the two ruling nations were only playing a game which might during the days of the Cold War have been called 'brinkmanship'. In reality neither of the two parties was prepared to break off a relationship which gave it a privileged position within a hierarchically organized community. This was especially true for the Hungarian part of the Monarchy, where the Magyar minority flagrantly suppressed the national aspirations of the Slav peoples, who had been loyal subjects of the Habsburg empire since time immemorial. The result was that small and backward Serbia began to exercise a growing attraction for the Serbs, Croats and Slovenes living under the Monarchy. The Austro-Hungarian Ministry of Foreign Affairs became increasingly nervous as distinctly centrifugal tendencies emerged. Economic measures directed against Serbia during the last decade of the century – the so-called 'Schweinekrieg' (pig war) – were but one expression of the escalating tension in this area.

In November 1913, the economist and journalist Gustav Stolper drew attention to the fateful dimensions of the southern Slav problem:

> Its solution is the very basis of our official relationship with Hungary. For the Magyar nationality problem cannot be solved by a greater or lesser degree of tolerance on the part of the ruling aristocracy. It is the natural consequence of the unnatural fact that in the twentieth century a minority, by no means outstanding on the cultural level, rules over a majority of the population which is making rapid progress in the realm of culture. . . . But as soon as the nationalities in Hungary achieve full political equality – and the conflict will not end before this happens – the Dual Monarchy will lose its purpose . . . For the Germans in Austria there are only two options, the pan-German or the pan-Austrian alternative, between which, as matters are developing now, they will have to choose. . . . And if they want to fulfil their historical task of being the representatives of the Austrian state . . . they will have to accept the fact that there is a Slav majority in the population of the Monarchy with which they will have to find a *modus vivendi* according to that very Austrian concept of the state.[52]

I want to add to Stolper's statement only that there were strong currents within the Austrian bourgeoisie and even stronger ones within the working class of Cisleithania which advocated a *modus vivendi* with the Slav majority, and were always looking for a suitable constitutional framework; among the Magyar population, on the other hand, there were few supporters of a policy of understanding and accommodation with the southern Slavs.[53]

Did the nationalities policy of the two ruling classes in the Monarchy exert an unfavourable influence on the economic development of Austria-Hungary? This has often been asserted, but conclusive evidence for it has never been produced. It is true that the Hungarian government started to pursue an independent economic policy from the 1880s onwards, aiming at more rapid economic development of Transleithania. These endeavours at first met with only moderate success. Only in the last decade before World War I did the industrialization of the Hungarian part of the Monarchy make considerable headway; this did not, however, have an adverse effect on the steadily increasing volume of sales of Austrian industrial goods on the Hungarian market. It must also be noted that Austrian capital played a dominant part in the founding of industrial enterprises in Budapest and in other Hungarian cities during this period.[54]

The occasional boycotts of German Austrian goods, advocated predominantly by Czech nationalists, had only an ephemeral influence on the general economic development. Their main effect was to accelerate the emergence of an indigenous Czech bourgeoisie establishing itself in the sugar, beer and spirits industries. During the last decades of the period important Czech entrepreneurs also became prominent in mechanical engineering and in other capital goods industries.

In so far as the nationalities conflict had a negative effect on economic development, it was mainly caused, as I have said, by the foreign-trade policy of the Monarchy, which hampered the importing of agricultural products from the Balkans, or even blocked it completely. This led to drastic counter-measures by the countries concerned, which primarily affected Austrian industry. The embargo on Serbian and partly on Romanian agricultural products as well was inspired chiefly by representatives of the Hungarian landowners, who often held strategic posts in the Austro-Hungarian Ministry of Foreign Affairs. Economic aggression against Slav peoples struggling for national independence increased the tensions within the Monarchy, until finally the view became dominant among the Hungarian higher nobility that a military conflict over the Balkans was inevitable

– not least because this seemed the most effective, even though the most reckless, way of putting a lasting curb on the insubordinate Slav nationalities, especially in the Hungarian part of the Monarchy.

This is by no means a complete account of the forces that hampered progress, but will perhaps explain none the less why the period of upswing before World War I – the long wave of the 1890s and the first decade of the twentieth century – took full effect in Austria at a relatively late date. Only during the last decade of its existence did the Monarchy achieve a growth rate comparable to, and temporarily even exceeding, the rapidly expanding western nations. But a period of slightly more than ten years was too brief to reduce substantially the lead which the well-established industrial nations had attained over Austria.[55]

The favourable economic trends of the last decades before World War I need not be described in detail here.[56] The rapid spread of the capitalist system to other continents, the impetus of new industries such as the automobile, oil, electrical and chemical goods industries, the increasing urbanization of western civilization and the development of the urban infrastructure were among the most effective influences on the so-called 'belle époque'. In Austria, too, forces gradually made themselves felt which overcame the apathy that had prevailed during the Depression of the 1870s. The public, alarmed by certain bourgeois newspapers and by leading representatives of the regime, became increasingly concerned at the ever-widening gap between Austria and the more advanced western countries. The large banks were repeatedly urged to take a more active part in founding industrial enterprises.[57]

We do not know if the pressure of public opinion would have sufficed to bring about a change in the attitude of the Austrian haute finance. But during the late 1880s and the 1890s several factors led to the business of industrial promotion being seen in a new light: first, there was a steady improvement in the financial status of the Austrian government, and consequently a spectacular increase in its creditworthiness on the capital market. Bank loans to public authorities, hitherto a profitable form of investment, lost much of their appeal. Secondly, the steady and sometimes remarkably rapid growth of Austrian industry caused the banks to seek ever closer relations with their client firms. They therefore encouraged, and, when the opportunity arose, fostered the transformation of private enterprises into joint stock companies. As a result, they not infrequently retained a part of the share capital involved in such transactions. Thirdly, not only was there a 'pull' emanating from the banks in the direction of permanent relationships with promising client firms, but also a 'push' in the same direction coming from the firms themselves. It must be remembered that in imperial Austria the borrowing of capital in the form of mortgages and other long-term credits was very expensive, since interest payments were heavily taxed by the authorities. Industrial firms tended therefore to keep long-term indebtedness at a minimum, and to broaden their capital base through the issuing of shares.[58]

The leading financiers of the Danubian Monarchy, to whom fell the difficult task of advancing the industrial development of a large empire, were children of the nineteenth century. With few exceptions they adhered to economic doctrines inspired by the prophets of liberalism – Smith, Mill and Bentham. These men were convinced that neither the state nor the banking system could take the place of the creative individual; their task as they saw it was to provide the financial and institutional framework by means of which the spirit of enterprise, badly stunted in Austria, could at last develop freely.

But Austria's economic development during the 25 years before World War I bore precious little resemblance to the concepts of liberal economics. Without a large, well-to-do middle class and with a public that had lost all interest in investing in industry as a result of the repeated panics on the stock market, the banks were left holding a large proportion of the shares acquired in the course of their promotional activities.[59]

In time the top managers and large shareholders of the banks came to view the permanent possession of such shares and other industrial securities as a strategy offering certain obvious advantages despite its unorthodox character. During the upswing that started in the 1890s the securities portfolio came to be appreciated as a source of considerable and, more importantly, of permanent capital earnings. The close relationship with industrial enterprises based on equity holdings also resulted in an increase of turnover on current accounts with the banks, thus contributing to a rise in their income.

But apart from these 'tangible' advantages, the result of a close relation between industry and finance, many indirect (that is, quantitatively difficult to assess) advantages soon became manifest. The period of close interaction between the banks and industrial enterprises began, greatly adding to the power of a relatively small number of individuals. This process, which could be observed in Germany and elsewhere as well, in Austria had two special features: first, the new phase in banking policy coincided with the emergence of Austrian large-scale industry, which from its very early beginnings was thus under the patronage of bank capital; and secondly, the relationship between finance and industry was determined, to a much greater extent than in Germany, by the predominance of high finance.

'These investment banks', an expert on the Austrian banking system observed,

> with their enormous capital resources conduct all types of current banking business as well as industrial financing. Having no clearly defined limits to their operations, they become influential in all areas of production. Without their consent and co-operation almost no transaction requiring a major allocation of money and capital can be carried out. They virtually set the limits of the activity on the free capital market, whose central organization is the Vienna Stock Exchange. Their monetary, credit and investment policies are decisive for the prosperity of thousands of businesses and of whole sectors of the economy.[60]

One has to consider the decisive part the banking system played in the economy of the Danubian Monarchy during the last two decades before World War I, to understand fully the empirical core of Schumpeter's credit theory, namely that capital is 'a fund of purchasing power' and that 'credit serves industrial development' (*Theory*, 120, 102). The 'fund of purchasing power' which enabled the Austrian entrepreneur to divert the means of production from their former uses, thus forcing the economy on to new tracks, was provided during that period mainly by the large banks in the form of industrial credit.[61]

Schumpeter's credit theory has a second interesting aspect: the inflationary consequences of the 'development loans' granted by the banks. Schumpeter's explanation of the temporary inflationary effect of such credit is, of course, well known:

> in so far as credit cannot be given out of the results of past enterprises or in general out of reservoirs of purchasing power created by past development, it can only consist of credit means of payment created *ad hoc*, which can be backed neither by money in the strict sense nor by products already in existence. It can indeed be covered by other assets than products, that is by any kind of property which the entrepreneur may happen to own. But this is in the first place not necessary and in the second place does not alter the nature of the process, which consists in creating a new demand

for, without simultaneously creating, a new supply of goods.
(*Theory*, 106)

The thesis of the close, and one is almost tempted to say 'organic', connection between economic development and inflation – a brilliant observation of the young theorist – also has its roots in Austrian economic reality of the first decade of this century. The continuous rise in the level of prices[62] was in fact the most discussed economic phenomenon of the last years of peace in the Monarchy. Generally it was explained by the fact that during that period Austria was forced increasingly to import foodstuffs and raw materials from abroad and that as a result of the high agrarian tariffs the then rapidly rising world market prices made themselves strongly felt in the domestic market.[63] But it can scarcely be doubted that the upward trend of prices was also caused by the extremely rapid development of Austrian industry and its rising demand for raw materials and investment goods.[64]

In spite of the brisk development of the Austrian economy during the first decade of the century, the Danubian Monarchy must be said to have been a large 'underdeveloped' economic area on the eve of World War I. With its population of 52 million, Austria-Hungary was among the most densely populated of European nations, but its relatively scant industrial resources and the low standard of living of the great majority of its inhabitants rendered its claim to be a great power rather dubious. In view of the rudimentary statistics available on the national income at that time, comparisons with the income of other nations are rather problematic. Nevertheless, an impression of the modest standing of Austria-Hungary among the great powers can be gathered from Colin Clark's estimate that in 1913 the per capita income of the labouring population in Great Britain was about 51 per cent and in Germany about 38 per cent higher than in the Danubian Monarchy.[65]

But it must be borne in mind that regional differences in income were considerable within the Monarchy. The big industrial centres were mainly in the German-speaking parts of the country, in Styria, in Lower Austria, in Vorarlberg and especially in the northern and western parts of Bohemia. The industrialized regions of the Monarchy had a population of about 11.5 million, less than a quarter of the total population.[66]

3 The intellectual roots of Schumpeter's theory of the entrepreneur

I want now to give a survey of the process of industrialization from the point of view of its most important participants. During the eighteenth and the first half of the nineteenth centuries five representative groups were involved in the process of industrialization: the state, the feudal nobility, the merchants, the private bankers and the craftsmen.

In the eighteenth century the initiative was as a rule taken by the state, which either itself paved the way for industrial ventures or was supported in these efforts by the feudal nobility and the great merchants. To run the manufactories, which were set up in the big cities (Vienna, Linz) and in the flat countryside, craftsmen and master mechanics were often recruited from abroad. Some of these foreign specialists established themselves in Austria and became important entrepreneurs.[67]

The importance of the feudal nobility for the industrialization of Austria visibly decreased at the beginning of the nineteenth century, mainly because the direct encouragement given businesses by the state, through monopolies, privileges and subsidies, began then to be withdrawn. Moreover, as Professor Arnošt Klima has shown, the nobility was incapable of transforming and modernizing its enterprises in an age of more rapid industrialization.[68] One can only speculate today on the relative importance of the other main participants in the process of industrialization (merchants, bankers, craftsmen, master mechanics). One thing is certain: many important clothiers, owners of manufactories and large factories started out as merchants. Among these were the commercial and banking firm Fr. Schey & Co., which contributed substantially to the development of the silk industry in Vienna; the trading firm J.M. Miller & Co., founded by Josef Maria von Miller-Aichholz, who set up a number of enterprises in the sugar, cotton, lambswool and paper industries; the entire business of Alexander von Schoeller, who built up an industrial empire which has survived to the present day; the trading firms Biedermann and Todesco, pioneers in the Lower Austrian textile industry; and many textile producers from the Sudeten region such as Blaschka, Dittrich, Fuchs, Epstein and Pribram.[69]

Among private bankers were some names important in Austria's industrial history, notably the bank S.M. v. Rothschild, which played a leading role in the development of railways and heavy industry. Bankers of secondary importance, such as Sina, Stametz-Meyer, Arnstein & Eskeles, Königswarter, Biedermann (mentioned above among the merchants) and others often paved the way for important industrial establishments. But it would be wrong to believe that the trading firms and banks were of crucial importance to the industrialization of Austria. Generally these institutions had a rather conservative influence on economic development. Industrial establishments were – in spite of the Chinese wall erected by the pre-revolutionary customs system against the entry of foreign goods – an extremely risky undertaking. On the other hand, by handling government bond issues and granting loans to the great aristocratic families it was possible for banks to make huge profits often without much effort or risk.[70]

The ambivalent role played by merchants and bankers did not apply to craftsmen, mechanics and engineers, and the self-made captains of industry. The latter had nothing to gain from the preservation of feudal methods of production and everything to gain by altering them. This is how the famous Marxian phrase characterizing the rise from producer to capitalist as the 'really revolutionizing way' (*Capital*, vol. III) must be understood.

Austria's industrial history offers, of course, countless examples of this, perhaps the most famous being the Leitenberg family. It can be traced back to the master craftsman Johann Josef, who founded what would today be called a 'textile group' in northern Bohemia in the last quarter of the eighteenth century. The Liebig brothers, too, who built up in northern Bohemia during the nineteenth century one of the largest textile groups of the Monarchy, were the sons of a modest master clothier. In the linen industry the transition to the factory system was owed above all to the work of Johann Faltis, son of a small shopkeeper, who built a linen manufactory and a cotton weaving mill at Trautenau at the beginning of the nineteenth century. Adolf Mautner, the inventor of artificial yeast, also came from Bohemia. In the 1840s he founded a spirit and yeast-pressing factory as well as a brewery in Vienna and thus laid the foundations for the still existing Mautner-Markhof Group.[71]

Foreign technicians who founded important and durable enterprises in Austria included in particular the Englishman Thornton (textile industry), the Scotsman Skene (textile industry), a man from Vogtland, Sueß (leather industry), a man from the Rhineland, Thonet (furniture industry), and a man from Passau, Philipp Haas, who established the biggest carpet and damask enterprise in Austria. Of course, the 'little men' who became the founders of large industrial concerns also included people from the Alpine region. Josef Werndl, for example, the son of a smith at Steyr, founded the famous arms factory Steyr, one of the centres of European arms production in the nineteenth century. Johann Nep. Reithoffer (Lower Austria, rubber industry), Franz Mayr-Melnhof (Styria, iron industry), Thaddäus Berger (Lower Austria, silk industry), Martin Theyer (Vienna, fancy goods and paper processing) et al. were also founders of big industrial enterprises.[72] But it is remarkable how many foreign (especially German) entrepreneurs and people from the Sudeten region were among the industrial pioneers in the late eighteenth and early nineteenth centuries. In his study of the beginning of the machine-building industry in the Czech lands, Arnošt Klima mentions a number of German and English master mechanics as having established the first specialized workshops for the construction of spinning machines, water wheels, shearing machines and, in the last decades of the pre-revolutionary period, of steam engines. Outstanding men in this field were the Germans Jan Reiff (originally Würtemberg), Alexander Luz (also Würtemberg), the Dutch machine-builder Peter Comoth, and a number of English master mechanics, among them Edward Thomas, Thomas Bracegirdle, David Evans and Joseph Lee.[73]

In the second half of the nineteenth century the importance of the three types of entrepreneurs mentioned above declined. Among the founders of businesses in that period we repeatedly come across the heirs to large fortunes, lawyers, academically trained technicians and members and descendants of the upper bureaucracy. Interestingly enough, the number of foreign (especially German) entrepreneurs who joined the ranks of the Austrian capitalist class remained very high.[74] In this way certain circles of the Austrian haute bourgeoisie developed an almost exaggerated dependence on the large neighbour to the north, which unfortunately left a distinct mark, though less pronounced, on later phases of Austrian history. Around the turn of the century this servile attitude was expressed in an interesting article in the Neue Freie Presse, representative daily of the Austrian bourgeoisie:

If Austria wants to have a big, strong industry she will only get it from the Germans. . . . What terrible and fateful political foolishness it is to attack the Germans in Austria on moral grounds just at the time when the German people are impressing other nations with their industrial efficiency, as they did by their prowess in battle in France. Their importance has never been greater, because

only from them and through them can a substantial Austrian industry emerge, in the same way as Grillparzer and Lenau followed
Schiller and Goethe, inspired and stimulated by the German in-
tellect.[75]

Under the circumstances the antithesis between the entrepreneur
and the great mass of static producers was a matter of common experience in Austria; it was hardly less so in Germany, where the situation was similar until well into the second half of the nineteenth
century. The most remarkable anticipation of Schumpeter's theory
can be found in the book *Österreichs Wiedergeburt*, published in Vienna
in 1876, whose author, the German economist Max Wirth, spent
many years of his professional life in Austria:

> This process [i.e. the cyclical upswing] is a shift in equilibrium
> among the various branches of production, therefore also between
> production and consumption. In this connection one has to take
> into account that only a few productive personalities create new
> products and establishments, and that the great majority of pro-
> ducers conduct business as their fathers did, or only imitate the
> measures of a few ingenious originators. When a new product
> brings extraordinary profits to the original entrepreneurs, this
> usually rouses the jealousy and greed of other producers so that
> they will apply themselves in large numbers to the production of
> the new product or to the marketing of it.[76]

Max Wirth then explains the onset of the economic crisis through
structural changes occurring in the course of the economic upswing. It
is remarkable that he recognized – very much as did Schumpeter – the
close connection between the capitalist process of development and
the cyclical movement of economic activity.

Max Wirth's novel theory did not, so far as I know, arouse any
direct response in Austrian and German economic literature. At that
time the micro-economic approach had begun to captivate people's
minds, creating a rather unfavourable intellectual climate for the re-
ception of Wirth's ideas. Not until a generation later was the idea of
the 'creative entrepreneur' again broached in the literature. Viewed
under the heading of the 'history of economic thought', the starting
point for the later discussion seems to have been the teachings of J.B.
Say.[77] Actually two factors rooted in contemporary history probably
had a much greater influence on economics: the growing need of the
bourgeoisie to 'surround the leading entrepreneurs with an aura of
heroism'[78] and mounting academic attempts at refuting Marxian poli-

tical economy.

Two distinguished economists and sociologists with whom Schumpeter was in personal contact largely anticipated his concept of the entrepreneur. In one of his essays Werner Sombart calls the entrepreneur 'the inventor of new modes of production, of transport and of distribution, the discoverer of new markets, the conqueror and organizer . . .'.[79] The great Austrian scholar F. Wieser expressed similar views in his lectures at the University of Vienna in the years before World War I.[80] It is uncertain if the theories of the French sociologist Gabriel Tarde, in vogue at the beginning of the twentieth century, were also important for the genesis of Schumpeter's theory. (Professor Lange denies this in a letter to the present author: 'My impression was', Lange writes, 'that Schumpeter did not know Tarde's work.')[81]

Fritz Redlich has referred in an interesting essay to the *'Geschichtsphilosophie des Helden'*, which 'immunized' a 'younger generation of German scholars' against the influence of Mill and Comte. In Dilthey's philosophy of history, Redlich adds, 'the outstanding individual became almost the basis of the historical process'.[82] Anyone who knew Schumpeter personally can testify that he had a thorough knowledge of theories of the élite of the late nineteenth century (Nietzsche, Pareto, Mosca, Michels, Le Bon) and took pleasure in flirting with such ideas. The conclusion suggests itself that his own theory of development was an attempt to give concrete economic substance to the vague theories of his time.[83]

4 Marx and Schumpeter

I have repeatedly mentioned the relationship of the Schumpeterian system to Marx's ideas. (See Chapter 1 for a detailed treatment of this subject.) There is no doubt that in his youth Schumpeter thoroughly studied Marxian theories. In many of his articles and in his best-known work, *Capitalism, Socialism and Democracy*, he refers repeatedly to the Marxian system and to fundamental problems of socialism.[84]

Although he dissociated himself from many aspects of Marxian theory (especially from the theories of exploitation, pauperization and increasing malfunctioning of the capitalist system), Schumpeter never failed to pay the deepest respect to the dynamic overall conception of Marx. In the work mentioned above he calls the theory of historical materialism 'one of the greatest individual achievements of sociology to this day' (*Capitalism*, 10). But an expression of even deeper respect was the fact that he incorporated many Marxian elements (accumulation, concentration, economic development by way of cyclical fluctuations, etc.) into his own system.

The affinity of the Schumpeterian system with that of Marx is, however, much closer than Schumpeter may have imagined at the outset. Even his basic notion, that capitalism has an inherent tendency towards innovation and that the innovator, by virtue of his achievement, gains a temporary monopoly position which becomes the source of profits, was repeatedly – and with admirable clarity – stated by Marx. I want first to quote a passage from the popular essay *Wage Labour and Capital*:

If now, by a greater division of labour, by the utilization of new machines and their improvement, by more profitable and extensive exploitation of natural forces, one capitalist has found the means of producing with the same amount of labour or of accumulated labour a greater amount of products, of commodities, than his competitors, if he can, for example, produce a whole yard of linen in the same labour time in which his competitors weave half a yard, how will this capitalist operate?   The capitalist will not, however, sell a whole yard as cheaply as his competitors sell half a yard, although the production of the whole yard does not cost him more than the half yard costs the others. Otherwise he would not gain anything extra but only get back the cost of production by the exchange. His possibly greater income would be derived from the fact of having set a larger capital into motion, but not from having made more of his capital than the others. Moreover, he attains the object he wishes to attain, if he puts the price of his goods only a small percentage lower than that of his competitors. . . . However, the *privileged position* of our capitalist is not of long duration; other competing capitalists introduce the same machines, the same division of labour, introduce them on the same or on a larger scale, and this introduction will become so general that the price of linen is reduced not only *below its old*, but *below its new cost of production*. . . . We see how in this way the mode of production and the means of production are continually transformed, revolutionized, how *the division of labour is necessarily followed by greater division of labour, the application of machinery by still greater application of machinery, work on a large scale by work on still a larger scale*. That is the law which again and again throws bourgeois production off its old course and which compels capital to intensify the productive forces of labour, *because it* has intensified them – the law which gives capital no rest and continually whispers in its ear: 'Go on! Go on!' This law is none other than that which, within the fluctuations of trade periods, necessarily levels out the price of a commodity to its *cost of production*.[85]

We know that Schumpeter, much like Marx, tried to formulate a general theory of economic development. Although at the beginning he was not aware of his intellectual affinity with Marx in this 'broader' sense (compare the passage on this question in his *Theory of Economic Development*), it seems plausible to assume that his early contacts with such prominent socialist theorists as Otto Bauer, Rudolf Hilferding and Emil Lederer deeply influenced his theoretical thinking. While in the period before World War I the Austrian marginal utility school was dealing mainly with problems of value, interest and distribution, the younger generation among the Marxist theorists passionately discussed the prospects for the development of capitalism. Bauer's and Grossmann's contributions to the breakdown theory, Hilferding's *Finanzkapital* and the works on modern imperialism by Rosa Luxemburg, Bukharin and Lenin reflected this long intellectual struggle.[86]

Schumpeter's view was that the trend towards innovation (in Marxian terms, the tendency towards the transformation of surplus value into capital, i.e. towards accumulation) can be found in more or less pronounced form at any stage of social development. Innovation, he held, is a trait inherent in economic life. But Marx (and the school of historical materialism founded by him) saw this trait or 'characteristic' not as a general but a *historical* category. It is, of course, true that man is faced in all social formations with the task of harnessing the natural forces; in fact, the embodiment of man depends on the degree to which this task is accomplished. The development of the productive forces is indeed the *primum agens* of the entire social process. But the millions and millions of farmers, craftsmen, engineers and scientists who have altered man's natural environment over the past thousands of years, and have received fresh impulses for the further development of the productive forces from the thus created 'artificial' environment, have done this only exceptionally with a view to achieving social ascendancy and attaining a powerful position in society. In pre-capitalist times ambitions of this kind had to be achieved through quite different methods.

The capitalist mode of production is the result of a great, century-long transformation (to use Karl Polanyi's famous dictum). Marx and Engels have not left us a systematic analysis of the period of transition from feudalism to capitalism. But in Marx's main work *Capital* and in the historical essays by Engels are many passages which provide insight into the decisive phases of that transition. Basing themselves on the suggestive work of Marx and Engels, Maurice Dobb, Paul M. Sweezy, Christopher Hill, E.J. Hobsbawm and other contemporary Marxists have made important contributions towards analysing the problems of the period of transformation.[87] Non-Marxian authors like Polanyi and Fernand Braudel have acknowledged their indebtedness to the Marxian school of historical development.

As we have seen, many contemporary authors, not as a rule those inspired by Marx, took a critical view of the Schumpeterian theory of development. In these circumstances it comes as no surprise that Schumpeter's influence on the current discussion of the ultimate driving force of economic development has been all but negligible in the West as well. One is tempted to observe that it was not Schumpeter who stimulated the fashionable discussion of development problems, but, quite to the contrary, the current discussion that has revived interest in his brilliant essays. Since the mid-1970s when the long post-war boom came to an end, Schumpeterian theory has been looked at afresh with a view to determining more clearly the role of the innovator in the process of capitalist production. In particular, Schumpeter's *Business Cycles* and his *Capitalism, Socialism and Democracy* have inspired a number of provocative policy contributions. Christian Seidl as well as others have held that Schumpeter must be counted among the founding fathers of modern supply-side economics.[88] Be that as it may, Schumpeterian economics is no longer in need of artificial respiration, as was the case in the long era of Keynesian-inspired economics.

1964/1983

Chapter 4

The Modern Theory of Imperialism

Lenin's theory of imperialism was the result of a year-long debate among prominent Marxist theorists on the left wing of the Second International: Hilferding, Bauer, Luxemburg, Bukharin and, last but not least, Lenin – who in his book *Imperialism, the Highest Stage of Capitalism*, wove the most important contributions to this discussion into a theoretical system of revolutionary impact.[1] It is worth noting that the Marxist theory of imperialism received a decisive impetus from J.A. Hobson, who may be seen as a forerunner of J.M. Keynes and the school of the liberal welfare state.[2]

In chapter 7 of his study Lenin characterized the main features of imperialism as follows:

> (I) the concentration of production and capital has developed to such a high stage that it has created monopolies which play a decisive part in economic life; (II) the merging of bank capital with industrial capital, and the creation, on the basis of this [finance capital], of a financial oligarchy; (III) the export of capital as distinguished from the export of commodities acquires exceptional importance; (IV) the formation of international monopolist capitalist combines which share the world among themselves; (V) the territorial division of the whole world among the biggest capitalist powers is completed.   (*Imperialism*, 525)

For a better understanding of Lenin's theory, two further points should be raised: the significance of capital export is explained by the fact that in the more advanced countries a 'huge capital surplus' has been built up, the ultimate cause of which is the 'unevenness of development' and the 'wretched state of the masses'. As if to support the thesis of 'capital surplus', Lenin adds that capitalism has become 'overripe' in some countries. (Ibid., 494-5) Some authors have concluded from this that he was trying to link the phenomenon of capital export to the Marxian hypothesis of the tendency of the rate of profit to fall. Finally, an essential point, Lenin saw an 'interrelationship of opportunism in the workers' movement and the imperialist features of English capitalism' (ibid., 545). He thought – in close agreement with Engels – that the bourgeoisie would be able to buy a proletarian upper class, the labour aristocracy, by means of the excess profits from the colonies.

Since it was formulated 70-odd years ago, Lenin's theory has been the subject of a long series of essays aiming at replacing one element or another to make its basis stronger, or, proceeding from anti-Marxist positions, to call into question the whole theoretical edifice. What follows is an attempt to set forth some of the issues over which bourgeois and Marxist opinions have divided.

To begin with a frequently posed historical problem: Is there any point in speaking about a phase of imperialism dominated by monopoly or finance capital? Lenin's view on this was affirmed, by and large, by Marxists of all shades.[3] The conditions of dependence have, of course, become more complex and less transparent in the post-war period since the rupturing of colonial ties. With regard to the time scale of imperialism, the bourgeois approach follows three main lines of thought. In one, the school of Social Darwinism proceeds on the assumption of the predatory instincts of the human herd and views modern imperialism (tanks and atomic bombs instead of clubs) as a technologically induced variety of a basically timeless socio-biological behaviour.[4]

In his theory of imperialism Schumpeter too ascribes to instinctive behaviour such as bellicosity and aggressiveness an important role in imperialist policies. He speaks explicitly of the existence of 'an arational, irrational, purely instinctive inclination to war and conquest'.[5] Unlike the Social Darwinists, however, he does not view these inclinations as biologically given but as 'acquired dispositions', rooted in certain social conditions of life, which have a tendency to consolidate as 'lasting types' and to go on existing even under altered circumstances. According to Schumpeter, imperialist wars differ from other wars in that they do not pursue a particular interest, materialistic or other, but as a rule degenerate into limitless expansion – 'conquest for its own sake'. Those who desire this expansion are always ruling classes whose main business is war and who are able to maintain their social power only through permanent warfare.

It is relatively easy for Schumpeter to prove that in most social structures of the past – he mentions nomadic peoples, slavery, feudalism and its various intermediate forms – there is an inherent disposition for a class of professional warriors to form and to function. The matter becomes more difficult when he comes to deal with 'modern imperialism', which Schumpeter treats as a special case. Here he faces the problem that while seeing the bourgeoisie (as well as the farmers) as a basically peaceful social class,[6] at least not oriented towards 'boundless expansion', he still has to explain the phenomenon of imperialism as being rooted in capitalism, a fact which he does not deny. Nor can he deny that this involves very solid, entirely concrete material interests, which he – like the Marxists – attributes to the replacement of competitive forms of business by 'trusts and cartels'.

Here, as so often, Schumpeter's relationship to Marxism turns out to be ambivalent. In his opinion the Marxists, especially Hilferding and Otto Bauer, had by then (1953) made the most serious contribution to revealing the class interests behind the imperialistic conflicts of the late nineteenth century;[7] yet, he continues, they had missed the ultimate cause of the phenomenon. For in reality, the emergence of trusts and cartels is not a tendency immanent in capitalist development; rather, they are the upshot of the protective tariff policy of the great powers, which is thus at the root of the causal connection. This is what led to the emergence of monopolies in the first place and, as a result, to 'export-monopolistic interests' charged with a high conflict potential which would not have existed in the peaceful world of free trade.

But what was the origin of the sudden wave of protectionism which seized the leading capitalist countries in the last quarter of the nineteenth century? Schumpeter's answer is as clear as it is unconvincing: he thinks that the prime mover is to be found not in the bourgeois-capitalist classes proper, but in the ruling classes that arose in the principalities of the mercantilist period, whose actions and beliefs, with their 'ingrained' disposition to war and expansion, were still in force in the new epoch. Schumpeter sees these qualities not as an ideological survival without a real social basis, but as the very concrete emanation of the, to his mind, still strong position of the aristocracy and the landowners in the prevailing social system: 'The present social pyramid is not composed of the material and laws of capitalism alone, but of two different kinds of social material and of the laws of two different eras.'[8]

It is not difficult to show the weaknesses of this none the less brilliantly argued position. Schumpeter does not explain why the ideas of a previous epoch should have asserted themselves at a late phase of the following epoch instead of becoming weaker in the course of time, as one would normally expect. His thesis of the double pyramid, which may to some extent be applicable to Germany, Russia and Austria, is completely inapplicable to England and America. So it is only logical that, in order to keep to his idea of a 'pacifist bourgeoisie', Schumpeter views British policy as predominantly defensive, serving only to protect the already acquired empire. At the same time, though in a different context, he stresses the aggressive element in the bourgeois consciousness – which is theoretically compatible with the above idea, but does not render his interpretation more plausible from a socio-psychological point of view.

Another serious weakness of Schumpeter's theory of imperialism is the focusing of its economic analysis on the interest of monopolistic exporters in exploiting the price gap between the protected home market and the world market. 'Export at dumping prices' becomes the be-all and end-all of the imperialist trade policy; the much more important aspects of capital export and the struggle for sources of raw material are mentioned only incidentally, and no effort made to integrate them into the analysis. As will be shown, the great imperialist conflict was over the sharing out of the African and Asian territories still free of colonial rule during the last quarter of the nineteenth century; what was at stake was not so much the opportunity to dump products produced at home as the drive to acquire and defend *protected* markets in new colonies and spheres of influence. .

As noted, Schumpeter's theory of imperialism proceeds from the conception of a pre-capitalist ruling class motivated by the abstract urge to conquer. It is thus in strange contrast to his theory of economic development, represented – as Schumpeter never tires of repeating – by a bourgeois class marked by the 'will to succeed' and the 'will to fight'. It seems paradoxical to ascribe to a feudal social class in the process of dissolution qualities such as chauvinism, a sense of mission and outward aggression, while at the same time attributing to the bourgeoisie a purely defensive attitude in relation to foreign affairs. The connection between outward aggression and the existence of very substantial material interests had already, incidentally, been described by Hobson with exemplary clarity:

Finance manipulates the patriotic forces which politicians, soldiers, philanthropists, and traders generate; the enthusiasm for expansion which issues from these sources, though strong and genuine, is irregular and blind: the financial interest has those qualities of concentration and clear-sighted calculation which are needed to set imperialism to work. An ambitious statesman, a frontier soldier, an overzealous missionary, a pushing trader, may suggest or even initiate a step of imperial expansion, may assist in educating patriotic public opinion to the urgent need of some fresh advance, but the final determination rests with the financial power.[9]

A number of economic historians and other social scientists have, while affirming the existence of a capitalist motive for imperialism, rejected as implausible the arguments Lenin put forward on behalf of a special monopoly–capital stage of development, thought to have started in the '70s of the past century.

Objections of this kind have been formulated with particular poignancy by W.H.B. Court, a British economic historian. Court thinks that the export of capital, seen by Lenin as a constituent feature of the imperialist period of capitalist development, was of considerable economic importance as early as the *first* half of the nineteenth century – that is, under the auspices of competitive capitalism:

> Lenin's book was written largely out of continental experience. Great Britain, however, as the largest foreign investor known, is the best test of this theory. He takes no account of the very large investments of the first half of the nineteenth century in an age when the economic organization of England was intensely competitive and colonial expansion much out of fashion with its people.

Then Court adds:

> Great Britain in the last century lent enormously, long before her industry or her credit system showed the least tendency in the world towards monopoly; but had there been no openings abroad for her capital, much of that capital would never have been saved at all. She had much to lend, because she lent indefatigably; only the economic developments abroad made possible by her loans brought about the further increases in her wealth out of which new loans were raised.[10]

I do not believe that Lenin would have tried to refute this analysis, because it would hardly have been unknown to him that in the railway era (that is, as early as the first half of the nineteenth century), capital export had become a new and increasingly important source of income for finance capital – which until well into the second half of the nineteenth century was provided mainly by Great Britain. Again, Lenin would hardly have shut his eyes to a second observation, that in England monopoly capitalism took root relatively late: 'The emergence of monopolistic firms in Britain was slow before the 1920s, yet most of the foreign capital in the world, at least before 1914, was British.'[11]

But if it is true that capital export was carried on by British finance capital relatively early, and moreover that it took on its most distinctive form in the pre-monopolistic phase of development,[12] can Lenin's theory of imperialism, as expressed in the five points mentioned above, be seen as plausible? Such doubts are confirmed when we note that the lion's share of the colonies annexed by the Great Powers in the last third of the nineteenth century fell to Great Britain.[13] Thus it was, paradoxically, the Great Power in which the tendency towards monopoly had been the least pronounced that pursued the imperialist policy of expansion most consistently.

Lenin saw modern imperialism, however, as a world system the inherent laws of which became effective simultaneously, in a greater or less emphatic form, in all industrially developed countries. The Great Depression of the 1870s was the first worldwide crisis of capitalism and was felt especially in the more recently industrialized countries like Germany, Austria-Hungary and the United States. Accordingly, far-reaching structural changes occurred particularly in the economies of these countries. The system of *laissez-faire* was replaced more or less promptly by 'organized capitalism' or 'monopoly capitalism'. This process was accurately described by Rudolf Hilferding and a number of other authors extensively cited by Lenin in his work on imperialism.[14]

More recently, Hans-Ulrich Wehler has described the economic and political impact of the Great Depression in Germany in these poignant words:

> Six years of the most severe economic depression were then followed in 1878-9 by the bitter quarrel over the protective tariffs, over the new conservative course of the Reich government, over the purge of the liberal bureaucracy and over the plans for state monopolies in industry. At the same time the National Party disintegrated, whereas the Social Democrats grew stronger each year.

Finally Bismarck recognized the integrating force of an imperialist policy:

Around 1880 Bismarck discovered the potential of overseas policy, both as a long-term integrating factor which helped to stabilize an anachronistic social and power structure, and as a tactical electoral gambit. He recognized that imperialism could provide a new objective for the Germans; he hoped 'to steer [the Germans] towards new paths' abroad, away from the numerous problems at home. Thus imperialism became an integrative force in a recently founded state which lacked stabilizing historical traditions and which was unable to conceal its sharp class divisions.[15]

The Great Depression seemed at first to have caused fewer structural changes in France than in Germany or in Austria-Hungary. But as so often in European history, the theoretical genius of the French proved more 'precocious' than that of its neighbour and rivals. In 1874 the well-known economist Paul Leroy-Beaulieu wrote in *De la colonisation chez les peuples modernes* – a book which won considerable recognition and acceptance in France as well as outside – that colonization was one of the most important functions of a country at an advanced stage of civilization; and in the Preface to the second edition of his book (1882) he argued that 'the true sinews of colonization are capital funds rather than emigrants. For France', he continued, 'colonization is a matter of life and death; France will either become a great African power, or in a century or two she will be no more than a secondary European power.' It was the French statesman Jules Ferry who later translated Leroy-Beaulieu's ideas into action.[16]

Influences of this kind also took root in Great Britain. It is true that until the end of the nineteenth century England stuck to the policy of free trade to which it owed its enormous economic rise. But as Michael Barratt Brown shows, the new imperialist policy was a suitable means of defending Britain's world-wide free trade: 'When Britain's world monopoly was challenged, the actual control of territory became increasingly important, to anticipate the moves of the rivals.'[17] Of course, the influence of personalities like Cecil Rhodes, who extracted a huge fortune from his African mines and the blacks sweating in them, on British expansion can hardly be overestimated; but Ensor is right that large strategic considerations figured in the agreements concluded in the 1890s, on the basis of which Africa was carved up politically among the Western European powers and Germany.[18] It must be added that Britain forced through this division so favourable to its own capital interests at a time when it had virtually lost the industrial dominance it had held for decades. 'This is a situation', Hilferding wrote four years before the outbreak of World War I, 'which must considerably aggravate the conflict between Germany and England and their satellites, a situation heading towards a violent solution.'[19]

Occasionally it is claimed that the annexation movement of the late nineteenth century was a 'poor' bargain because the annexing countries soon realized that most of the newly-won Asian or African territories were relatively poor in raw materials and were markets with a limited capacity to absorb foreign goods. This shows, it is usually added, that one does not get very far with a purely economic approach to such a complex problem. But it is questionable whether the annexation of South Africa, Rhodesia, the Congo and parts of West Africa can be called a bad bargain. The main point, however, is that already mentioned by Ensor: the establishment of a colonial empire requires a strategy that takes into account political and military aspects as well as purely economic considerations. In retrospect, the acquisition of one colony or another, or even of a large amount of unlawfully acquired territory might prove a 'loss', but this would hardly disturb those who profit from colonial property, because the costs of administration and defence of the empire is borne by the community as a whole – that is to say, not only by the inhabitants of the 'mother country', but also by those of the colonies.[20]

The argument that imperialism is a 'bad bargain' is related to the objection frequently raised that Lenin's theory attaches too much importance to the export of capital to underdeveloped countries and as a result overlooks the fact that a high percentage of the capital of the 'mother countries' will have been invested in industrially advanced nations. Thus one of the more recent critics of the theory writes, apropos the views expressed by Herbert Feis in *Europe, The World's Banker, 1870-1913*, that only about 25 per cent of the capital exported by Great Britain before World War I can be considered as investment of the 'colonial' type; and that more than half the capital invested abroad by France and Germany was exported to other European countries.[21]

But Lenin did not misjudge the complex character of the capital export of the leading imperialist nations, as the following passage shows very clearly:

How is this capital invested abroad distributed among the various countries? *Where* is it invested? Only an approximate answer can be given to these questions, but it is one sufficient to throw light on certain general relations and connections of modern imperialism.

Distribution (Approximate) of Foreign Capital in
Different Parts of the Globe (*circa* 1900)

	Great Britain	France	Germany	Total
	(000,000,000 marks)			
Europe	4	23	18	45
America	37	4	10	51
Asia, Africa and Australia	39	8	7	44
Total	70	35	35	140

The principal spheres of investment of British capital are the
British colonies, with large investments also in America (for
example, Canada), not to mention Asia, etc. In this case, enormous
amounts of capital go chiefly to the larger colonies. . . . In the case
of France the situation is different. French capital exports are invested mainly in Europe, primarily in Russia (at least 10,000,000
francs). This is mainly *loan* capital, government loans, and not
capital invested in industrial enterprises. Unlike British colonial
imperialism, French imperialism might be termed usury imperialism. In the case of Germany, we have a third type; colonies are considerable, and German capital invested abroad is divided chiefly
between Europe and America.   (*Imperialism*, 497)

Here it becomes clear that the imperialist policy of annexation – as
Lenin sees it – involves not merely the incorporation of underdeveloped agricultural areas by the industrially more developed nations.
Lenin stresses this point in his polemic against Kautsky's theory of
imperialism:

This definition is worthless because it is one-sided, *i.e.* it deals arbitrarily with the national question only . . . arbitrarily and *incorrectly*
it connects this question *solely* with the industrial capital in
countries which annex other nations; in an equally arbitrary and
incorrect way it pushes into the forefront the annexation of agrarian
regions.   (ibid., 527)

And, to make certain of being understood, Lenin goes on:

The characteristic feature of imperialism is precisely that it strives
to *annex not only* agrarian but also the most highly industrialized
regions (the German designs on Belgium; the French on Lorraine),
first, because the fact that the world is already divided up makes it

necessary, in the event of a *re-partition*, to reach out for *any* kind of territory, and second, because an essential feature of imperialism is the rivalry among a number of great powers striving for hegemony, that is, each seizing territory, not so much for its own direct advantage as to weaken its adversaries and undermine *their* hegemony. . . .   (ibid.)

As I have said, Lenin regards capital export as a constituent element in modern imperialism. In this respect, too, he follows Hobson. The main cause of such export, he indicates, is the 'huge capital surplus' which develops under the conditions of the monopoly capitalist mode of production. This leads me to one of the most difficult and perhaps most controversial hypotheses of Lenin's theory.

Although Lenin does not quote directly Hobson's thesis as to the inequality in distribution of incomes under monopoly capitalism, his reference to the 'starvation of the masses' may be understood in this sense. From here the path leads to the Marxian theory of crises, which we cannot go into here. I agree with Sweezy that it is to be seen mainly as a 'theory of underconsumption',[22] summed up in the following frequently quoted observation: 'The ultimate reason for all real crises always remains the poverty and the restricted consumption of the masses as opposed to the drive of capitalist production to develop the productive forces as though only the absolute consuming power of society constituted their limit' (Marx, *Capital*, III. 484).

The periodic trade crisis (or recession) is, of course, a phenomenon that has accompanied industrial capitalism since its earliest days.[23] Thus it would hardly be logical to argue for a causal connection between the crises of underconsumption occurring at more or less regular intervals in the past and modern imperialism. The depression of the 1870s was, however, not a conventional trade crisis but a deep rift in the development of world capitalism which, as I have noted, led to the monopolistic restructuring of the economies of the industrially developed countries.[24] Endeavours were made to cope with the depressing, and, as was at one time believed, permanently cramped state of the domestic market by means of two strategic weapons: protective tariffs, which were intended to provide a barrier against foreign competition, and the establishment of a privileged position in foreign markets, where efforts were increasingly directed towards selling capital goods. Annexed areas are, of course, well suited for establishing such a privileged position. This is certainly one, though not the only, reason for the competition among the industrial nations over the still unclaimed overseas territories in the last quarter of the nineteenth century.

The world depression lasted until well into the 1880s. Monopoly capital in its various aspects – giant corporations resulting from mergers, cartels, branches of industry with oligopolistic structures – has since taken possession of almost every area of the economy. A number of Marxist authors, among whom I would mention particularly Baran, Magdoff and Sweezy, have analysed Lenin's theory of the close interrelation between monopoly capital and the export of capital. Baran and Sweezy in particular rely on the pioneering study by Joseph Steindl, *Maturity and Stagnation in American Capitalism* (1952). Steindl's theory can I think be condensed into the following basic thesis: Under conditions of free competition, capacity shortages and surpluses can be eliminated fairly easily by the free play of the market mechanism. The amount of profits realized will always be sufficient to produce the savings required for planned investment. Not so under conditions of monopoly capitalism, in which, as price competition is largely eliminated, a tendency develops towards over-capacity and excess profit.[25]

A retarded rate of investment and chronic over-capacity doubtlessly increases the tendency towards capital export, but these are not, according to the authors mentioned above, the primary cause of the perpetual efforts of the giant corporations to find new investment opportunities in foreign markets. For the export of capital, Baran and Sweezy argue, has in the long run proved to be a method 'of pumping surplus out of underdeveloped areas, not as a channel through which surplus is directed into them'.[26] This was demonstrated by the British economist Alec Cairncross, who showed that Great Britain's income from foreign investment totalled £4.1 billion in the years 1870 to 1913, while its exports of capital amounted to only £2.4 billion over the same period.[27] A similar balance may be struck for the United States for the post-war period. From these observations Magdoff draws what I consider an unwarranted conclusion, namely that 'it does not follow that the export of capital was stimulated primarily by the pressure of a surplus of capital'.[28]

Magdoff, like Hilferding and Rosa Luxemburg,[29] thinks that 'the desire and need to operate on a world scale is built into the economies of capitalism', but he deduces this tendency from the business strategy of the trusts, which soon after their formation in the leading industrial countries begin to act on an international scale in accordance with the principle of maximization of profit. Thus the monopoly triggers off an acute phase of the internationalization of capital. Magdoff describes the most important strategies of the giant corporations: (1) opening up of new sources of raw materials in the overseas territories and establishment of the required infrastructure; (2) jumping over tariff walls erected by rival nations by way of founding subsidiaries; (3) establishing a dominant position in foreign markets; (4) emergence of an international capital market enabling the monopolies to raise capital quickly for purposes of investment at home and abroad. Then Magdoff points out that the giant American corporations finance their subsidiary companies chiefly by raising local loans and re-investing undistributed profits. He adds: 'And that is hardly what one would expect on the basis of a theory that the main reason for foreign investment is the pressure of a superabundance of capital at home.'[30]

So Magdoff, although for reasons different to those of Baran and Sweezy, arrives at the conclusion that the thesis of capital surplus, which had been introduced into the imperialism debate by Hobson, is of secondary importance, or even less. From the passage just quoted one has the impression that Magdoff is prepared to accept the causal connection between monopoly and capital surplus mainly on the grounds of tradition. But it is wrong, I believe, to assign a high rank to the frontier-crossing character of monopoly ('internationalization of capital') and a low rank to the traditional thesis of capital surplus. In reality the two are closely related. Baran and Sweezy argue that in the period before World War I, Great Britain's income from capital invested abroad was considerably larger than the flow of capital in the opposite direction. This is seen as 'proof' of the fact that the export of capital cannot be attributed primarily to the pressure of surplus capital. But it should be clear that the behaviour of the *individual* entrepreneur cannot be deduced from certain macro-economic data. On the contrary, the macro-economic data demonstrate only the plain fact that the individual transactions of British investors on foreign markets were extremely profitable and that successes of this order must have given a strong impetus to more intensive capital export. W.H.B. Court, whom I quoted above, argued in a similar way that the economic development made possible abroad by British loans led to an increase in Britain's wealth, providing the basis for further exports of capital.[31]

A system tending towards over-capacity, slower growth and stagnation will of necessity develop a propensity to capital export. This does not mean, however, that the business strategy of the individual enterprise will be directly determined by this fact. As a rule the investment decisions of monopolies depend on profitability considerations, beginning with the presumed amount of *extra* profit expected from a particular capital investment. The costs of raising capital may also influence investment decisions considerably; the fact that 'local' credits are used says nothing about the actual source of the borrowed capital, given the international connections of finance capital. Finally there are business strategies based not so much on short-term profit expectations as on the attempt to anticipate the offensive 'move' of a competitor.[32] But as the profits are transferred to the 'mother country', the direction of such transfers being dictated by the ownership structure of the enterprise, the pressure of the surplus capital and thus the tendency towards export of capital grows.

The export of capital is, however, not the only 'safety valve' built into monopoly capitalism. Agreeing with Hilferding, Lenin regards militarism as primarily an attribute of the imperialist state, enabling it to pursue an expansionist policy. He neglects the *economic* function of militarism, which plays a more important role in absorbing the capital surplus than in the export of capital.[33] In Lenin's time this sin of omission was pardonable for two reasons: first, military spending, even just before World War I, was far below the level it reached in the period of the Cold War,[34] and secondly, the decade before World War I was generally characterized by full employment, so that no specific public spending policy was required to mobilize idle labour and resources. By contrast with later periods, most segments of the population felt military spending to be a heavy material burden, acceptable only at a time of acute threat from outside.[35] Since the end of the 1920s the situation has changed completely in this respect. A few years after the end of World War II the German sociologist Friedrich Pollock tried to calculate the percentage of the labour force in the United States whose employment was owed to the level of military spending. He arrived at the surprising figure of 15 per cent.[36] This result was confirmed by other social scientists, so at the beginning of the 1960s the United Nations assigned a scientific committee to investigate the problem of whether a far-reaching reduction of military spending was possible without causing serious economic and social disruption. Although the most renowned economists from East and West (among them the Pole Oskar Lange and the American W.W. Leontief) arrived at a definitely optimistic result, military spending has considerably increased since then, both in absolute and in relative terms.[37]

Investigations of this kind have however not prevented the apologists for the armament economy from denying that there is any connection between military spending and the tendency of the capitalist mode of production towards under-consumption and capital surplus. So the American economist Mark Blaug writes:

> How often are we told that post-war prosperity in the United States is utterly dependent upon armament spending, since military hardware does not come on to the market for sale. The fact that such expenditure since 1945 has been almost entirely financed by taxing current income, so that the net expansionary effect may well be nil, is simply forgotten. Moreover, the prosperity of capitalist countries such as West Germany, Holland, Belgium, Norway, and Sweden, all of which have spent very little on arms, is conveniently explained always as being a 'special case'.[38]

In the United States, a budget deficit has become almost a secular phenomenon. But even if it is true that military spending has been financed out of current income, by means of taxes, it should be clear that in an under-employed economy additional spending which leads to an incremental growth in income could also have been financed out of current income – without having recourse to a budget deficit. The essence of this process is given in the following description:

> This creation of effective demand can take the form of direct government purchases of goods and services, or of 'transfer payments' to groups which can somehow make good their claims for special treatment (subsidies to businessmen and farmers, doles to the unemployed, pensions to the aged, and so on). Thanks largely to the work of Keynes and his followers, these possibilities first began to be understood during the depression of the 1930s. For some time it was widely believed, however, even among economists, that government could create additional demand only if it spent more than it took in and made up the difference by such forms of 'deficit financing' as printing more money or borrowing from the banks. The theory held that the total increment in demand (government plus private) would be some multiple of the government deficit. The strength of the government stimulus was therefore believed to be proportional not to the level of government spending as such but to the magnitude of the deficit. Thus no amount of government spending could exercise an expansionary effect on total demand if it was matched by an equivalent amount of taxation. This view is now generally recognized to be wrong. Where there is unemployed labor and unutilized plant, government

can create additional demand even with a balanced budget. A simple numerical example will illustrate the point. . . . Suppose that total demand (= Gross National Product, GNP) is represented by the figure 100. Suppose that the government share of this is 10, which is exactly matched by taxation of 10. Government now decides to increase its purchases of goods and services – say, for a larger army and more munitions – by another 10 and to collect additional taxes of the same amount. The increased spending will add 10 to total demand and (since there is idle labor and plant available) to total output as well. The other side of the coin is an increase of income by 10, the equivalent of which can be drained into the public treasury through taxation without affecting the level of private spending.[39]

Another point raised by Professor Blaug should be mentioned here. The post-war prosperity of West Germany, Sweden, Norway, *et al.* can be regarded as a 'special case' only in so far as the growing activity of the Western European bourgeois state, by contrast with the USA, has its origin in 'welfare' rather than 'warfare', owing to the greater political weight of the European labour movement. But 'American conditions' have become firmly established in Western Europe as well over the past years.

Lenin paid only marginal attention to the *sociological* aspects of militarism. It is true that in a well-known passage he notes the close relationship between the business of armament, banks and government,[40] but he fails to examine more thoroughly the role of the military establishment in preparing war. A successful attempt at this can be found in Schumpeter's theory of imperialism. In his book *The Power Elite*, the American sociologist C. Wright Mills has thoroughly analysed the qualitative changes in the socio-political position of the military oligarchy in the United States – changes which had become manifest particularly during World War II and the period of Cold War:

> Most representatives of liberalism . . . assumed that the growth of industrialism would quickly relegate militarism to a very minor role in modern affairs. Under the amiable canons of the industrial society, the heroic violence of the military state would simply disappear. . . . But the classic liberal expectation of men like Herbert Spencer has proved quite mistaken. What the main drift of the twentieth century has revealed is that as the economy has become concentrated and incorporated into great hierarchies, the military

has become enlarged and decisive to the shape of the entire economic structure; and, moreover, the economic and the military have become structurally deeply interrelated, as the economy has become a seemingly permanent war economy; and military men and policies have increasingly penetrated the corporate economy.

The interpenetration of economic and military spheres is bound to produce a result which Mills describes as involving 'a coincidence of interests and a co-ordination of aims among economic and political as well as military actors'.[41] The permanent maintenance of the military apparatus and the perpetuation of a political situation justifying its maintenance becomes a categorical imperative scarcely requiring further explanation.

From Lenin's observation cited above, that the capitalist system has become 'overripe', some authors have drawn the conclusion that he explained the export of capital mainly by the Marxian law of the tendency of the rate of profit to fall.[42] This is the law which states that in the course of the accumulation process the qualitative composition of capital changes, with capital (means of production), the constant component, continuously increasing at the expense of the variable component (labour). The result is that unpaid work – the surplus value – decreases relative to the value of the total capital advanced. As the rate of profit is 'the driving force in capitalist production', sooner or later a situation must arise where the 'stimulating fire' of this mode of production will be extinguished.

The law of the tendency of the rate of profit to fall is weakened in its effect by some opposite tendencies. In this context Marx attaches great importance in particular to the 'increase in the degree of the exploitation of labour' and to the 'cheapening of the components of constant capital'. But foreign trade and capital export are also among the most effective opposite tendencies. On the latter Marx writes: 'On the other hand, capital invested in colonies, etc., may yield a higher rate of profit for the single reason that the rate of profit is higher there on account of the backward development, and for the added reason, that slaves, coolies, etc., permit a better exploitation of labour' (*Capital*, III. 279)

It appears that Marx was expecting an almost revolutionary effect on the economy of a colonial country, and thus on the political future of a suppressed people, from the export of capital:

I know that the English millocracy intend to endow India with railways with the exclusive view of extracting at diminished expenses the cotton and other raw materials for their manufactures. But when you have once introduced machinery into the locomotion of a country, which possesses iron and coal, you are unable to withhold it from its fabrication. You cannot maintain a net of railways over an immense country without introducing all those industrial processes necessary to meet the immediate and current wants of railway locomotion, and out of which there must grow the application of machinery to those branches of industry not immediately connected with railways. . . . Modern industry, resulting from the railway system, will dissolve the hereditary divisions of labour upon which rest the Indian castes, those decisive impediments to Indian progress and Indian power.[43]

As we know today, Marx ascribed to the export of capital an effect which has not materialized in the classic colonial countries up to today. It must be added, however, that in the first volume of *Capital* (1867), as well as in later works, he subjected the theory of the revolutionizing role of capital export to a fundamental revision. The relevant passage in *Capital* runs:

A new and international division of labour, a division suited to the requirements of the chief centre of modern industry, springs up and converts one part of the globe into a chiefly agricultural field of production, for supplying the other part which remains a chiefly industrial field.[44]

I think Lenin was well advised not to refer explicitly to the law of the tendency of the rate of profit to fall. This 'law' seems to have applied only to a rather brief period connected with the transformation of an economy based chiefly on small farmers and craftsmen into a mode of production based on factories. At the same time, the antiquated infrastructure (energy, transport and communications) was completely revolutionized, so that the capital goods industry was able for a long time to achieve a volume out of all proportion to the comparatively moderate development of the consumer goods industry.[45] Marx's often-quoted observation well applies to such a singular transformation of the economy: 'In spite of the lower cost of individual components, the cost of machinery as a whole rises enormously, and the increase in productivity is reflected in the constant increase in the quantity of machinery. . . .'[46]

In the twentieth century the basic conditions under which the law would apply to my mind no longer exist. As some Marxist authors have explained, since the end of the period of transformation, during which the capital goods industry was in a way capable of developing independently of the consumer goods industry, the qualitative composition of capital has remained relatively constant.[47] Where changes did occur, these had in all probability rather negative consequences for the constant component of capital, as a result of the capital-saving nature of many innovations (increased use of control mechanisms, more efficient use of raw materials, etc.). Also, many statistical analyses have shown that during recent decades the share contributed by wages to the national income in western countries has remained fairly stable.[48]

As Kazimierz Laski has recently pointed out, Joseph Steindl was probably the first to demonstrate a certain inconsistency of logic in the Marxian argument. Laski and Steindl both believe that these analytical difficulties can be overcome by the introduction of the capital coefficient (ratio of total capital to net product). But even when operating with this concept, hardly anything can be done about the tendency of the rate of profit to fall, as Laski argues with reference to Steindl's view:

> Marx was critical of the explanation offered by Ricardo, who only pointed out the diminishing returns derived from land. But the assumption of a rising capital coefficient goes much further than Ricardo's assumption. To preserve the logical consistency of the law of the tendency of the rate of profit to fall, Ricardo must be called in to help, and in an amplified form at that. In fact, a rising capital coefficient means a fall in the productivity of capital and presupposes the extension of the law of diminishing returns from land, which plays a certain role in agriculture, to the whole economy.[49]

I want to deal briefly now with the concept of the 'labour aristocracy', already introduced into the discussion by Engels, and its corrupting effect on the labour movement. Engels's remarks on this problem were anything but consistent. In the letter of 1858 quoted by Lenin, Engels wrote, 'this most bourgeois of all nations [i.e., England] is apparently aiming ultimately at the possession of a bourgeois aristocracy and a bourgeois proletariat *alongside* the bourgeoisie'.[50] Obviously he did not at that point differentiate between an aristocratic upper class of workers and the other strata of the proletariat. In 1881, however, Engels spoke of 'those most terrible English trade unions, which sell themselves to the bourgeoisie or at least let themselves be directed by people paid by it'. Finally we read, in his 1892 preface to the English edition of *The Condition of the Working Class in England*, of a privileged group of skilled workers organized in trade unions:

> They form an aristocracy among the working class; they have suc-
> ceeded in enforcing for themselves a relatively comfortable posi-
> tion, and they accept it as final. They are the model working-men of
> Messrs Leone Levi & Giffen, and they are very nice people indeed
> nowadays to deal with, for any sensible capitalist in particular and
> for the whole capitalist class in general.

And after this passage Engels predicts the collapse of England's industrial monopoly and the loss of privilege of its working class:

> The truth is this: during the period of England's industrial mono-
> poly the English working class have, to a certain extent, shared in
> the benefits of the monopoly. These benefits were very unequally
> parcelled out amongst them; the privileged minority pocketed
> most, *but even the great mass had, at least, a temporary share now and then.*
> And that is the reason why, since the dying out of Owenism, there
> has been no Socialism in England. With the breakdown of that
> monopoly, the English working class will lose that privileged posi-
> tion; *it will find itself generally* – the privileged and the leading minor-
> ity not excepted – *on a level with its fellow-workers abroad.* And that is
> the reason why there will be Socialism in England again.[51]

It should be noted that in his last comment on the problem of a
working-class aristocracy, Engels explicitly stresses that the great
mass had 'at least a temporary share now and then' in England's industrial monopoly. And he sees this as the ultimate cause of the
modest attraction of socialism for the English workers, even for the
mass of the less privileged and unprivileged among them. The clearly
perceived decline of the English industrial monopoly was thought by
Engels to be the material basis for the renaissance of the English
labour movement. But he was careful not to make any predictions as
to the nature of the regenerated English socialism.

Not so Lenin. He proceeds from the assumption that the division of
the world is complete and that 'the struggle of a small number of imperialist powers for a share in the monopoly' has replaced the uncon-
tested English monopoly. And he adds the following forecast:

> Opportunism cannot now be fully triumphant in the working-class
> movement of one country for decades as it was in Britain in the
> second half of the nineteenth century; but in a number of countries
> it has grown ripe, overripe and rotten, after having completely

merged with bourgeois policy in the form of 'social chauvinism'.

(*Imperialism*, 546 f.)

We know that what Lenin called the 'opportunistic' tendency within the working-class movement has remained dominant in Western Europe until now. Euro-Communism, too, has largely been integrated tactically and programmatically in the opportunistic front which Lenin considered moribund. I do not think this phenomenon can be satisfactorily explained by referring to the continued existence of a labour aristocracy which corrupts the working class. Another of Engels's observations may be more helpful here, namely that under the conditions of Western industrial monopoly the great mass of workers have 'at least a temporary share now and then' in this monopoly.[52]

Thus we arrive at the *present significance* of Lenin's theory of imperialism. Michael Barratt Brown holds that developments in the inter-war period confirm the 'prophetic character' of that theory:

> The establishment by Britain, France and the United States of exclusive trading areas in the 1930s drove Japan, Germany and Italy to seek their own alternative spheres of influence. Japan followed the programme laid down by her militarists in the Tanaka memorial of 1927; first into Manchuria, then China and finally South-East Asia. Italy moved into the Balkans, North Africa and Abyssinia; Germany through south-east Europe to the Middle East. The great monopolies, which dominated the governments of these countries, unable to find an outlet for their greatly expanded capacity, particularly in heavy industry, turned once more to war.[53]

After the end of World War II we enter a world which can only inadequately be grasped with the analytical methods worked out by Lenin and his predecessors. Of the political and economic changes of the past few decades, sometimes referred to summarily as 'neo-imperialism', the most important new political fact is the emergence of several rival world systems. While in the inter-war period the Soviet Union was still a peripheral political power, unable decisively to influence the intra-imperialist conflict, today three rival centres of power have become established outside the sphere dominated by the old capitalist Great Powers: the Soviet Union and its allies; China; and finally the so-called '77 non-aligned nations', which are trying to work out a joint foreign policy and economic conceptions (the 'New Economic Order').[54] The operational scope of the old imperialist powers has become narrower; their aims collide with the emancipatory aspirations of the newly established centres of power for which the political and economic categories developed above will hardly be valid.

Another political novelty closely allied with the above-mentioned one is the collapse of the old colonial system. To be sure, only one former colonial territory, China, has achieved a degree of independence that allows it to reorganize its political and social relations while safeguarding its full sovereignty. The old relations of dependence have been replaced by new, more complex, and often harder to recognize, unequal relations among countries and groups of countries. While the old intra-imperialist contrasts are receding, the conflicts between East and West as well as between North and South are growing more acute and more dangerous.

The economic and political laws determining the behaviour of the old imperialist powers in the periods before World War I and between the two world wars are still to a great extent effective: monopoly capital, export of capital, use of economic, political and military power to maintain and expand exclusive spheres of influence – which have, however, lost their former colonial character – are the major external features of capitalism in its neo-imperialist stage of development.

After World War II, however, some important qualitative changes have occurred. The hegemonic role has been taken over by the United States, which is practising, to a much greater extent than the former hegemonic power, Britain, the export of capital in the form of direct investment. Again the main thrust of economic expansion is directed today towards industrially advanced countries such as Canada, Britain and continental Europe, while investment in the underdeveloped regions is mainly aimed at increasing production of raw material, food and oil. The offensive by American 'multinational' companies, which reached considerable proportions during the 1950s and '60s, has recently been replaced with a counter-offensive by European and Japanese trans-national corporations.[55] That the economies of the leading capitalist nations show a high and still increasing degree of interlocking I regard as the characteristic feature of the neo-imperialist period of development.

That intra-imperialist conflicts have not completely vanished can be proved by many recent examples.[56] But I think it would be wrong to conclude that there is serious danger of a split in the imperialist front. Two developments would seem to favour a process of increasing cohesion within the old imperialist camp: the challenge by the new non-capitalist centres of power, and the increasing tendency towards internationalization of capital. In fact, a development is emerging which Karl Kautsky (on the basis of a rather inadequate analysis of the world political situation caused by the First World War) as early as 1915 described as conceivable – namely the development of an 'ultra-imperialism'. Instead of the various national financial capitals fighting each other, Kautsky thought, there would be 'joint exploitation of the world through an internationally allied financial capital'.[57] Lenin termed Kautsky's hypothesis of ultra-imperialism 'ultra-nonsense'. It is highly improbable that he would dismiss the argument in the same way today. But he would, I think, argue that ultra-imperialism must not be identified with a position of undisputed dominance as held by the United States.

What changes have occurred in the Third World since the collapse of the colonial system? As we have noted, only the great power China has been able to pursue a completely independent course in remodelling its economic and social order. As regards the developing countries not belonging to the sphere of influence of either the Soviet Union or China, one can say generally that they have tried to overcome their state of poverty and backwardness by imitating the highly industrialized capitalist countries. The industrial breakthrough was expected to be achieved by means of development aid intended to work as a 'primer'. To the extent that a national capitalist class would emerge, it was thought that the stream of development aid could be replaced by a stream of savings accumulating in the hands of the entrepreneurs in the course of the industrialization process. From these considerations the conclusion was drawn that the objective of a just distribution of income must be subordinated to that of rapid economic development. As Professor Harry Johnson has expressed it, 'In particular, there is likely to be a conflict between rapid growth and an equitable distribution of income; and a poor country anxious to develop would probably be well advised not to worry too much about the distribution of income.'[58]

Pakistan was one of the many countries where this concept of development was tried out – successfully, as it seemed at first. During the 1960s industrial production increased about 10 per cent annually, GNP more than 5 per cent and per-capita GNP about 2.5 per cent. But this high growth rate was accompanied by an enormous concentration of income and wealth in the hands of a small minority. The situation of the vast majority of the population seems to have deterio-rated during that period, not only in relative but also in absolute terms.[59] As far as the masses of the people were concerned this produced the impression, detrimental to further development, that the policy was being followed only for the purpose of enriching a small privileged class. Pakistan first pursued a policy of 'import substitution', which was only partly successful because the amount of consumer goods imported is still considerable. The transition to a second stage of development, namely the shift from import substitution to the exporting of consumer goods must be viewed as a failure for the time being, because Pakistan's light industry has not as yet managed – despite massive support by the state – to secure an appreciable share of foreign markets. Needless to say, under these circumstances the third stage of the policy – the building up of a domestic capital-goods industry – can be considered a thing of the far-distant future. The limited success of the export policy has considerably increased Pakistan's dependence on foreign development aid, especially since the so-called 'Yom Kippur' War.[60]

The case of Pakistan, chosen here as representative of many other underdeveloped countries of the Third World, seems to make it clear that a poor country's path to economic and thus to political independence cannot be found by following strictly the western model of development. Countries like Taiwan and South Korea, which receive massive support from the USA and Japan in the form of capital, can certainly be seen as exceptional cases.

Can imitation of the Soviet model of development and dependence on Soviet development aid be recommended to a backward country as a sure-fire recipe for success? The reader may find a clue to this problem in Lenin's Preface to the *uncensored* Russian edition of his study:

> In order to show the reader, in a guise acceptable to the censors, how shamelessly the capitalists and the social-chauvinists who have deserted to their side (and whom Kautsky opposes so inconsistently) lie on the question of annexation; in order to show how shamelessly they *screen* the annexations of *their* capitalists, I was forced to quote as an example – Japan! The careful reader will easily substitute Russia for Japan, and Finland, Poland, Courland, the Ukraine, Khiva, Bokhara, Estonia or other regions peopled by non-Great Russians, for Korea. (*Imperialism*, 434)

One assumes that Lenin – were he still alive – would agree with the Trotsky-Djilas-Bettelheim-Sweezy hypothesis, namely that the expansionist foreign policy of the Soviet Union must be attributed to its 'new class' and its need for legitimation.   1983

Chapter 5

The Crisis of the Tax State*

Joseph A. Schumpeter's brilliant essay, *Die Krise des Steuerstaates (The Tax State in Crisis)*,[1] was intended primarily as an appraisal and a critique of Rudolph Goldscheid's *Staatssozialismus oder Staatskapitalismus* (1917);[2] in this work Goldscheid dealt with sociological and financial problems, viewing the Austrian national debt, which had increased enormously during World War 1, and ways of settling it as a challenge to future-oriented social reformers. Schumpeter recognized the primacy and the urgency of innovative attempts at social reform; but he saw the levy on property, to which he ascribed strategic importance, as did Goldscheid, chiefly as a means of reorganizing a national budget that had got into almost total disarray through the unrestrained spending policy of the country at war. Almost a year later, in a letter addressed to Karl Renner shortly before leaving the Austrian cabinet in which he had been Minister of Finance, Schumpeter stressed the 'conservative' nature of his reorganization programme, based mainly on the capital levy.[3]

Schumpeter's *Tax State in Crisis* contains, however, a number of observations which go far beyond matters of immediate concern, and almost prophetically anticipate the course of financial policy in the decades to come. We shall look first at two of its cognitive premises. Like Goldscheid, Schumpeter viewed the financial policy of a country as a reflection – perhaps the most essential of all indicators – of a community's social orientation. 'One will always have to credit Goldscheid', Schumpeter writes,

as being the first to draw attention to this approach to financial

* Prepared in collaboration with Hans Kernbauer, and first published in W. Weigel, E. Leithner, R. Windisch, *Handbuch der österreichischen Finanzpolitik* (Vienna, 1986), 501-13.

history, for publicizing widely the truth that the budget is the very
skeleton of a country, completely stripped of deceptive ideologies –
a mixture of hard facts, which have yet to be incorporated into the
field of sociology. Above all, the financial history of any country is
an essential part of its general history. . . .

(*Die Krise*, 331)

In his later works Schumpeter refers again and again to the idea
that the budget is the skeleton of a country stripped of all deceptive
ideologies. He elaborates this idea in his essay 'Finanzpolitik', where
he says that the budget is

> always the summation of all social, political, cultural, economic
> and external living conditions and relations of a people; its success
> or failure, its correctness or incorrectness, its greatness or inade-
> quacy depend on whether or not it is based on a correct diagnosis of
> all these things and translates this diagnosis properly into the
> financial sphere. But its function extends beyond that. Financial
> policy not only needs to translate into the language of budget and
> tax legislation what is true today, but also what will happen tomor-
> row, and it must prepare, enable and facilitate what will have to be
> done with regard to foreign affairs, and in the economic and social
> fields.[4]

But the view he shared with Goldscheid of the sociological dimensions of public finance is only one of the two basic premisses which
make Schumpeter's early financial analysis (it was written during
World War I) remarkably relevant to the present day. The second
premiss is Schumpeter's interpretation of the changes in economic
history to which the tax state has been subject since it originated at
the end of the Middle Ages. Colbert, Peel, Miquel and Böhm-Bawerk
mark different stages in the development of the tax state. While Peel
and Gladstone designed and executed a fiscal policy that was tailored
almost ideally to the needs of the rapidly developing free-market
economy of the United Kingdom,[5] Miquel's and Böhm-Bawerk's fiscal policy showed that a modern tax state could not be burdened
beyond certain limits.

As we know, Eugen von Böhm-Bawerk held the post of Finance
Minister in the Danubian Monarchy three times. Shortly before his
death in 1914 he wrote a series of newspaper articles describing most
vividly the social mechanism causing an increased tax load on a
democratic community. Böhm-Bawerk deals first with the gradual
change in the spending policy of the Austrian state:

It is said, and it may well be true, that in our country at present many private persons live beyond their means. But it is certain that for quite some time many of our public bodies have been living beyond their means. First the state itself. It is hardly an accident that those decades during which our balance of trade was constantly favourable roughly coincide with the era in which our economy was marked by a rigorous austerity heavily criticized at the time; of course, austerity is never popular. But the change in our balance of trade – the exact date is of no concern here – occurs at approximately the time when there is a change of attitude towards the way our economy is managed. We have undoubtedly become slack and inattentive as regards our public spending.[6]

Böhm-Bawerk then goes on to ask why this has come about:

A whole book could be written about that, which would have to deal with the internal history of the last decade and especially its *internal political* history, because in our country financial policy was the whipping boy of politics. We have seen in countless forms the futile endeavour to create political contentment by material concessions. While in former times parliament was the guardian of thrift, nowadays it has become its sworn enemy. Today the political and national parties . . . almost regard it as a duty to covet all kinds of advantages, at public expense, for their members or constituencies, and if the political situation is favourable – that is to say, unfavourable for the government – political pressure can be applied to obtain the desired advantage. But, as carefully calculated rivalry and jealousy exist among the individual parties, often enough a concession made to *one* party has also to be granted immediately to other parties by way of compensation: a single expensive concession instantly becomes a whole cluster of expensive concessions. . . .[7]

With these apt remarks Böhm-Bawerk characterizes what are today called the rules of a 'pressure-group democracy'; it may be left open here as to whether the growing weight of public expenditure before the outbreak of World War I can be attributed solely to the covetousness of the political parties.[8]

As a professional observer of the financial scene in Austria, Schumpeter followed the developments outlined by his teacher Böhm-Bawerk with growing concern. But only in *The Tax State in Crisis*, four years later, did he draw the conclusions from the observations of his teacher

that came to seem so prophetic. His basic concern was with the increasing discrepancy between the traditional sources of income of the
bourgeois tax state, on the one hand, and the proliferating needs, expectations and demands of its individual representatives, on the other.
The concept of the 'revolution of rising expectations', a term coined
only recently, was largely anticipated in Schumpeter's study:

> The financial efficiency of the tax state is limited, not only in the
> obvious sense, which would apply to a socialist society as well, but
> also in a much narrower sense, more embarrassing for the tax state.
> Now, if the popular will is directed towards ever-greater public
> spending and an ever-increasing quantity of funds is used for pur-
> poses not those for which they were created by the private in-
> dividual, if an ever-growing power is behind that will and finally all
> sections of the population begin to rethink their views on private
> property and ways of life – then the tax state will be overcome and
> society will depend on economic motives other than those of in-
> dividual selfishness. This limit – and thus the crisis which the tax
> state could not survive – can certainly be reached: no doubt, the tax
> state *can* break down.   (*Die Krise*, 351-2)

Schumpeter stresses the fact that the World War of 1914-18 did not
set off this development, but only accelerated it: 'The war itself did
not create any new problems, but only aggravated an existing situation, and it would be superficial to claim that the viability of the tax
state – or of any other social institution for that matter – is linked to
war' (ibid., 353).

He may be right that basically the war did not create a new situation, but we believe he would have agreed that the financial strain
caused by four years of military conflict exposed the limits to which a
tax state could be burdened more clearly than the experience of previous years. Another passage in his study seems to confirm this:

> The closer the tax state approaches these limits, the stronger the re-
> sistance to it and the losses from friction caused by this state of
> affairs. The civil service machinery required to administer the tax
> laws becomes larger and larger, tax collection becomes more in-
> sistent and enforcement measures assume ever more unbearable
> proportions. This absurd waste of energy shows that the purpose of
> the tax-state organization is to preserve the autonomy of the private
> economy and of private life and that it loses its purpose as soon as it
> can no longer respect this autonomy.   (Ibid., 378n.)

Schumpeter's concept of the crisis of the tax state would be called 'structural' by latter-day authors, because this crisis – caused by the 'revolution of rising expectations' – cannot be coped with even through radical and large-scale fiscal reforms. Christian Seidl argues that Schumpeter's explanation of the phenomenon of rapidly increasing public expenditure has a sociological cast, whereas the stagnation of tax revenue must be attributed to the historically conditioned fact that there is a limit to the *economic* endurance of the taxpayer. Following Jonathan Swift, Adam Smith, and drawing on the notion of the Laffer curve, recently much discussed, Seidl believes that any effort to raise taxes above this maximum limit must lead to diminishing revenues.[9]

Schumpeter dealt repeatedly in his later works with the problem of the 'maximum limit' of endurance of the individual taxpayer. Neither the household nor the firm, nor the income tax which had become the pillar of the tax state in the course of the nineteenth century, seemed to him an adequate basis for the steadily growing pyramid of demands made by large parts of the public (and by the political parties representing them) on public spending. Thus he wrote in an essay in the late 1920s:

> But finally the income tax can only work in the way it is intended to if its rates are felt to be moderate – which, if it is to contribute a considerable part to government revenue and to be of importance for the budget, means that *public expenses* themselves must be *moderate*, i.e. they must be the expenses of a *'Nachtwächterstaat'* ['Nightwatchman' or caretaker state] of the liberal era. For only in this case can the above-mentioned advantages be attributed at least approximately to the income tax: an income tax which is so moderate that it has no appreciable influence on production or consumption by the people, nor on their propensity to save, will for this very reason not entail a noticeable shift and will actually place the ultimate tax burden on the taxpayer. But if the tax takes a fifth, a quarter or an even greater proportion of the income, then it will transform the *homo oeconomicus* and everything he does. It will become the cause of economic disturbance, the lever of general disorganization, the source of precisely the evils it was introduced in the first place to mitigate. . . .[10]

As we have seen, Christian Seidl holds that historically there is an upper limit to the taxpayer's endurance. Seidl was able to base this observation on the experience of half a century which had seen a formerly unheard-of increase in the tax rate (average as well as margi-

nal) in every Western country. According to calculations by Ewald
Nowotny, the tax and social-insurance ratio (that is, taxes and social-
insurance contributions as a percentage of the GNP) in the Austrian
half of the Monarchy was approximately equivalent to religious tithes
around the middle of the nineteenth century, and then grew by 1982 to
about 42½ per cent; it must be added that by that time countries like
Sweden and the Netherlands had exceeded the 'magic' limit of 50 per
cent.[11] We need not go into detail here as to the rhythm at which taxes
and social-insurance contributions rose during this long period of
time. For our purposes it is enough to state that the average annual increase between 1950 and 1982 was approximately 0.5 percentage
points, indicating a considerable long-term increase and an
astonishing change in attitude (the 'revolution of rising expectations'). The threshold of the individual taxpayer's endurance has
proved to be substantially higher than Schumpeter imagined in his
Tax State in Crisis.[12]

But it must not be overlooked that this almost continuous increase
in tax and social-insurance contributions occurred in the years after
World War II under unprecedentedly favourable economic and political circumstances. The years between 1945 and 1975 were remarkable in two respects: they comprised the longest period of economic upswing modern capitalism had known, and they were marked
by enormous social reforms. During this period a new social entity
emerged, the welfare state, but it must be emphasized that the pattern
of spending in Scandinavia, in Central Europe and in the Anglo-
Saxon countries differs in many ways. What all these countries have
in common, however, is that they have granted to the modern
Leviathan rights of intervention which earlier generations would have
denounced as being alien to the system or possibly even as 'socialist'.
It is interesting that Schumpeter in fact followed this line of argument
in his last essay, 'The March into Socialism', characterizing state
intervention based on the Keynesian recipe for full employment as a
phenomenon responsible for the turn towards socialism.[13]

One might argue that the 1980s, during which economic growth
declined perceptibly, are no longer marked by a 'revolution of rising
expectations', but by a counter-revolution of rebellious taxpayers and
anti-interventionist ideologies. The Schumpeterian tax state has indeed entered on a critical phase, but it has not – pessimists would say;
not yet – broken down; it has developed various ways of adjusting to a
stagnant economy. To simplify matters we shall speak here of an
American and an Austrian model of adjustment; but it must be admit-

ted that the reality cannot be explained in such simple terms.

Dieter Bös has developed a theory of the tax state in crisis which obviously reflects certain recent phenomena in the United States. He thinks that a crisis occurs as soon as a majority of the voters decides in favour of procuring most goods and services through the market mechanism, rather than drawing on tax-financed public supply of these items.[14] This essentially Californian model is only partly reflected in American federal policy. Massive tax reductions initiated by President Reagan have not been combined with complementary measures in the area of social services, primarily because the dismantling of the American type of welfare state has met with unexpectedly strong resistance. But one should not rashly assume that this means the end of the attempt at mastering the crisis of the American tax state at least partially by conservative methods – i.e. by drastically reducing social services. Account must be taken of the fact that not only have these efforts been initiated by Reagan and his Republican Party colleagues, but they are supported by a substantial part of the propertied population, including the petty bourgeoisie, who are definitely against the system of publicly financed social services.

Except in Britain, the European tax state has nowhere been exposed to such a massive attempt at liquidation as in the United States. What has been observed since the beginning of the 1980s, not least in Austria as well, is a slow process of internal erosion, clearly reflected in budget revenue and expenditure. When in the second half of the 1970s a distinct slow-down of economic growth became apparent also in Austria, efforts were made – initially with undeniable success – to combat stagnation by an increased use of public funds. The rapid growth of the public debt was accepted quite deliberately, obviously on the assumption that one was up against a temporary cyclical slump. In accordance with popular Keynesian doctrine, it was announced that the rapidly growing deficit would soon vanish in the upswing expected in the near future.

This light-hearted – one is almost tempted to call it 'Viennese' – interpretation of the business cycle had to be abandoned at the beginning of the 1980s. By that time it had became clear that around the mid-'70s a change had taken place in the economic climate which would prove to be the determining factor for the rest of the century. By contrast with Reagan and Thatcher & Co., this realization did not lead to the conclusion that a long period of stagnation must be dealt with by a more or less extensive dismantling of the welfare state. On the contrary, the strategy adopted in Austria was that of a limited and orderly retreat.

Before looking more closely at the effectiveness of such a concept, a few words should be said about the structural peculiarities of the Austrian budget. Data on expenditure by the federal government and the federal provinces (except Vienna) for the period 1973-82 provide some interesting indications as to future developments in the most important areas of spending by Austrian territorial authorities. As Gerhard Lehner points out, the 'traditional' functions of government (internal and external security, central administration) gradually lose their significance. This also applies to the 'classic' areas of spending on the infra structure, such as road-building.[15] But one should not overlook the fact that the old governmental functions are suffering from a disorder generally, in economics, termed 'cost-disease' of the public sector. The term points to the widely-known fact that cost increases in the service sector are above average because productivity in that sector lags behind that of the rest of the economy, while wages increase at the same pace as in all other sectors. This is the main explanation of why the proportion of spending on central administration rose considerably at current prices during the 1973-82 period, while at constant prices it did not change very much. The phenomenon of 'cost-disease' is not likely to alter fundamentally in future, although more intensive efforts to rationalize – especially through the use of data-processing systems – may lead to considerable opportunities for saving money also in the service sector.

Contrary to theories of the classic functions of government, whose uselessness has become apparent over the past decade, a perpetual increase in expenditure on social insurance must be faced in coming decades, caused by the shift in demographic structure already manifesting itself. Attempts have been made over the past few years to meet this challenge by a certain, though by no means serious, cut in national insurance benefits for the retired part of the population. But such a course will have to be considered carefully, for it could lead to the emergence of a new pariah class. In the nineteenth century Disraeli spoke of the existence (or coexistence) of two nations, the rich and the poor. The systematic reduction of insurance benefits would give his words a new, previously unthought-of topicality.

Finally another item of expenditure, in what Moislechner and Nowotny regard as the most expansionary area of the public sector today. They are, of course, referring to the fact that the government assumes financial functions which clearly reflect the interventionist character of the welfare state. It emerges from the studies of these two authors that the proportion of loans and guarantees subsidized by the Austrian government in the period 1970-4 amounted to 36 per cent of the total gross private investment. The figure then rose in 1975-9 to an impressive 73.2 per cent. A good part of these financial funds was raised by public-sector borrowing, and, as Nowotny explains, the considerable interest charges had to be paid out of current revenue as well as through further borrowing by the public sector.[16] Those who speak idly of the necessity for the state to withdraw from the economy should become aware of the growing importance, and the consequences, of these transactions.

How was public spending, with its continuously upward trend, financed over the past decade? In that period taxes and social insurance contributions, expressed as a proportion of GNP, rose by more than 4 percentage points, with taxes in the narrower sense accounting for the smaller part of this increase. But the relatively moderate increase in the tax ratio has involved a further shift of the tax burden on to the lower-income groups (through value-added tax, wage tax), as a result of which the Austrian tax system today has a clearly *proportional* character that is hardly in keeping with the generally held view of the burden to be imposed progressively on high-income earners by the welfare state. Moreover, it has become increasingly clear, especially since the beginning of the 1980s, that in times of slow and occasionally static economic growth, a growing resistance by the population to any form of additional taxation has to be reckoned with. One is reminded of Schumpeter's gloomy statement at the beginning of the Depression:

> If . . . income tax becomes the largest item of expense, its assessment the most important economic act of the year, if the taxpayer feels deprived and his psychology becomes that of a hunted animal, all this gives rise to the paralysing and wasteful situation in which the best and most humane tax becomes the worst and most inhumane.[17]

A further increase in taxation will become rather problematic under such conditions. The public reacts to measures of this kind with various strategies of tax-avoidance and sometimes tax-evasion, but also – what may be of even greater weight – with forms of tax-shifting difficult to keep track of. The tax system is increasingly becoming an arena for a free-for-all, violating more and more often one of the imperatives of a fair tax system: the identity of the taxpayers with those who ultimately bear the tax burden. But a higher levy on capital by means of a withholding tax, or some modified version of such a tax, proves to be a relatively unproductive fiscal measure – which is, of course, a necessary consequence of the extensive freedom of movement of capital in the western world. Finally the increasing trend towards 'moonlighting' has become a popular method of tax evasion for many beneficiaries of the welfare state.

The Austrian type of welfare state seems to have reached a deadlock. The possible extent of vertical redistribution of income has always been limited, not least because people with high incomes have learnt to practise the many forms of legal tax avoidance with considerable skill. Of far greater importance has been the horizontal type of redistribution, whose ethical precondition is solidarity among working people. It must be said that a sense of solidarity of the employed with the unemployed, the healthy with the ill, and the young with the old, has been put to severe ideological tests during the past few years. The forces that campaign – and a campaign indeed it has been – against the welfare state have used two plausible arguments: the inefficiency of some of the institutions of that state, and the occasional abuse of those institutions by a minority, however small, of its beneficiaries. Although the grounds for these two grievances cannot be denied, and the need for remedying them as far as possible should be beyond argument, the public awareness of such shortcomings has scarcely led to the system as a whole being discredited – at least until now.[18]

The threat of a slow erosion of the welfare state seems, however, to come from another quarter. As Günther Chaloupek observes, the comparatively high standard of living in Austria – the gross annual income of a worker's household in 1984 averaged about 330,000 schillings – is in many instances based on the employment of both partners.[19] The author rightly draws the conclusion that a high level of employment plays a considerable role in a policy of distribution. Until very recently Austria was able to a remarkable degree to check unemployment by means of an investment-oriented budget policy, which may be seen as the most important aspect of the so-called 'Austro-Keynesianism'. The budgetary leeway for continuing this policy has considerably narrowed during the past few years, both on the revenue side, where as we have seen a tendency towards stagnation can be observed, and on the expenditure side, which is extensively blocked by social services, public consumption and debt service. A point seems now to have been reached where a further stepping on the budgetary accelerator might have negative consequences for the external position of the Austrian schilling.

In his *Tax State in Crisis* Schumpeter sees tendencies at work which lead more or less inevitably to a new order of things. At the end of the study he writes:

> Gradually private enterprise will lose its purpose as a result of economic development and the expansion of social sympathy this entails. This manifested itself and was in accord with tendencies of the second half of the nineteenth century, probably the last aberration of which was all that culminated in the World War. Society rises above private enterprise and the tax state – not because of but in spite of the war: *this* too is certain.   (*Die Krise*, 370-1)

Schumpeter predicted, as we have seen, the tendencies which were to pose an acute threat to the tax state in this century. But contrary to his prophecy, the western world has not risen above that state but has experimented with various ways of reforming it. The Anglo-Saxon model amounts to a fundamental departure from the western-type welfare state set up over half a century. Tax reduction for the rich and the gradual dismantling of social achievements are aimed at pushing certain politically defenceless sectors of the population 'to the verge of society'.

The Austrian model, we have shown (and with certain modifications the Swedish model as well), signifies not a turning away from the welfare state but an attempt to modify it in an era of slow growth. The strategy pursued up to now provides for occasional slight increases in public revenue, with the main emphasis on raising social insurance contributions. However, it seems unlikely that the fiscal burden will be further shifted towards indirect taxes. On the expenditure side, the scope for anti-cyclic controlling measures has become desperately narrow. To get the rising unemployment under control, other short- and medium-term strategies will have to be devised.

In accordance with the Swedish model, an occasional 'softening' of the Austrian hard-currency policy seems indicated so as to offer temporary support to the export industry. It appears questionable to make a fetish of stable exchange rates as has been the case in Austria for the past two decades. Another measure to be copied from the Swedish model would be a widening of the range of re-training courses and of further education, since rapid technological progress is accompanied by increasing unemployment in certain areas, in contrast to a growing labour shortage in others.

Long-term measures would include focusing greater attention on Austrian research and education policies. It is the common opinion that public expenditure on research still lags considerably behind that of the leading industrial nations. As regards future education policy, one of the most important reforms would be to extend the compulsory period of schooling from nine to ten years. The spectacular technological changes of the recent past, the so-called 'Third Industrial Revolution', clearly require a new type of worker able to adapt promptly and easily to changing economic processes. The working lives of tomorrow's generation will require a *continuous learning process*. Moreover, the extension of the schooling period would also help to ease the strain on the labour market. Therefore a marked reduction in working hours could be sensibly combined with the school reform.[20]

The slow-down in economic growth in the light of which the above comments were written will, it can be assumed, remain in force throughout the following years if not decades. One can expect in the near future neither a revival of the strong technological impulses to growth of the post-war period, nor that the strongest western economic power, the United States of America, will continue its function as the economic 'engine' to the extent that it did in the period 1983-6.

It is, of course, conceivable that the countries devoted to the guiding principles of the welfare state will unite to form a more or less solid economic bloc capable of steering an expansionary and anti-inflationary course, even if one or other of its member states is thereby exposed to pressure from a temporary foreign trade imbalance. A decisive international dimension would thus be added to the idea of solidarity, on which the welfare state is based. However, in the years to come the Austrian welfare state and similar structures (for what has been shown here may also apply *mutatis mutandis* to the Scandinavian model of the welfare state) will, in our view, have only one practicable option: that of an orderly and limited retreat in the terms outlined above. It is to be hoped that this policy will proceed on the principle that the sacrifices to be imposed on the citizenry are distributed fairly, i.e. according to the ability of those bearing the ultimate tax burden.

1986

PART TWO

Schumpeter
and the Austrian Economy

Chapter 6

Schumpeter's Vienna; or the 'Bauer-Mises-Schumpeter' Controversy[*]

In the last decades preceding World War I, which were marked by the political death struggle of the Hapsburg Monarchy, intellectual and especially artistic life in Vienna was in full bloom, reminiscent of Athens at the time of Pericles or of Florence under Lorenzo il Magnifico. This brief colourful spring, which was not to be followed by a summer's rich harvest, has recently been the subject of much speculative comment and of studies, particularly by non-Viennese authors.[1] Some of Vienna's cultural significance may have resulted from the coexistence, however uneasy, of the great number of nationalities in the city, from the increasing wealth of the bourgeoisie, from the gradually strengthening intellectual freedom that followed the breakdown of neo-absolutism, and perhaps also from the awareness of internal disintegration and the threats from outside.[2]

Vienna at the time of the *belle époque* was very fertile soil also for economic theory. Two schools established themselves there which were soon to gain worldwide reputation: the so-called 'Austrian' or 'marginal utility' school of economics, the most important representatives of which were Karl Menger, Eugen von Böhm-Bawerk and Friedrich von Wieser, and the Austro-Marxist school, represented most notably by three relatively young men – Rudolf Hilferding, Otto Bauer and Karl Renner. Schumpeter, who published his main work before World War I, tried – as can easily be demonstrated – to blend ele-

* First published in *Das geistige Leben Wiens in der Zwischenkriegszeit*, ed. Norbert Leser (Vienna, 1981).

ments of the two schools into a fruitful synthesis, particularly in his *Theorie der wirtschaftlichen Entwicklung (The Theory of Economic Development)*, first published in Leipzig in 1911.

The two currents of economic thought functioned as theoretical antipodes, one sometimes taking note of the other in polemical articles which tried to explain the real world from completely different intellectual positions.[3] The problems the two schools were dealing with differed considerably. The triumvirate of the Austrian school – Böhm, Menger and Wieser – believed they could explain certain basic concepts of economics, such as capital and interest on capital, entrepreneurial profit, the process of distribution of original incomes, etc., in a new way, while the young protagonists of Austro-Marxism tried to apply the economic tools developed by Marx to the interpretation of modern socio-economic phenomena such as monopoly capitalism, finance capital, imperialism and the economic aspects of the conflict of nationalities under the Danubian Monarchy.[4]

The two schools, existing in close proximity yet so different intellectually, had one rather important feature in common, namely the Olympian calm and thoroughness with which their respective representatives were producing their principal works. Never before, and unfortunately never afterwards, did Austrian economists write with such commitment and with such craftsmanship. This was also true of the essays of the young Schumpeter which appeared before World War I.[5]

The Austria that emerged from the horrors of World War I bore little resemblance physically to the country that had preceded it – the western part of the Monarchy only – still less so intellectually. This was true of the little world of economics even more than in other fields of knowledge. Of the leading representatives of the Austrian school, Wieser was still alive at the end of the war; he was giving his didactically brilliant lectures at the University of Vienna until the mid-1920s. Of the younger adepts of the Viennese school, Ludwig von Mises in particular had made himself a certain reputation in the last years before the outbreak of war,[6] but he and his colleagues Hayek, Haberler, Morgenstern and Machlup all eventually left their native country, which had become narrow and impoverished, to work in the 1930s at one or another of the famous universities of the West.

The Austro-Marxist school, too, never fully recovered from the blood-letting of World War I and from the trauma of the collapse of the Monarchy. Rudolf Hilferding left Vienna even before the outbreak of war and embarked on a spectacular political career in the Weimar

Republic, which ended in 1940 with his martyr's death at the hands of the Gestapo. After 1918, Karl Renner too devoted himself to political tasks and party politics, and only occasionally ventured into the field of socialist theory. Otto Bauer, cast in the difficult role of leading politician and parliamentarian of the Austrian Social Democratic Party after Victor Adler's death, was still able to produce several well-grounded economic and sociological essays as well as countless minor articles. But Bauer's most important work in the inter-war period was written during the enforced leisure of his exile in Brno.[7] The younger socialist publicists included in particular Käthe Leichter, Otto Leichter, Otto Neurath, Emil Lederer and, last but not least, Karl Polanyi. The latter, who owed many intellectual impulses to Austro-Marxism, later – as a professor at Columbia University in New York – went his own way, clearly dissociating himself from Marxian orthodoxy.[8]

It is impossible to provide, in the space available, an adequate impression of the lively economic discussion of the inter-war period. Its principal feature, I think, was its concentration on the acute economic difficulties of the present and on possible ways of overcoming these in the not too distant future. Among important topics discussed were inflation and its social consequences, the problematic viability of the new Austria, the functioning of a fully socialized economy, the possibilities and dangers of the wave of rationalization starting in the 1920s, the reasons for the cyclical fluctuations of the economy, and the question of how to combat chronic mass unemployment.[9]

I want to deal here only with the debate on socialization of the early post-war period, not merely because it reflected the gravity of the political and social crisis, but also because its impact was felt far beyond the Austrian borders and continues to be felt up to the present. After the end of World War I, the whole of Central Europe was shaken by a wave of social uprisings. The collapse of the old monarchic system of government in Germany and in Austria, as well as the October Revolution in Russia, set off social movements which resulted in the formation of workers' and soldiers' councils, in the occupation of factories, in local rebellions, and finally in the foundation of Soviet Republics in Bavaria and Hungary. As in the revolutions of 1848 and 1789, the remodelling of the old and by then already brittle social structure became a hotly debated subject, finding its most vivid expression over the issue of socialization in the late autumn of 1918.[10]

What traditions and theoretical studies did the Austro-Marxist school have to rely on in attempting to work out a concept of socialization? It is easy to show that the leading forces in the Austrian Labour Party did not expect, even after the Russian Revolution, to be confronted with similar developments in the foreseeable future. In the years 1917 and 1918 the right wing of the party was absolutely convinced that the Danubian monarchy was viable if it was subjected to a thorough constitutional reform. Even Otto Bauer, who rejected Karl Renner's narrowly conceived national programme of reform, could write in the spring of 1918:

> Austria's existence is secured for the future by the results of the war. The nations can obtain their right of self-determination only in so far as it is possible within the given governmental framework. Renner presents national self-government within the borders of present-day Austria as the most ideal, and under any circumstances the best and most perfect solution for all nations. . . . We think this has not been proved and cannot be proved. But we, too, view it as the only solution possible under the present power relationships in Europe.[11]

The deeper causes of the lack of revolutionary preparedness must be traced back to the period before 1914 and doubtless resulted from the pragmatic political line which had become dominant in the period of pre-war prosperity – the economic matrix of the *belle époque*. As Otto Bauer was to say many years later, people just did not dare to draw 'the final tactical and strategic consequences' from the basic reformist attitudes.[12] The socialist economic constitution of the future was defined by the empty notion of the 'socialization of the means of production', which could be filled with co-operative, syndicalist or Utopian ideas depending on individual attitudes.[13]

The discussion about socialization had reached an equally unsatisfactory stage at the end of World War I. Karl Kautsky's *Sozialdemokratische Bemerkungen zur Übergangsgesellschaft*, published in the last year of the war, can be seen as symptomatic. Kautsky, regarded as the undisputed and final authority on Marxism in Austria at the time, wrote in a pamphlet that the transition to socialism, which would take place only at some remote date, was not a current issue. So he confined himself to discussing the transition of the war economy to a peace-time economy under the existing socio-economic conditions.[14]

But Kautsky's position was soon abandoned by the left wing of the Social Democratic Party, in view of the rapid growth of a revolutionary mass movement after the end of the war. Even for those on the Left, however, the sudden change of mood among the workers, which occurred soon after the collapse of the Monarchy, came as an utter surprise, as can be seen from a remark by Max Adler: 'Socialism cannot, *as we have always believed*, simply take over the capitalist economy in its undisturbed development and at its full height, but must try to set up this economy anew under the whip of hunger [wielded by] the imperialistic victory of the Entente.'[15]

Otto Bauer realized at a relatively early stage the qualitative change in the outlook of the Austrian workers. His draft of an election manifesto, which he submitted to the party's executive committee on 28 December 1918, contained a demand for socialization;[16] a little later, from 5 to 28 January 1919, he published a series of essays in the *Arbeiter-Zeitung (Workers' Daily)* in which he presented his plan for socialization to the public. Soon afterwards the essays were published in a pamphlet entitled *Der Weg zum Sozialismus (The Road to Socialism)*.

Bauer's short study, which – as he said later – was written in great haste, has found a permanent place in the history of ideas of socialism. It was the first systematic scheme for transferring the means of production to social ownership, by stages, and contained a plan that was original, though based on syndicalist ideas as well as on those of the English 'guild socialists', for the internal and external organization of socialized industries.[17]

Under the impact of the fundamental social changes which had taken place in Hungary and Bavaria, but which proved to be of short duration, the Austrian Social Democrats were forced to act. In March 1919 a commission on socialization was established which included, besides Bauer, the leading Christian-Social politician, the prelate Ignaz Seipel. The commission met and conferred for only six months. With the decline of the revolutionary mood among the masses, especially evident after the collapse of the Hungarian Soviet Republic in August 1919, Austrian efforts towards socialization were deprived of their strongest political foundation. Of the few laws which owe their existence to the commission on socialization, only that on works councils has survived to the present day, though in modified form. But, contrary to Otto Bauer's expectations, the councils have not gone down in Austrian history as the 'grand school of proletarian self-government in the production process'.[18] The nationalization laws of the Second Republic are the product of a political constellation in which the existence of works councils provided no decisive momentum.

In Bauer's plan the process of socialization was to start in the mines and in heavy industry and be gradually extended to other branches of the economy. The immediate socialization of coal and iron-ore mining as well as the iron and steel industries had two important reasons behind it: firstly, the strategic importance of these industries for the economy, and secondly, their high degree of concentration, which made it seem practicable to manage production from a central location.

The administration of the socialized industries was not to be put into the hands of the government, which Bauer thought to be bureaucratic and thus a bad manager, but into the hands of bodies comprised of representatives of the producers, the consumers and the government, with each group providing one third of the members. The representatives of government were to reconcile the interests of the producers with those of the consumers. For those branches of production which, because of their small-business structure, were not yet ready for socialization Bauer suggested the formation of 'federations of industries', similar to cartels, following the pattern of the central offices and industrial boards that had developed during the war. Workers and entrepreneurs as well as representatives of the consumers and the government were to have an equal share in managing these big associations under public law.

Bauer's *Road to Socialism* must be seen above all as an attempt to confront the communist model of socialization, which is based on the 'dictatorship of the proletariat' and thus on the total deprivation of power of all political groups opposing socialization, with a social-democratic counter-model. The 'revolution' Bauer and his party comrades had in mind was to be a gradual and orderly change, an act – or rather, a series of acts – of 'creative legislation' which could be pushed through, they hoped, without dictatorial measures. Bauer rejected the concept of a violent total socialization for reasons of *Realpolitik*, and still more so for basic political reasons. Prussian socialism in the fashion of Plenge or Spengler and Bolshevism were both, to his mind, manifestations of the same superstition about an omnipotent state which wants 'to force the obedient masses to develop higher forms of life'. He contrasted this misconceived socialism, forced upon the people by an élitist minority, with democratic socialism, at the root of which, as he put it, 'is the desire for liberty of the individual, its source the independent activity of the masses and its aim self-government by all the workers. . . .'[19]

In Bauer's opinion another important argument in favour of a gradual socialization was that the social apparatus of production in Western and Central Europe was far more complicated and susceptible to disorder than in backward Russia. Thus a revolution backed by European workers would have to take care, as Bauer expressed it, 'not to disrupt the social metabolism'. It must not 'destroy any capitalist organization ... before the socialist organization exists which is supposed ... to take its place'. For all these reasons Bauer expected a 'long transitional period which will last for generations' and in which 'capitalist and socialist enterprises will exist side by side'. In much the same way as remnants of feudalism survived into the capitalist era, there would be traces of capitalism within a socialist society. Socialism would be a 'social order of mixed forms'.[20]

I have dealt at some length with Otto Bauer's thought because it had a considerable influence on the long debate about socialism within Austrian Social Democracy, which reached a provisional close in 1932 with Walter Schiff's study *Die Planwirtschaft und ihre ökonomischen Hauptprobleme (The Planned Economy and Its Main Economic Problems)*. Obviously Bauer's programmatic publications, confining themselves to problems of the external and internal organization of the socialized sector of the economy, left open a number of important questions. Notable among them are:

(1) On what kind of information concerning the pattern of demand can a central planning authority rely if it is to function almost completely without the signals of a free market?

(2) How rational is a system which in the allocation of its necessarily scarce resources lacks the controlling functions of the market?

The two questions are, of course, in close logical relation to each other. One may make allowances for the fact that Bauer was not particularly interested in devising an efficient controlling mechanism for the planned economy he aimed at; the utter destitution of the early post-war period made it essential to meet the basic needs of the population with what means were available. Walter Schiff, too, whose above-mentioned book was published in the very trough of the world economic depression, believed that what mattered was to use the unemployed manufacturing facilities, thus making it possible 'to give to the economic plan a static character to some extent'.[21] The question of national accounting under socialism may have seemed of relatively little interest in 1918 or 1932, but nevertheless must be considered a key problem of any *dynamic* economy. Thus it is no surprise that the theoretical and ideological counter-offensive of the Austrian bourgeoisie launched by Ludwig von Mises centred around this open question.

Ludwig von Mises, whom I have mentioned as a younger representative of the Austrian school of economics, in the spring of 1920, while Bauer's proposals for socialization were still being actively discussed, published an essay in the renowned periodical *Archiv für Sozialwissenschaft* of which little notice was taken at the time. Two years later he enlarged his essay into a book which must be seen as an ambitious attempt to refute all the theories so far advanced that had demonstrated the efficiency and ethical soundness of a socialist economic and social system.[22] *The Road to Serfdom,* the anti-socialist treatise published by Friedrich von Hayek shortly after World War II, which became known all over the world, was anticipated in its main points by Mises's book.

Briefly, in his study Mises proceeded from the system of economic distribution *in natura* practised during World War I, which was reflected particularly in the works of Otto Neurath,[23] to postulate that in consumer-goods markets there would be complete freedom of choice for the consumer. The situation would be different in markets for capital goods, where socialist managers confronting one another have to act according to the directions of the central planning office. In such a situation a market in the traditional sense cannot develop, and thus no system of pricing which would make it possible to act rationally. In other words, the valuation of capital goods in terms of money would become impossible, and hence the efficiency of investment decisions could no longer be ensured.

So Mises, following the logic of his argument, concluded that only a system based on private ownership – or special ownership (*Sondereigentum*) as he termed it – of the means of production, as well as on the totality of the exchange relations originating in private property, would guarantee a rational allocation of the limited resources of a particular economy. He drew an emphatic contrast with the view, held by socialists, that capitalism was basically marked by anarchy. 'Liberalism', said Mises, 'does not demand that property belong specially to the owners of capital but to the public at large; it holds that the maintenance of the capitalist social order is in the interest not only of the owners of capital, but of all members of society.'[24] In a socialist society there would be none, or only slight inequalities in the distribution of income. But as under socialism less is produced, the sum total of what can be distributed would be considerably smaller; everybody would get less than even the poorest receive now.

Mises raised what he saw as another grave objection to the prevailing socialist doctrine represented chiefly by Bauer: this doctrine was aimed, he said, at perpetuating the stage of production reached before socialization because it was 'unable to admit that in economic matters nothing is more permanent than change'. Looking ahead and making provision for the future, introducing new methods of production, he stated emphatically, 'has always been the concern of the few, the leaders'. Socialism, on the other hand, is 'the economic policy of the masses, of the many who are strangers to the nature of business ...'.[25] A short time later, as we shall see, Schumpeter was to publish an essay in the *Archiv für Sozialwissenschaft* which very effectively demolished this second pillar of the liberal position.

Meanwhile Mises's assertion concerning the fundamental irrationality of the socialist planned economy had a varied response in professional economics circles. He had overlooked – or perhaps deliberately ignored – the work of the Italian economist E. Barone who, basing himself on the ideas of the renowned theorist Walras, from Lausanne, had defended the rationality of a socialist system in the period before World War I.[26] Among the Austrians, only Walter Schiff treated explicitly the question of national accounting under socialism and tried to solve it by referring to the labour theory of value, as set out in the often-cited passage from Engels's *Anti-Dühring*:

> From the moment when society enters into possession of the means of production and uses them in direct association for production, the labour of each individual, however varied its specifically useful character may be, is immediately and directly social labour. The quantity of social labour contained in a product has then no need to be established in a roundabout way; daily experience shows in a direct way how much of it is required on the average.[27]

The discussion of the 1930s, which by then had taken on a truly international character, challenged Mises on his own terms – those of the 'marginal utility' school.[28] The eminent Polish economist Oskar Lange, in a logically tight and brilliantly formulated response, held that the price is not necessarily the result of exchange relations in the market but can also be laid down by the central planning authority as a 'calculation price'. So that this price may make possible an efficient use of resources, the top management of a given public enterprise is obliged to apply certain rules: first, to minimize the cost of production for each product and, secondly, to fix the volume of production at the level indicated by the equivalence of price and marginal costs. The calculation price fixed by the planning authority will, in a process of gradual approximation, lead finally to a clearing of the markets and will thus display all relevant features of an 'equilibrium price' which,

under conditions of free competition, is arrived at through the interplay of supply and demand.

The central planning authority has another important function,
namely to establish the economic rate of accumulation, that is the
ratio between the production of capital goods and that of consumer
goods. So the dynamics of this system are, in the final analysis, determined by the political will of the community, finding expression in the
decisions of the planning authority. With the long series of essays that
culminated in Lange's study, cited here,[29] the ideological counter-
offensive of Ludwig von Mises and associates was effectively demolished.

What then followed was a rear-guard action, chiefly conducted not
by Mises himself but by his disciple Friedrich von Hayek. The immediate response of Hayek to Barone and Lange's line of reasoning
was to attribute to a socialist system the theoretical but not the practical ability to apply its resources in an optimal way. The central planning authority, Hayek thought, must

> take into consideration all the interdependent factors (the quantity
> of goods produced, prices, production coefficients, etc.) and solve
> the equations for all goods and services – a system composed of
> hundreds of thousands of equations, with hundreds of thousands of
> unknown quantities, the underlying assumption being always that
> the latest data are used. As it can hardly be assumed that these re-
> quirements can be met, a rational socialist economy, although
> theoretically conceivable, cannot exist in practice.[30]

At a time of increasingly mechanized and automated business
accounting, Hayek may have realized that this line of argument was
not based on very solid ground. In his polemical pamphlet *The Road to
Serfdom* he therefore shifted the main emphasis of his argument into
the sphere of politics. He concluded that a community which entrusts
final authority in the field of economic policy to a central agency
would sooner or later be forced to transfer the formulation of its political will to a hierarchically organized team of leaders. Conversely, the
free interplay of market forces would also guarantee the free interplay
of political forces. Thus Hayek, in relying on a vulgarly materialistic
philosophy, established a direct connection between a private-enter-
prise economic system and a liberally organized society. In this respect, he was following certain ideas expressed by Mises as early as
1922, when he said that

> Marxism does not, in spite of some remarks on the historic achieve-

ments of liberalism, understand the importance of the ideas of liberalism. It does not know what to make of the liberal demands for freedom of conscience and freedom of opinion, the basic acknowledgement of any opposition and of the equality of all parties. Wherever it is not in power it claims all the basic liberal rights to the greatest extent possible because it is only through these rights that it gains scope for the action urgently needed for its propaganda activities. But it can never understand their nature and it will never bring itself to concede them to its opponents when it is in power.[31]

It would appear that in demonizing Social Democracy, leaders of both liberal and conservative opinion knew how to give each other their cues.

Otto Bauer may have been too preoccupied with his political duties to pay much attention to the ideological counter-offensive by Mises, Hayek and their associates. Thus it must have come as a surprise to him to receive support from someone he had used to count among those in the rival camp. In 1921 Professor Joseph Schumpeter published an essay, 'Sozialistische Möglichkeiten von heute', in the same periodical in which Mises, shortly before, had launched his anti-socialist offensive. The essay shows very clearly that Schumpeter by no means rejected a socialization programme under *favourable* historical circumstances – and to him the year 1919, when Austria was completely dependent on relief measures from abroad, seemed a rather unfavourable moment.

By way of introduction Schumpeter notes that political action aiming at the socialization of the means of production 'can only be successful when a historical process of automatic socialization, inherent in the course of events, has already set in, that is, if the social development itself is moving in the direction of socialism'. 'We owe this realization', Schumpeter added, 'especially to Karl Marx.'[32]

Schumpeter explains this 'inherent' process of socialization through the tendency towards concentration in capitalism – paying explicit tribute, also in this context, to Marx's theoretical system. But in contrast to Marx's disciples, Kautsky and Hilferding, Schumpeter thought that monopoly would not necessarily have to reach its highest stage of development; in his opinion – and this was confirmed by the subsequent development – the process of concentration could terminate at an earlier stage: at that of oligopoly. In any case, he says, a competitive economy develops 'out of its own necessities' a tendency 'unmistakably pointing towards socialism: it has "rationalized" the economy and business management'.[33]

How is the Schumpeterian concept of 'rationalization' to be understood? While in the era of the competitive economy the continuous re-organization – or, as we would say today, the re-structuring of the economy – was a function of entrepreneurial innovation or creative destruction, today it has become 'the subject of a systematically pursued scientific process'. To put it in Schumpeter's words, economic expedience has 'made itself independent, economic progress has become more and more impersonal'.[34]

Many years later, in his widely known book, *Capitalism, Socialism and Democracy*, Schumpeter devoted much more space to this idea. He thought that in the era of monopoly capitalism the creative entrepreneur had been supplanted by a collective of managers (or a 'technostructure', to use a Galbraithian term), and the highly individual acts of innovation of former days gave way to collective acts by a managerial team. The function of the continuous recreation of the productive potential of society has in recent times been turned into a scientific pursuit and has become 'bureaucratized'.

It is, however, not only in the position of the manager of the means of production, but also in that of the owner of capital that a far-reaching socio-economic change takes place, as Marx observed.[35] Schumpeter argues that

> the ownership of an inherited factory is gradually replaced by the ownership of a parcel of shares; the lively contact with all the people and things involved in production is gradually replaced by management from a board room, in particular by the management of employees. Today's typical industrial magnate is president or managing director of a stock corporation; his position is essentially temporary, in no case hereditary.

Thus Schumpeter draws the conclusion that 'at the centres of capitalist life a step towards socialism is taking place – more effective through the force of facts than any deliberate action could be'.[36]

In his 1921 essay Schumpeter implied that, from the point of view of the public interest, socialism should be seen as a much more efficient economic system than capitalism. In *Capitalism, Socialism and Democracy* he explicitly affirms the same idea. But 'Of course', he says there,

> all that I have said so far refers exclusively to the logic of blueprints, hence to the 'objective' possibilities which socialism in practice may be quite unable to realize. But as a matter of blueprint logic it is undeniable that the socialist blueprint is drawn at a

higher level of rationality. (p. 196)

Then he mentions some reasons why socialism is to be seen as a more rational economic system than capitalism. He thinks socialism will be able to eliminate almost completely the cyclical fluctuations characteristic of capitalism, and that thereby unemployment, the permanent scourge of capitalism, will be largely banished. But the elimination of unemployment will never be complete under capitalism, even under a variation on this system controlled by means of modern economic instruments.

Schumpeter emphasizes that socialism offers the preconditions for a systematic introduction of technological innovation as well as, simultaneously, the elimination of obsolete methods of production. But he adds a warning which todays sounds rather prophetic:

> Of course, the likelihood of this particular advantage, whether great or small, being realized by a bureaucracy is another matter; a decent bureaucracy may always be relied on to bring all its members up to *its* standard, but this says nothing about what this standard itself will be. That possible superiorities might in practice turn into actual inferiorities must be kept in mind throughout.
> (*Capitalism*, 197)[37]

As we have seen, Oskar Lange and Schumpeter, in their counter-attacks on Mises's position, proceeded from different assumptions. Lange had constructed the model of a socialist *market* economy and presented it convincingly as logically consistent. But it could justifiably be claimed that his logically incontestable abstraction was no closer to realization than the model of his adversary Mises, which he so stringently criticized. Schumpeter rightly pointed out that the atomized free market economy had long ago been replaced by a highly monopolized economy which had an inherent tendency towards socialization; and further that the innovative function of the industrial entrepreneur – which Mises regarded as the decisive advantage of an economy oriented towards capitalism – had gradually been taken over by a managerial team and thus become bureaucratized. But later he added, as we have noted, the warning that a bureaucracy could perform this function either efficiently or inefficiently. The superiority of a socialist system over its historical predecessors was not guaranteed under any and all circumstances.

The Bauer-Mises-Schumpeter controversy of the inter-war period, in which many other hardly less competent and articulate economists took part, leads us right into the continuing and persistently pursued discussion about socialism. Today there seems hardly any need to demonstrate that socialism is a system which works, as Schumpeter always stressed. Whether it should be organized mainly along the lines of a market economy, as Oskar Lange thought, or as an economy more or less rigorously controlled from above, which Schumpeter seems to have had in mind, is an issue still hotly debated today. Finally, most of the socialist systems in existence today are of a mixed type, in which a market and a planned economy are combined in various proportions.

The question of 'proportion' is, of course, not a purely technical one nor – to use the customary jargon – a technocratic one. The more rigorously the central plans are put into effect, the more powerful will be the bureaucratic structures required to carry them out, and the narrower will be the limits imposed on the initiative of the working population. As the Russian example has demonstrated, a centrally controlled economy may even be able, under certain circumstances, to make up a serious lag in development within a relatively short time, and to mobilize to a great extent the material and human resources of a country to this positive end. But such a system of tutelage, no matter how paternally and popularly conceived it may be, will necessarily have a tendency to perpetuate itself. No class of officials, even if initially it is committed to a socialist – or pseudo-socialist – objective, will be prepared to accept the gradual atrophying of its functions, as would be in keeping with a philosophy of the 'withering away of the state', on the contrary, it will invent excuses, like the paranoid notion of a constant encirclement and a permanent threat to the country from outside, to cling to its influence, prestige and privileges, even at times when there are hardly any objective reasons for the continued manipulation of the masses.

But with the permanent installation of a paternalistic system its initial advantages turn into disadvantages which are bound to become increasingly manifest. The governing apparatus, which according to Parkinson's Law is continuously expanding, sees itself as isolated from the great mass of the people, which, as the level of education rises, becomes more and more alienated from the ruling system. The growth rates of productivity at the place of work, in the laboratory and in the institutes of higher education and the arts visibly decrease, finally jeopardizing the competitiveness of the system as a whole.

The question of the relationship between plan and market, self-initiative and control from 'above', bureaucracy and determination from below, is in the final analysis not a technical or a technocratic but a highly political problem. Bauer certainly realized this at a very early date, when, as we have seen, he rejected both a Prussian and a Bolshevist model of socialism. Austro-Marxism conceived of socialism and political freedom as an inseparable entity. Mises and his pupil Hayek, on the other hand, have denied that any reconciliation between socialism and democracy could ever be brought about. History has not yet delivered its final verdict on this issue.

1981/1983

Chapter 7

The Periodization of the Austrian and German Economies[*]

Schumpeter prefaces his book *Business Cycles* (1939) with the statement that 'Analyzing business cycles means neither more nor less than analyzing the economic process of the capitalist era' (p.v). He thought it necessary to study the development of the capitalist system as a whole in order to extract from it a theoretical construct of its cyclical oscillations. The historical material available to him at the time was the more or less well-trodden economic history of Western Europe and of the United States. Relatively little research had then been carried out on nineteenth-century Central Europe and the Danubian Monarchy; Austria-Hungary in particular was a blank space on the historiographic map.

Fortunately the picture has changed greatly over the past 20 years. During this period a number of Austrian and American economic historians have dealt very thoroughly with the process of industrialization in the Danubian Monarchy; however, considerable differences have emerged in the interpretation of the historical material.[1] In what follows Schumpeter's theories of economic growth and of the business cycle will be tested by applying them to two countries which were given relatively little attention in his monumental work.

Let us first make a short side trip into Schumpeter's theory of the

---

[*] A revised and enlarged version of the essay, 'Das Wirtschaftswachstum in Deutschland und Österreich von der Mitte des 19. Jahrhunderts bis zum 1. Weltkrieg: Eine vergleichende Darstellung, first published in *Historische Konjunkturformen*, ed. Wilhelm H. Schroeder and Reinhard Spree (Stuttgart, 1980).

114

business cycle. How – and this is the question tackled at the outset by the young Schumpeter in his early work, *The Theory of Economic Development* (1911) – do periodic disturbances of a stationary state of equilibrium occur? The essence of the Schumpeterian theory is that a disturbance of equilibrium, which usually occurs after a more or less extended period of relative peace, characterized by relative stability of prices and costs, is caused by the introduction of new productive combinations. Or, put more simply, his theory of the business cycle is based on the concept of innovation.

A successful act of innovation as a rule encourages imitation. In this way the state of equilibrium is disturbed, not by a single shock but by a series of similar shocks, leading to a general change in price and cost relations. In his *Theory of Economic Development* Schumpeter stresses the emergence of 'clusters' of entrepreneurs (or of entrepreneurial achievements) which become the starting-point of a cyclical upswing. This primary wave of upswing is soon followed by a secondary one, sustained by a number of factors, above all by increased demand for capital and consumer goods resulting from the first wave.

As entrepreneurial profits, originally high, are subject to a gradual process of erosion – through competition from imitators, on the one hand, and through increased prices of elements in the cost, on the other, to mention two of the most important recessionary tendencies[2] – the economic boom increasingly loses force. Finally an upper turning-point is reached, leading to a calming down and consequently to a shrinking of business activity. We thus enter a phase of recession, which, if one goes along with Schumpeter, is not necessarily superseded by a period of depression. It may be added here in parentheses that the period of upswing is accompanied by inflation caused by increasing demand for personal and material resources. In the ensuing recession prices move in the opposite direction.[3]

In *Business Cycles* Schumpeter distinguishes between three cycles (each named for the prominent theorist who 'discovered' it) of different duration: the 60-year Kondratieff, the 10-year Juglar, and the short 40-month Kitchin. There are about 18 disturbances of equilibrium of varying duration within a single Kondratieff cycle. As Schumpeter sees the introduction of new combinations as the cause of all disturbances of equilibrium, we have to assume that the shortest of all waves, the Kitchin wave, has the same causal nexus. At first sight this would seem to be a purely mono-causal approach. The Schumpeterian theory may be correct in the case of the long Kondratieff and the 10-year Juglar, because radical changes in the production

function, of the stage-coach/railway type, necessarily lead to large
shifts in the structure of prices and costs. Schumpeter himself conceded that such explanations do not apply to the short Kitchin cycle.
It may, instead, be regarded as a process of adaptation caused by
'secondary waves'. *External* shocks such as wars, crop failure or the
discovery of gold are also identified by Schumpeter as factors causing
crises, sometimes leading to long-term oscillations in the economic
process.[4]

It is hardly fair, therefore, to reproach him for taking a purely
mono-causal approach. The duration of the Kondratieff and Juglar
cycles, too, is seen by him as an *empirical* phenomenon. He would
certainly not have denied the observation made frequently today that
the span of the Juglar cycles has become shorter over the past decades
– possibly because of the escalation of innovative processes. And
finally, he would not have objected, I think, to the criticism occasionally advanced that he did not succeed in establishing a close link
between statics and dynamics. Schumpeter knew very well that reality
is more complicated than any model of it, however sophisticated. And
so he wrote in *Business Cycles* of the 'chronic disequilibrium of
reality'.

Does Schumpeter's model of growth, with the 60-year Kondratieff,
comprising 6 Juglars and 18 Kitchins, have any bearing on Austrian
economic history in the 60 years leading up to the outbreak of World
War I? I shall try to answer this question at the end of this chapter,
noting here, however, the paucity of the available data. The research
done thus far on Austria's economic history in the era of the Emperor
Francis Joseph still shows considerable gaps – lacking, for example,
statistical data on Austria's economy (or, to be more precise, on the
Cisleithanian half of the Danubian Monarchy) such as W.G. Hoffmann and his colleagues have compiled for nineteenth-century Germany. In tracing business cycles one can therefore rely only partly on
quantitative information, and has to use, especially for the period up
to 1870, individual indicators and qualitative information provided by
contemporary authors.

1 The economies of Austria and Germany c. 1850

Around the middle of the nineteenth century the states of the German
Zollverein were doubtless more advanced economically than Austria;
according to estimates by Nachum Gross, based on the first industrial
census of 1841, the per capita income in Austria at that time was about

75 per cent of that in Germany.[5] Cisleithania's relative backwardness can be demonstrated by a number of economic indicators, although some branches of the Austrian economy, such as the cotton industry, still had a lead over Germany around 1850.[6] The structure of employment, too, shows a higher degree of industrialization in Germany: a comparison of data collected in a survey of employment in Austria in 1869 with the corresponding data for Germany indicates that the proportion of industrial workers was 19.7 per cent in Austria, but as high as 27.6 per cent in Germany. At that time about two-thirds of the Austrian population was still employed in agriculture, compared with only about one-half in Germany.[7] The markedly higher level of development in Germany around 1850 was the result of the comparatively rapid economic development from about 1800 onwards, when the states of the later German Zollverein and Austria had started from almost the same economic level.[8]

The development of modern large-scale industry had begun in Austria at about the same time as in the rest of continental Europe, that is towards the end of the eighteenth century. The move towards large-scale industrial production was then fostered through a series of measures on the part of the central government: protectionist tariffs on imports from foreign countries and removal of the customs frontiers between individual parts of the Empire (with the exception of the tariffs between Austria and Hungary), as well as by loans granted at low interest rates for the establishment of new industrial enterprises. The beginnings of industrialization were favoured by a high standard in handicrafts and manufactories as well as by immigration of entrepreneurs and master mechanics from the West.[9] Further development was adversely affected, however, by the unfavourable location of coal and iron-ore deposits, an inadequate transport network, and the lack of domestic markets capable of absorbing the goods produced.[10] Moreover, the absolutist regime of the pre-revolutionary era viewed industrialization as a threat to its social basis and so, by contrast with the mercantilist economic policy of Maria Theresa and Joseph IX, did little to promote the modern factory system.

The sparse statistical material that is available on the first half of the nineteenth century does not permit any exact periodization of Austria's economic development, but growth probably proceeded through the following phases: The Napoleonic wars initially stimulated the Austrian economy, but this was followed by a long period of stagnation after the 'national bankruptcy' in 1811. It was only around the middle of the 1820s that a new upswing started, which lasted until about 1830 and was supported by a considerable expansion of the iron as well as woollen and cotton industries. These three branches recorded an average annual growth of 5.2 per cent.[11] After a slow-down in the first half of the 1830s, influenced by the cholera epidemic brought in from China, another upswing set in around the middle of the decade, caused in particular by railway construction and lasting – with few interruptions – until well into the pre-revolutionary era.

We need not deal here in detail with the early phase of industrialization in Germany.[12] In spite of favourable conditions, partly resulting from the proximity of coal and iron-ore deposits, the process of industrialization could only fully take hold in the wake of the institutional and economic changes in the first half of the nineteenth century: the political reorganization after the Napoleonic wars, the Stein-Hardenbergian land reform, the formation of the German Zollverein as well as the expansion of the transport systems – road building, railways, ships – created the basis for the industrial revolution in Germany, which began around 1850 and was to lead the country, by the outbreak of World War I, to top rank among the industrial nations of the Old World.

2 Economic growth between 1850 and 1913

Paul Bairoch's calculations of the per-capita gross domestic product for the major European countries may serve as a rough indication of economic growth.[13] If Austria's per capita gross domestic product in real terms is compared with the corresponding figures for Germany, the growth differential of the two countries can clearly be seen.

*Real per capita income in Austria
in % of the German figures*

1850	1860	1870	1880	1890	1900	1910	1913
74	67	61	60	57	54	57	57

Source: P. Bairoch, A. Kausel

From 1850 to 1913 average economic growth in Germany surpassed that of Austria in all decades except one; the upswing setting in in Cisleithania after the turn of the century was decidedly stronger than that in Austria's northern neighbour. We have therefore, elsewhere and with some justification, called this period a second *'Gründerzeit'*.[14]

An outline of the development of per capita income gives only a very general idea of economic growth: to obtain a more accurate picture of the factors determining growth, we must look at the cyclical development in Germany and Austria, and, after that, at the most outstanding structural changes in the two economies from 1850 to 1913.

3 The development of the Austrian economy from 1850 to 1913

An outline of Austrian economic development can be based on yearly estimates of the gross domestic product only from 1870 onwards; for the period from 1850 to 1870, quantitative data exists only in the form of indicators for individual branches of industry and estimates relating to certain years in which censuses were taken.[15] The calculations by Gross of the growth of industrial output must be revised, however, in the light of more recent research: Th. F. Huertas has shown that the data for 1865, on which Gross's estimates are based, stem from an industrial census conducted ten years earlier. If this correction is taken into account, the picture of industrial expansion differs somewhat from that presented by Gross, because the industrial upswing of the 1850s took a course considerably more pronounced than has emerged from the studies carried out so far.[16]

The works of März and Matis suggest the following periodization of economic growth between 1850 and 1870:[17]

The first half of the 1850s was characterized in Austria by a slight economic upswing, briefly interrupted by the Crimean War (1854). The years 1856 and 1857 were marked by strong business activity, followed by a long period of stagnation which was finally overcome by the boom of the 'Gründerzeit'. The unsatisfactory development between 1858 and 1866 can be attributed to a number of economic and political factors, the most important of which are doubtless the deflationary monetary and budget policies of the then Minister of Finance Ignaz v. Plener. By severely reducing the quantity of notes in circulation, Plener hoped to do away with the disagio of the paper gulden against the standard coin,[18] an undertaking which was, however, defeated by the war against Prussia (1866). Railway construction, too, slackened towards the end of the 1850s: the government, impeded by its acute financial troubles, was unable to compensate for the lack of private initiative.[19] From 1855 to 1860 the Austrian railway network was extended by about 1,439 km, but in the subsequent five years by only about 771 km (−46 per cent).[20] The cotton crisis caused by the American Civil War, and the silk crisis ensuing from the loss of Lombardy (1859), aggravated the recessionary tendencies of the early 1860s. The indices worked out by Rudolph for three sectors of industry illustrate the crisis-like development of the Austrian economy: the index of metallurgy increased only from 71 to 73 in the period 1859-63; the index of textile production fell from 60 to 37 in the period 1857-65 (1880=100); while mining was stagnant between 1857 and 1867.[21]

The economic upswing that began in Austria in 1867 lasted almost seven years and came to an end with the crash of 1873. The impetus for improvement in business activity was provided by the 'miracle harvests' of the years 1866-7 and 1867-8. As Western Europe had bad harvests in those years, Austrian exports of grain to the West increased considerably, thus greatly improving the profitability of the railway companies. The favourable earnings position of the railways led to stronger efforts in the railway sector; in 1866-78 2,514 km, and in 1871-5 4,225 km of track were opened to traffic in Austria.[22] Starting with the railways, the upward economic trend first took hold in major branches of the capital-goods industry and then spread to almost all branches of the consumer-goods industry. Part of the demand resulting from railway construction was lost to foreign companies as a result of inadequate production capacity at home, as can be seen from the rising capital goods imports.[23] The last two years before the crash of 1873 were characterized by the establishment of a large number of new banks in the financial sector, many of which were of a speculative nature and had to be liquidated during the ensuing depression. Neuwirth, Schäffle and Wirth have left us vivid descriptions of the feverish founding activity and of the crash.[24]

Summarizing the period from 1848 to 1875, one can say that it was characterized by three cycles of approximately equal duration which, from lower turning point to lower turning point, lasted from 1848 to 1854, from 1855 to 1866, and from 1867 to 1875.

The further development until 1913 can now be analysed on the basis of the data compiled by Kausel.[25] We shall divide this period into years of upswing and stagnation, with the growth of the gross domestic product in real terms serving as the unit of measurement.

Years of upswing (U) and years of stagnation (S) in
the Austrian economy 1871-1913

	U	S	years
	(average annual growth rate in %)		
1871	6.3		1
1872-1875		0.7	3
1876-1878	3.0		3
1879-1880		−0.2	2
1881-1884	2.5		4
1885		−0.2	1
1886-1891	2.7		6
1892-1893		0.7	2
1894-1898	3.2		5
1899-1900		0.7	2
1901-1907	3.1		7
1908-1909		0.7	2
1910-1912	2.8		3
1913		−0.4	1

Source: A. Kausel; author's own calculations

If one combines periods of upswing with the subsequent years of stagnation into a business cycle, five such cycles can be distinguished, each with an average duration of just under seven years, in the period 1876–1909.

Growth cycles of the Austrian economy

	years
1876-1880	5
1881-1885	5
1886-1893	8
1894-1900	7
1901-1909	9

Until well into the second half of the nineteenth century agriculture was the dominant sector of the Austrian economy: the living conditions of the major part of the population were more dependent on crop fluctuations than on the cycles of the capitalist industrial system. Between 1881 and 1882 the contribution of industry and trade to the real gross domestic product overtook that of agriculture and forestry, though employment in the agricultural sector remained higher until World War I.

The growth cycle from 1876 to 1880 shows clearly the still-dominant position of agriculture: although industry and trade had shown positive rates of growth since 1874, it was only from 1876 onwards that a higher net value added by agriculture gave rise to a general economic upswing. The recovery of industry after the crisis of the *'Gründerzeit'* was mainly characterized by increases in production in the textile industry as well as in mining, while metallurgy reached the level of 1873 only at the beginning of the 1880s.[26]

The business cycle between 1881 and 1885 saw the rapid expansion of industrial production: particularly high growth rates were achieved in mechanical engineering and metal production, but the textile industry and the sugar industry also recorded considerable increases in production. The index for agriculture and forestry shows a stagnating volume of production in this period.[27] The relative share of industry (including small trades) in the gross domestic product now made the development of this sector the decisive factor in overall business activity from the 1880s onwards.

Mechanical engineering and metal production were the growth branches of the Austrian economy during the 1886-93 cycle. During the six years of upswing from 1886 to 1891 industry expanded its production by almost 30 per cent, compared with the rather modest growth of agriculture and forestry of just under 12 per cent.

The last two business cycles before World War I were marked by periods of strong upswing, each interrupted by only two years of slower growth: from 1894 to 1898 the gross domestic product increased rapidly, the average annual growth rate of 3.2 per cent recorded during that period being the greatest increase in the last 40 years of the Monarchy. During the seven years from 1901 to 1907 economic growth in absolute terms reached its highest level: the average growth rate in that period amounted to 3.1 per cent. The years from 1905 to 1907 were boom years, with real growth rates of 6.6 per cent, 4.1 per cent and 4.8 per cent.

The increase in the volume of production from 1894 to 1907 was determined by the development of industry, which grew by about 58 per cent during that period, while agriculture and forestry expanded by only about 28 per cent. Within industry, the sectors of heavy industry registered higher growth rates than the consumer-goods industry.[28]

This survey of economic activity in Austria, outlined here in rather general terms, has now to be contrasted with the corresponding data for Germany in order to gain insight into the industrialization process from a comparison of the two countries.

4 Economic development in Germany 1850-1913

The development of Germany's economy has, as we have said, been far more thoroughly studied than that of Austria; in what follows we shall mention only the most important data relevant to a comparison of economic growth.

If the statistics assembled by Hoffmann and others[29] for the real value added in Germany are taken as a yardstick for distinguishing between years of upswing and stagnation, one arrives at the results shown in the table below. The growth pattern of the German economy in the years after 1880 clearly differs from that of the take-off period: on average, the years of growth record higher growth rates until 1880; the periods of stagnation in the 1850s and '60s are distinctly longer than in the period of high industrialization that follows the depression of the second half of the 1870s. The turning away from competitive capitalism, the 'organizing' of markets through the formation of cartels, may have contributed to the steadying of the business trend.[30]

Years of upswing (U) and years of stagnation (S) in the German economy

	U	S	years
	(average growth rates in %)		
1850-1855		0.3	6
1856-1857	6.6		2
1858-1859		0.0	2
1860-1864	3.7		5
1865-1867		0.5	3
1868	5.9		1
1869-1870		0.2	2
1871-1874	5.5		4
1875-1880		0.1	6

Table continued on page 124

	U	*S*	*years*
	average annual growth rate in %)		
1881-1885	2.9		5
1886		0.6	1
1887-1890	3.5		4
1891		0.0	1
1892-1900	3.9		9
1901		0.0	1
1902-1907	3.6		6
1908-1909		1.9	2
1910-1913	4.0		4

Source: W.G. Hoffmann; author's own calculations

From the data in the above table, business cycles can be derived which are compared below with the results arrived at by Spree.

Business cycles of the German economy

(1)	(2)
1856-1859	1848-1859
1860-1870	1859-1879
1871-1880	
1881-1886	1879-1886
1887-1891	1886-1892
1892-1901	1892-1901
1902-1909	1901-1908

Source: (1) W.G. Hoffmann; (2) R. Spree[31]

The agreement in the periodization from 1880 in spite of the use of different methods comes as a surprise: Spree dates the business cycles by comparing the turning points of 15 indicators of economic development and by means of a diffusion index.[32] The results differ most markedly in the way the 1870s are classified: while Spree views the four years of upswing from 1871 to 1874 as a partial period of a twenty-year cycle (1859-1879), we think of the upswing after the Franco-Prussian War as the starting-point of a new business cycle.[33]

5 Comparison of economic development in Germany and Austria

In the period from 1850 to 1913 the growth rate of the German economy was higher than that of the Austrian: in Germany the real value added increased at an annual rate of 2.6 per cent, while Austria's gross domestic product in real terms reached annual growth rates of only 1.8 per cent on average.[34] German industry expanded at the rate of 3.8 per cent per year, while Austrian industry lagged behind at 3.1 per cent.

If one compares the individual business cycles in the two countries, the big disparities in economic growth during the 1860s are conspicuous: the Austrian economy stagnated from 1858 to 1867, but in Germany during that period the volume of production increased considerably. The disparities in growth are most marked in industry: from 1860 to 1874 the gross domestic product of industry and trade in Austria increased by a mere 33 per cent, while in Germany the real value added by industry and trade rose by about 87 per cent. Austria was unable to close this enormous industrial gap until World War I. From about 1880 onwards the growth of both countries followed a similar pattern, although Germany had higher rates of growth during that period,[35] while the lag in Austria's economic development, dating from the 1850s, became ever more pronounced during the decades before World War I.

The weaker overall performance of Austria resulted from a combination of economic and political factors. As I have recounted elsewhere, with the beginning of railway construction, the iron and steel industry along with mechanical engineering displaced the textile industry from its leading role in the process of industrialization. At that stage the availability of coal and iron ore in sufficient quantity and quality, as well as of cheap transport, became a precondition of rapid development. Compared with Germany, Austria was at a disadvantage as to the supply of raw materials. While there were large amounts of cokable coal and considerable iron-ore deposits in Cisleithania, the coal mines were far away from the ore deposits. The iron industry was adversely affected by the high cost of transport of coal and ore, and was capable of expanding only behind high customs barriers.[36] In Austria the prices of iron and coal were considerably higher than in Germany.[37] Besides the cartel policy of the Austrian iron producers,[38] the relatively high transport costs helped to account for the difference in prices compared with Germany. According to Milward and Saul, in the Ruhr area the transport costs of one ton of coal decreased between 1820 and 1850 from 40 pfennigs to 2.[39] Calculations of this kind are not available for Austria, but it may be considered certain that the extension of the railways, which did not start on a large scale until the *'Gründerzeit'*, did not lead to comparable cost reductions.

The unfavourable location of the deposits of strategic raw materials, as well as the relatively high transport costs, may have been among the factors responsible for the structure of Austrian industry, which was characterized until 1913 by the dominance of the consumer-goods industry. Its share in total industrial output was still about two-thirds in 1880, and at 49 per cent in 1911 it was clearly higher than the contribution of the typical capital-goods industry, which reached 38 per cent.[40] The data for Germany compiled by Spohn show a distinct preponderance of the capital-goods industry in 1913, which produced nearly 42 per cent of the total value added, as against the consumer-goods industry with a contribution of less than 32 per cent.[41]

Apart from economic factors, there were political and socio-psychological causes considered to have contributed to Austria's slower economic growth in the nineteenth century.[42] These include the numerous wars in which Austria was engaged between 1848 and 1866, the remarkably high volume of military spending even in times of peace, and the anti-capitalist climate prevailing in the Monarchy. The Austrian entrepreneurs were never able fully to assert themselves against feudal traditions nor against the guild mentality of small trade. Moreover, the large-scale enterprises organized in the form of joint-stock companies were clearly discriminated against by the tax system,[43] and so the economic structure was under the dominance of small-business units until the end of the Monarchy.

The fact that the patterns of growth in Germany and Austria began to converge from 1830 onwards can be explained by Austria's increasing integration into the overall European process of industrialization by way of foreign trade. Economic growth is causally connected with an increasing internationalization of the markets and at the same time with the emergence of a unified trading area within individual countries. During the fifty years before World War I, the world economy expanded to an extent hitherto unknown, although business cycles international in scope can be observed as early as the first half of the nineteenth century.[44]

Austria's foreign trade was oriented primarily towards Germany,[45] whose business trends were among the most important external factors of economic growth in Cisleithania, Around the turn of the century more than 50 per cent of Austro-Hungarian exports flowed to Germany. Although this proportion had decreased to 40 per cent by the outbreak of the war, it was still nearly five times as high as that to Great Britain, the second largest buyer of the Monarchy's exports.[46]

Approximately two-fifths of Austro-Hungarian imports came from Germany, and this proportion was to rise slightly in the decade before World War I.

For Germany trade with the Habsburg Monarchy was of far less importance: only about 10 per cent of its total exports went to Austria-Hungary; this percentage rose slightly from 1900 onwards. Conversely, the proportion of goods imported by the German Empire from Austria-Hungary decreased from about 12 per cent to just above 7 per cent during the same period. This tendency in Austro-German foreign trade, unfavourable from the Monarchy's point of view, led in 1909 to the first deficit in Austria-Hungary's trade with Germany.

The transmission of cyclical impulses through foreign trade cannot be analysed here in detail. But a rough indication of the significance of exports for economic growth may be seen from the share commodity exports contribute to the gross domestic product. In 1911 the export ratio (proceeds from the export of goods as a proportion of the gross domestic product) was about 13 per cent;[47] the ratio of commodity exports to the value of the output of agriculture and forestry as well as of industry and trade amounted to just under 23 per cent at that time.[48]

Comparative figures for the middle of the nineteenth century should be treated with great caution, because estimates of the gross domestic product are especially unreliable. Estimates by the statistician Schwarzer indicate that the export ratio for 1860 was 6 per cent;[49] expressed as a percentage of output (agriculture and forestry, industry and trade) exports totalled almost 10 per cent in that year. In 1863, 32 per cent of total exports of commodities went to the German Zollverein, whence came 27 per cent of Austria's imports.[50] A comparison of these data with corresponding figures of 50 years later shows the growing importance of exports and of the German market for Austria's development.

The diffusion of business cycles from one country to another can take place not only by means of trade but also through movements of international capital. There are almost no records of the flow of

capital out of and into Austria in the nineteenth century; the first estimates of foreign capital invested in the Monarchy were made during
World War I.[51] From these it can be seen that in 1912 about half of the
foreign capital invested in Austria came from Germany. The greater
part of this capital – about 90 per cent – was invested in government
bonds,[52] thus contributing indirectly to the economic development of
the Monarchy. The bearing of capital imports on the simultaneity of
economic development in Austria and Germany can scarcely be
proved, from the scanty statistical material, but it would seem to have
been negligible. This is not to say however that the import of capital
from Germany during the period of high industrialization had no economic significance. The introduction of new industries with an excellent growth potential, such as the chemical industry, mechanical
engineering and the electrical industry, was undoubtedly helped
along by German capital as well as technical know-how; the second
factor particularly influenced the economic development of the Monarchy in the period from 1880 to 1913.

6 The Schumpeterian scheme of development in its application to Austria

Can the scheme of development put forward by Schumpeter, following the ideas of Nikolai D. Kondratieff, be applied to the period of intensive industrialization in the Danubian Monarchy – i.e. to the six
decades before the outbreak of World War I? Yes, we would say –
although with reservations. A long wave of 45 years – not the 60 years
posited by Kondratieff – seems to have lasted from 1848 to 1893. This
wave may be divided into two clearly demarcated periods of stronger
and weaker growth. The first of these, comprising three cycles of
approximately equal duration, lasted from 1848 to 1875 (from lower
turning-point to lower turning-point). It seems sensible to regard
these 27 years as a particular epoch in Austrian economic history, as
they were marked by an impetus that was historically unique: the
rapid extension of the railway system, with its specific 'linkage effects'.

The much shorter period, 1876 to 1893, was characterized by relatively weak economic growth. This becomes especially clear from the
indices of production calculated by Professor Richard Rudolph, which
show a continuous upward tendency.[53] In the recovery phase, from
1881 to 1884, the gross domestic product may thus have grown hardly
more than 2 per cent. The cyclical development of the 1880s and the
early '90s was not given such a strong impetus as in the previous

decades. Railway construction, which was again promoted by the government, entered a new phase of expansion, but, as Matis states, it no longer held the 'key position of the previous epoch'.[54] Other activating impulses came from the sugar, paper, textile and chemical industries. The mining industry, too, began to be more active, especially from the mid-1880s. That period also saw the beginning of the electrical industry, which grew, however, at a faster rate only during the last decade of the century. But this 17-year period of development was characterized by the depressed state of the world economy, and by a continuous fall in prices.

After a short set-back in the years 1892 and 1893, the Austrian economy experienced a period of upswing lasting for almost two decades, justifiably called the *'belle époque'*. In that time the Austrian part of the Monarchy achieved growth rates of the gross domestic product which exceeded those of neighbouring Germany. But the shortcomings and sins of omission of a century could not be overcome within two short decades. At the outbreak of World War I the Monarchy was the weakest among the leading European industrial nations.

The *belle époque* of the Austrian economy has to be seen against the background of a rapidly expanding world economy that favoured an upswing in numerous branches of industry, such as iron and steel, cement, glass, machines, sugar and textiles. Relatively new industries, especially for the manufacturing of electrical goods, chemicals, automobiles and oil, were increasingly determining the pace of development. Three other trends in the last two decades of the Monarchy: the growth of the cities, the expansion of the infrastructure linked to this phenomenon, and finally the enormous efforts in the field of armament, all contributed substantially to the economic upswing in Austria, particularly after the Balkan crisis of 1908.

The phenomenon of rapid urbanization can be demonstrated by taking Vienna as an example: in 1869, i.e. at the beginning of the *'Gründerzeit'*, the population of the capital was 850,000 (the figure includes the suburbs which had been incorporated into the city before 1914). By about 1900 the population had increased to 1.7 million. In 1913 the number of people living in Vienna amounted to 2.1 million, not including the large military forces quartered in the city. The number of people in the Austrian capital had thus increased by two and a half times since the *'Gründerzeit'*.[55]

The above observations would seem to permit the conclusion that around the middle of the 1890s a new long cyclical wave had begun, the basis of which lay in a 'swarm-like' series of trail-blazing innovations. At the beginning of the cycle Austria was a passive 'partaker' of the economic upswing. In the course of time it made its own contribution to the favourable business trend, with the large commercial banks holding a key position during the very strong upswing in the decade before World War I. Vienna's commercial banks not only provided the financial 'fuel' but also fostered the emergence of efficient large-scale enterprises by intensively promoting mergers.[56] Under the impact of this development, Schumpeter in his early work assigned to the banker an especially exalted role in the capitalist process of production: 'He makes possible the carrying out of new combinations, authorizes people, in the name of society as it were, to form them. He is the ephor of the exchange economy.' (*Theory*, 74) In his later works it is no longer the commercial bank that is at the centre of the process of economic development, but the big corporation.

1980/1983

Chapter 8

Schumpeter and the Austrian School of Economics[*]

In economics as a scientific discipline the view has come to be widely accepted that our century has produced two outstanding theorists: John Maynard Keynes and Joseph Alois Schumpeter. Schumpeter would hardly have been surprised by this fairly unanimous vote; but I believe he would have been in favour of adding another fixed star to this binary configuration – his teacher and mentor Eugen von Böhm-Bawerk, whose principal work, *Kapital und Kapitalzins, die Positive Theorie des Kapitals*, was published towards the end of the nineteenth century; though it was not until 1909, when the third edition appeared, that the work took on its final shape and gained its present recognition.

Soon after Böhm-Bawerk's death in 1914, Schumpeter tried to pay tribute to his life work as a scientist in a systematically set out and brilliantly worded essay (collected later in his *Ten Great Economists*),[1] which I personally find the best concise presentation of the main ideas of the Austrian school as developed by Böhm-Bawerk. In it Schumpeter endeavours to present a literal exegesis of his teacher's doctrines and carefully avoids the slightest hint of antagonism, even when dealing with subsidiary matters. One has the impression that by prostrating himself intellectually before the great departed, Schumpeter was striving to underline the inner consistency and the greatness of Böhm-Bawerk's doctrines, and to state his own allegiance to Böhm-Bawerk as a student and the heir to a remarkable scientific legacy. It is tempt-

* From 'Joseph A. Schumpeter und die österreichische Schule der Nationalökonomie' in Norbert Lesser ed., *Die Wiener Schule der Nationalökonomie* (Vienna, 1986).

131

ing to ask whether under the impact of his teacher's tragically sudden death, Schumpeter had not succumbed to a temptation to play down, or to regard as insignificant, the criticism he had formerly expressed of some of Böhm-Bawerk's theories.

Schumpeter's admiration for Böhm-Bawerk's theoretical achievement seems sincere and all but unqualified. He holds that, taking Menger's new ideas as his point of departure, Böhm-Bawerk has provided us with an all-embracing theory of the economic process on the scale of the classics or of Karl Marx. The central point of Böhm-Bawerk's analysis is the phenomenon of interest or net return on capital, which for Schumpeter was the most difficult, most important and, until then, an unsolved problem in economics. Schumpeter believes that all of our insight into, and our whole attitude towards, capitalism depends on our view of the function of interest and profit. Before Böhm-Bawerk only Marx had clearly understood the theoretical importance of this phenomenon, for the core of Marx's system was nothing but a theory of interest and profit. Everything else would follow conclusively from this theory. (*TGE*, 147.)

In his essay Schumpeter refers a second time to the relationship between Böhm-Bawerk and Marx. Having underlined once again the outstanding achievement of his teacher, he then says (*TGE*, 153) that in this connection a comparison with Marx has always forced itself upon him. This may seem strange, he adds, but only because the political passion which has always surrounded Marx has obscured his real scientific achievement. The two great theorists are linked not only by their efforts to analyse scientifically the phenomenon of interest and profit, but also by their almost Faustian search for the elements of a consistent and logically plausible economic theory based on division of labour from which forecasts can be derived. Schumpeter thinks that the most important element of such an economic system is a sound theory of value, because value is not only the prime mover of the economic cosmos, but also the form in which its most essential phenomena can be made comparable and measurable. The phenomenon of value is thus the key to a theoretical understanding of any economic order. And here Schumpeter adds (*TGE*, 151) that the *second* fundamental task concerns the development of a theory of interest and profit.

In his numerous writings Schumpeter always stressed the fact that his own theory was based on the fundamental ideas of the marginal utility school in its Austrian mould. In his essay 'Epochen der *Dogmen- und Methodengeschichte*' Schumpeter mentions two essential points in which he thinks the marginal utility school differs from the classical school. First, he says, the former stresses 'the explanation of the essence of pricing and income and thus was from the beginning different from the classical theory'. Then he adds: 'In this way a different, much "purer" economic theory was created, containing far fewer concrete facts and therefore offering far fewer concise, practical results, but which is much more well-grounded.'[2] Schumpeter then mentions a second 'essential difference', namely that the new theory dispenses with 'the aspect of the amount of labour as a regulator and measure of the value of goods . . . and stresses and elaborates the factor of utility'.

He believes that basing economics on the 'subjective theory of value' offers four advantages:

> It is more correct because the various cost theories have at best only approximate validity and they never reduce the phenomenon of costs to its actual source of explanation. It is simpler because the value theory of labour requires a number of auxiliary constructions, which can simply now be omitted. It is more general because in the first instance all cost theories refer only to commodities produced under free competition and partly only to 'freely augmentable' commodities; in addition they are only valid for periods of a certain duration, while the subjective theory of value encompasses both monopolized and non-monopolized commodities, both augmentable and non-augmentable commodities, as well as long and short periods of time. Finally it renders the results of economics more relevant, because for most problems the state of satisfaction of wants and its alteration is much more important than the quantity of labour and the alteration thereof contained in the commodities, the consumption of which creates the above-mentioned satisfaction.[3]

It would be easy to add to this quotation similar passages from Schumpeter's other work. It should be said that Schumpeter presents the supposed advantages of the subjective theory of value in virtually the same words in what is perhaps his most important and most popular book, *Capitalism, Socialism and Democracy*. There he ends by stating that, on the assumption that work is the only factor of production and that the laws of completely free competition prevail, the labour theory of value can be seen as a special instance of the subjective theory of value.[4]

This is what Schumpeter wrote in the publication intended to be read by his colleagues and by a wider public. During his Harvard seminars, in which I took part as a student writing a dissertation, the great expert in the history of economic theory took a more objective position, so that his listeners sometimes had the impression that the Ricardian and Marxian versions of the classical labour theory of value had undeniable merits. He stressed particularly in his lectures, that the labour theory of value has different qualitative aspects under different socio-economic conditions. For example, if labour itself becomes the subject of exchange, then the value composition of the commodity changes. However, on this level of economic development the new ingredient of surplus value is added to the value structure of the commodity.

A touch of this more objective attitude towards the classical labour theory of value can be traced in Schumpeter's posthumous work, the *History of Economic Analysis*, where he writes explicitly that 'there is nothing mystic or metaphysical about the Marxist theory of value. Its central concept in particular, absolute value, has nothing to do with the meanings we attach to this word in some parts of philosophy. It is nothing but Ricardo's real value fully worked out and fully made use of.' But at the end of this paragraph he adds that, '. . . To use a Marshallian phrase, for Ricardo time was the greater disturber of his analytical pattern. But it was also, though less overtly, the great disturber of Marx's.' (*History*, 598)

In much the same way as Marx derives the category of surplus value from his special form of the labour theory of value, Schumpeter finds a direct connection between the subjective theory of value and the phenomenon of interest and profit. The agio theory is based on the premiss that present goods are valued higher than those which become available in the future, though they are exactly the same and thus fit for satisfying wants of the same kind and the same intensity. But Schumpeter adds that this fact is not outside the principle of value. It is, rather, the discovery of a particular property of valuation – occasionally anticipated before Böhm-Bawerk, and presented systematically only by Jevons. Schumpeter summarizes this reflection by stating that the theory of interest follows from the marginal utility principle.[5]

Subsequently, however, Schumpeter makes it clear that valuing present goods higher than goods of the same kind which become available only at some point in the future involves phenomena in two different spheres: the individual psychological sphere, rating the satisfaction of present needs higher than that of future needs, which are felt to be less urgent and cannot be clearly foreseen; and the material and technological sphere, where a given stock of commodities is multiplied by applying roundabout production. A capitalist who is able to make available a stock of commodities for roundabout production can logically claim the resulting surplus product. This makes it clear that the source of *consumptive interest* – which may be called a timeless phenomenon – is completely different from that of *productive interest*, which is rooted in the material world of technology. Schumpeter in his 1914 article elegantly passes over Böhm-Bawerk's double-track way of arguing; but as we shall see his great dispute with his teacher and intellectual idol was mainly caused by this aspect of Böhm-Bawerk's theory of interest. This dispute shows with exemplary clarity Schumpeter's ambivalent relationship to his original intellectual background – the Austrian school of economics.

In 1912 Schumpeter published what is perhaps his most brilliant work, the *Theorie der wirtschaftlichen Entwicklung [Theory of Economic Development], eine Untersuchung über Unternehmergewinn, Kapital, Kredit, Zins und den Konjunkturzyklus.*[6] He clung to the most important ideas of this book, with minor modifications, throughout his life. In 1913 Böhm-Bawerk made this early work of his gifted pupil the subject of a thorough analysis, which must be seen as a definite and clearly formulated rejection of the new, dynamically designed theory of interest which is at the centre of Schumpeter's study.[7] When Schumpeter replied, Böhm-Bawerk made it clear to him and to the academic community at large that, contrary to what Schumpeter believed, his own, Böhm-Bawerk's, views were by no means close to those of his disciple. This riposte ends with a statement very embarrassing to Schumpeter: 'A highly versatile, perspicacious and able author has fallen victim to a cause which simply cannot be properly defended.'[8]

Schumpeter's starting-point in the *Theory of Economic Development* is the abstract model of a stationary economy, to which he attributes a certain real content, pointing out that 'economies without development' are a 'fact and not mere fiction' (*Theorie*, 113). The realistic approach to his model derives mainly from the fact that economic development does not proceed continuously and that temporary phases of growth alternate in periodic succession with static conditions in the economy as a whole (ibid., 430 ff.).[9] In a concise historical survey, an appendix to the first chapter of the *Theory* in its original edition, Schumpeter attempts to prove that this static approach is common to the three great schools of economics: the physiocrats, the classical, and the school of marginal utility – thus implying that there is a direct genealogical link between his own static model and the mainstream of economic theory developed before Schumpeter.

It is well known that each of the three great schools has its own special way of explaining the phenomenon of interest. In his essay on Böhm-Bawerk, which one is tempted to call a funeral oration for his great teacher, Schumpeter differentiated among three groups of theories of interest: the so-called productivity theories, the weakness of which lies in a confusion of 'value productivity' and 'physical productivity'; the 'wage deduction theories' or 'exploitation theories', which fail because they do not show why the forces of competition will not sweep away the exploitative surplus value; and finally those theories which deduce the *'produit net'* from the phenomenon of value. Schumpeter numbers the so-called 'agio theory' in this third group.[10]

In this connection Schumpeter avoids dealing in greater detail with his own static model, which is based on the assumption that the gross national product is divided ultimately between the two original factors of production: labour and land. In the *Theory of Economic Development*, however, Schumpeter admits that even when the circular flow is stationary the parasitic form of consumptive interest may develop, and that occasionally profit and loss may appear which is of an accidental nature. But as to what Böhm-Bawerk considers the main source of the *'produit net'*, i.e., the surplus yielded by more roundabout production, there can be no question of such a relationship because in a static economy there is no such option. The economy, Schumpeter says, goes its own way. It is adjusted to certain processes of production. The current process of production must be completed by whatever means; economic subjects (*Wirtschaftssubjekte*) have no choice at all between present and future.[11]

In the static model described by Schumpeter the entrepreneur and the capitalist are alien phenomena. As Böhm-Bawerk summarizes it in his review, it is clear

> that as a matter of principle the static producer is already in possession of, and does not need to acquire, the means of production which he needs for continuing this static process of production, and of the 'purchasing power' required to obtain these means of production; because it is offered to him automatically by the proceeds from the products of the preceding economic period.

Later Böhm-Bawerk notes that 'the result of all these explanations is the fact that in a static economy no interest on capital is possible'
(*Zeitschrift* XXII, 8,9).

Böhm-Bawerk proves easily that Schumpeter's highly individual model contrasts oddly with certain forms of permanent interest income, which can be found even in chronically stationary, non-developing economies. He draws attention to house rent, which exists also in static economies. Following Schumpeter's logic, this would not mean 'rent' in the usual sense of the word, but only ground rent and a wage for administration. Here Böhm-Bawerk makes the polemical point:

> Does Schumpeter really want to make us believe that nowadays blocks of flats as a rule permanently yield only wages for the administrative effort and ground rent, but do not bear interest on the actual building capital, as Schumpeter has seriously and expressly maintained, at least in respect of static periods?(*Zeitschrift* XXII, 46)

The Achilles' heel of Schumpeter's model is seen by his distinguished critic in the pricing of pieces of land and other goods of practically infinite useful life. In this connection Böhm-Bawerk observes that for a permanent source of income, such as a piece of land, Schumpeter's theory would, in a static period, require the value of infinity. Schumpeter tries to refute this objection by assuming that in a static economy real-estate transactions would take place only in exceptional cases. This provokes Böhm-Bawerk to administer what is perhaps his sharpest rebuke to his disciple: 'I think this is no way out but a simple act of violence. In order to avoid having theory clash with the facts, an effort is made to cancel the inconvenient facts with a stroke of the pen' (ibid., 50).

I think that what has been said so far makes it clear that Schumpeter's construction of a static economy is aimed implicitly at negating the marginal theory of interest supported by Böhm-Bawerk. From his essay on Böhm-Bawerk's life work the unbiased reader would gain the impression that the student identifies himself unconditionally with each and every element of the great edifice of thought. But Schumpeter's *Theory of Economic Development* is based on ideas fundamentally different from Böhm-Bawerk's teachings, which may explain the annoyance with which the old master calls his gifted but highly individual student to order.

Of what do these so different ideas consist? Schumpeter has repeatedly given an answer, perhaps in greatest detail in a footnote to the second chapter of his *Theory*. There he deals first with the views of J.B. Clark who, following the ideas of J.S. Mill, explains the dynamic character of an economic process through disturbances. Schumpeter agrees, but adds that among the five causes of disturbance Clark mentions, two are of special importance. He then writes:

> But the other two [changes in technique and in productive organization] require special analysis and evoke something different from – though also in addition to – disturbances in the theoretical sense. The non-recognition of this is the most important single reason for what appears to us unsatisfactory in economic theory. From this insignificant-looking source flows . . . a new conception of the economic process, which overcomes a series of fundamental difficulties and thus justifies the new statement of the problem . . . more nearly parallel to that of Marx. For according to him there is an *internal* economic development and no mere adaptation of economic life to changing data.   (*Theorie*, 92 n.2)[12]

And Schumpeter concludes this reflection with a bow to Marx's genius: 'But my structure covers only a small part of his ground.' This gesture may not have been seen as exactly a matter of course in the academic environment in which Schumpeter had come to maturity.

In Schumpeter's stationary model the painstaking and continuous attention to detail, characteristic of the working environment of the average businessman, is assigned to the so-called circular-flow producer (*Kreislauf-Wirt*). If there are any changes here, they are made by countless small steps taken in response to external data, e.g. to a growth in population. Schumpeter ascribes the dynamization of a static economy to the pioneer and innovator, to whom he chooses to apply the term 'entrepreneur'. The final cause of economic progress is for him the entry of the entrepreneur into the static circular flow, which leads to spontaneous, discontinuous changes in the process of production of the type stage-coach/railway, conventional electrical energy/atomic energy, etc. The qualitative leap from the static to the dynamic economy secures for its initiator a temporary monopoly, which is gradually eroded when imitators appear who follow the innovator's successful example. However, it is not so much the prospect of commercial profit, which is anyway in constant danger of being eroded, that we have to regard as the ultimate motivation of Schumpeter's entrepreneur, as the elementary urge, prevailing again and again in all social formations, to assert a claim to economic and social leadership. The pleasure derived from being creative and from pushing through sporadic innovations is the prime factor, from which the acquisition of economic power is derived.[13]

In passing, let me remark that this glorifying view of the innovative entrepreneur is in contrast to the classical tradition, which since the days of Adam Smith has seen the activity of *homo oeconomicus* in a more sober light. Smith thinks that man is mainly motivated in all that he does by self-interest; and he adds that this is not to the discredit of mankind, but on the contrary to its benefit, because everyone who pursues his own interests 'is led by an invisible hand, to promote an end which was no part of his intention'. Smith sees the world order as based on the principle of 'sympathy', stemming not from altruistic motives and actions but from the pursuit of self-interest. The idea is stated very precisely in a frequently quoted passage: 'It is not from the benevolence of the butcher, the brewer, or the baker, that we expect our dinner, but from their regard to their own interest.'[14]

It is hardly surprising that Böhm-Bawerk, who is in many respects very close to the classical tradition, looks on a method of dynamizing the static cycle which proceeds from the glaring contrast between innovation and routine with undisguised dislike. In the review I have been quoting, Böhm-Bawerk points out that 'the enormous streams of interest on capital not only flow intermittently in individual periods of upswing, but continuously and without interruption also during depressions, with their volume reduced somewhat but not very sharply and at any rate not to the extent that Schumpeter's explanatory hypothesis would require'. As to Schumpeter's thesis that the 'big, regular flow of goods on which the capitalist class lives' has no source other than 'the transient, temporary entrepreneurial profit and the surplus of recent innovations', Böhm-Bawerk points out that when a process leading to static conditions begins, costs and proceeds again become equal, and thereby 'the profits of the entrepreneur and the source of interest on capital vanish' (*Zeitschrift* XXII, 54, 55). Böhm-Bawerk's point of view may be summarized – though simplified – by saying that the permanence of the phenomenon of interest cannot be deduced from the very narrow conceptual basis for the exceptional, heroic type of entrepreneur who is endowed with a special ability to force through his designs.

It may be objected that Schumpeter wanted to make the permanence of the phenomenon of interest dependent not solely on the phenomenon of the exceptional entrepreneur, but also – and hardly less so – on the existence of large numbers of mere 'imitators'. But here Böhm-Bawerk argues, I think correctly, that a strict conceptual distinction between the pioneering innovator on the one hand and the 'mere' imitators on the other is misleading. Schumpeter attributes to the entrepreneur who deviates from the beaten track of daily routine a number of characteristics the originality of which seems, as Böhm-Bawerk observes, to defy description. 'And which can', as he says, 'of course never have anything to do with the "great mass", which Schumpeter often and emphatically contrasts with the leading élite.' On the other hand, Böhm-Bawerk believes that Schumpeter could hardly have meant seriously the distinction he draws between those who 'almost entirely imitate' and the so-called 'leaders in the field', because he had to reckon 'the demand of this retinue as a quite indispensable component in that demand which is prepared to set aside a part of the entrepreneurial profit in the form of interest on capital' (*Zeitschrift* XXII, 32-4).

Looked at from this angle, is Schumpeter's antithesis between 'innovators' and 'imitators' logically tenable, and if it is not, does not this produce fatal consequences for Schumpeter's theory of development? Böhm-Bawerk describes Schumpeter's dilemma in these impressive terms:

> If he seriously believes in the existence of the rare type of strong leader who is gifted with creative and innovative power and who abstains from common hedonism – then it is not plausible that this rare type should become a mass phenomenon in Chapters 5 and 6. But if the idea of the mass phenomenon is correct, this would mean that in Chapter 2 Schumpeter is describing not the type of the entrepreneur in general, but only a small though in fact leading group *among* entrepreneurs. If this is the case, the only thing that distinguishes the great number of his genuine entrepreneurs from the static producers is the word 'almost', which Schumpeter uses to describe behaviour of the former which is otherwise exactly the behaviour of the static producers. . . .   (Ibid., 34)

One could go further than Böhm-Bawerk and confront the Romantic concept of the spontaneous and original achievements of the entrepreneur, as A.P. Usher and Fritz Redlich have done, with the fact that great innovations are the result of processes lasting for centuries and in which generations of inventors, businessmen and sometimes even adventurers have taken part. If innovation and its commercial exploitation are normally the achievement not of a single person but of generations, then to contrast the leader with the imitator seems irrelevant, as Fritz Redlich has pointed out with admirable clarity:

> It is impossible to differentiate the innovator from the imitator in a

way [disparaging to the latter] which states that special outstanding qualities are essential to the role of the innovator and that the qualities of those who intend to follow in the steps of the innovator are less important. Reality is not as simple as that. Transferring what was originally an innovation to a different area or to another industry ... requires in many, though not in all, cases abilities as great as does the innovation itself.[15]

As we have seen, in Schumpeter's static circular flow the gross product is fully shared between the original factors of production: land labour; and under these conditions the phenomenon of entrepreneurial profit, and of savings derived from it, can be only accidental. If a radical regrouping of the factors of production is to take place under such a constellation, the logic of this model dictates that the innovative entrepreneur obtain the financial means he needs for his projects only by using the banks' power of creating money. With the help of this mechanism he is able to transfer resources from traditional uses to new profitable ventures. Thus in Schumpeter's system adopting new productive 'combinations' does not depend on the previous accumulation of an adequate stock of goods.

This assumption by Schumpeter again violates a fundamental tenet of Böhm-Bawerk, who bases his positive theory of capital on the assumption 'that only the availability of *stocks of goods* adjusted to the needs of production makes it possible to carry out more profitable roundabout production and to get a higher return' (*Zeitschrift* XXII, 22). A key passage from his main work, *The Positive Theory of Capital*, makes even clearer Böhm-Bawerk's point of view concerning the strategic importance of accumulated stocks of goods:

> It is necessary to possess only enough capital of any kind that its gradual transformation into consumer goods meets the demand for such goods in the present and in the near future, to free current productive power for investment in intermediate products of the required kind. It would be even more correct to say that consumer goods are necessary to pursue roundabout production, whether in the form of stocks of finished consumer goods, or in the form of intermediate products.[16]

Note that in Böhm-Bawerk's system the adoption of more profitable roundabout methods of production depends on the existence of stocks of goods; it does not matter whether these stocks are made available by a single capitalist or by a collective. It is only possible to break out of Schumpeter's static circular flow, however, if, through an inflationary process of creating money, productive resources are diverted from traditional methods of production to new productive uses.

Of course, Böhm-Bawerk was right to be sceptical about, and even openly to reject, Schumpeter's antithesis between creative innovators on the one hand and imitators and static producers on the other. But in his negative reaction to Schumpeter's theorem of the inflationary financing of new production processes he seems to have been clinging to certain dogmatic positions. If he had looked more closely at the empirical evidence, Böhm-Bawerk might have arrived at different conclusions: genuine savings within and outside the business sector have contributed, *along with* the money-creating power of the banks, to the process of industrial development, even though the relative importance of each has varied from place to place and from time to time. Schumpeter's emphasis on the strategic importance of the commercial banks for the financing of 'combinations' was probably influenced by the special circumstances characterizing industrial development in the Austro-Hungarian Monarchy during the last two decades before the outbreak of World War I.[17]

This is not to be seen as a vindication of Schumpeter's theory of economic development. Of course his assumption that the dynamic entrepreneur occasionally outstrips his less able competitors is based on hard empirical facts. Marx in particular repeatedly and emphatically voiced Schumpeter's basic idea, that capitalism has an inherent tendency towards innovation and that owing to this the efficient innovator gains a temporary monopoly which becomes the source of profits. See for example the following passage:

> Hence, the capitalist who applies the improved method of production, appropriates to surplus-labour a greater portion of the working-day, than the other capitalists in the same trade. He does individually, what the whole body of capitalists engaged in producing relative surplus-value do collectively. On the other hand, however, this extra surplus-value vanishes, so soon as the new method of production has become general, and has consequently caused the difference between the individual value of the cheapened commodity and its social value to vanish.   (*Capital*, I.318-19)[18]

It is remarkable that Marx writes about the occasional occurrence of an 'extra surplus value', implying of course that even in periods where traditional methods of production prevail, entrepreneurs can count on a traditional return, as it were, on the invested capital. However much

Marx's and Böhm-Bawerk's viewpoints may differ, neither based his ideas on a stationary model, in which interest on capital tends to become zero. I believe Marx would have aligned himself with Böhm-Bawerk's statement in his polemic against Schumpeter: 'Schumpeter denies that interest on capital can exist in a static economy. But no-where and – as far back as my knowledge of economic history goes – never has there been a real economy in which interest on capital has not existed' (*Zeitschrift* XXII, 39).

In his essay on Böhm-Bawerk Schumpeter makes the significant statement that the latter's theory of interest is organically connected with the principle of marginal utility. And he adds that the agio theory is, '*kat exochen*', the value theory of interest (*TGE*, 175). Thus the question arises to which group of interest theories Schumpeter's dynamic conception belongs. During his controversy with Böhm-Bawerk and also later on, Schumpeter himself stressed his close re-lationship to the Austrian school of marginal utility. But having made this excursion into the history of economic dogma, I believe it must have become clear that there is an antithetical relationship between the theory of interest developed by Schumpeter and that of his teacher. Whereas the Austrian school deduces the phenomenon of in-terest from the relatively high valuation of present goods as compared with future goods, Schumpeter reverses the causal connection and ex-plains the agio phenomenon by the existence of interest on capital. One is tempted to say that it would be easier to establish a close re-lationship between the dynamic theory of interest and Marx's theory of exploitation, or Ricardo's wage deduction theory, than between Schumpeter's theory and that of his admired teacher Böhm-Bawerk. I imagine, however, that Schumpeter would hardly have come to such an heretical conclusion.

PART THREE
Schumpeter the Man and the Politician

Chapter 9

Schumpeter as Austrian Minister of Finance[*]

In 1919, for little more than half a year, Joseph A. Schumpeter held
the post of Austrian Minister of Finance or, as it was called at the
time, State Secretary of Finance. It can safely be said that the young
Professor of Economics had excellent qualifications for the post.
Shortly before the outbreak of war, before he had reached the age of
thirty – the 'age of sacred fertility', as he was to call it later – he had
published two of his most brilliant works, which demonstrated his
profound knowledge of economic theory as well as his talent for opening up as yet unexplored theoretical territory.[1] During the war years
he studied the sociological and financial problems of the conflict between the Great Powers which sapped their material as well as moral
resistance. He summarized his conclusions in two papers which were,
I believe, largely responsible for his nomination as Minister in the
Renner government that spring.[2]

The desperate economic and financial plight of the Republic of
Austria during her first years of existence has been extensively
described.[3] In the first few months of 1919 the weekly consumption of
meat in Vienna amounted to no more than 400,000 kg, which constituted a scant 10 per cent of the average consumption in the last pre-
war year.[4] The daily bread ration of 165 g (approximately 6 oz.),
which the Viennese people were accorded during the last year of the
war was gradually increased until it reached in August 1919 the substantially higher but still insufficient quantity of 235 g per day. That

* This essay originally appeared in English, in *Schumpeterian Economics*, ed. Helmut Frisch (New York, 1982).

autumn the bread ration had to be reduced once again, and ranged in December of the same year between 100 and 170 g. The Allied Relief Administration estimated that the Viennese derived from their daily food rations during the critical period of spring and summer of 1919 no more than 1,270 calories, rather than the prescribed minimum of 2,300.[5] The situation in the provinces was somewhat more favourable than in Vienna.

The critical situation of the year 1919 had several causes. The harvest of the last year of the war was even less adequate than the notoriously poor harvests of the previous years. The difficulties caused by low stocks of grain were aggravated by the fact that the new national states, soon after coming into existence, imposed severe restrictions on exports of foodstuffs and coal. Again, the blockade by the Allied Powers which had been generally expected to be lifted at the end of hostilities, remained in force until well into the spring of 1919. Lastly, there was the sudden asserted aversion towards Vienna of the agrarian provinces, which were disposed to supply the capital city with foodstuffs only on the basis of strict reciprocity.[6]

The severe shortage of coal not only intensified the suffering of the urban population, but led to the shut-down of the greater part of industry and of transport. The curtailment of production due to the scarcity of coal, the sudden halt in the manufacture of arms, and the influx of war veterans on to the labour market caused a steady increase in unemployment. In December 1918, according to an official count, the number of unemployed stood at 46,203. Two months later the figure was well above 162,000, of whom two-thirds lived in Vienna. In May 1919 unemployment reached the unprecedented total of more than 186,000.[7]

Suffering on such an enormous scale soon undermined the faith of the people in the viability of the new state. The ensuing discussions divided the country into two hostile camps and weakened the moral resistance of the inhabitants to foreign influences. Closely associated with the problem of viability was the socio-economic orientation of the country. Under the influence of the October Revolution in Russia and the social upheaval in neighbouring Hungary, large segments of the Austrian working class clamoured for a fundamental reform of the existing social order. The Social Democratic members of the government took account of these demands by instituting a so-called 'Socialization Commission', composed in equal parts of socialists and conservative politicians. The Commission was to make a thorough study of the conditions, possibilities and perspectives of socializing the

Austrian economy. After the revolutionary emotions had calmed down, in the summer and autumn of 1919, the Socialization Commission vanished from the political scene without having had any perceptible effect on the prevailing economic order.[8]

The desperate financial plight of the Austrian state during World War I had inspired Schumpeter to comment:

> . . . The financial history of a nation must be seen as an essential part of its general history: the destiny of nations is decisively affected by the economic blood-letting, which public needs require, and by the way in which the results of this procedure are employed. The immediate impact of the financial requirements and of the financial policies of the state upon the further development of the economy and thereby upon all social and cultural modes of life is in certain periods of history the key to the understanding of all major social trends. . . .   (*Die Krise des Steuerstaates*, 6)

The acute emergency of the year 1919 was reflected, of course, in the state budget. During the first six months of 1919 only two-thirds of total expenditure could be covered by tax revenue. The resulting deficit had to be covered through the issue of unbacked paper currency, a practice that had begun during the war and was largely responsible for the ever-accelerating pace of inflation. In 1919 and over the following three years the Austrian government continued to rely on the printing presses for the financing of its principal needs.

The unbalanced state of the budget had four main causes: (1) the interest and amortization requirements of the Austro-Hungarian war debt; (2) the funds needed to support the unemployed; (3) the food subsidies, needed to underwrite the difference between the price of food when acquired by the government and the price actually paid by the consumer; (4) the funds required to maintain a state bureaucracy tailored to the needs of a great empire as well as to the heavy tasks accruing from four years of total war.

At first it seemed that the financial obligations the new Austria had inherited from its imperial predecessor were more onerous than the emergency expenditure on food and on the unemployed. In the spring of 1919 the Finance Ministry had to appropriate 530 million crowns to meet interest and amortization payments.[9] However, the burden grew progressively lighter as a result of a long-drawn-out inflationary process, especially since the authorities refused to consider the full or partial valorization of all war and pre-war debts, proclaiming the principle 'the crown remains the crown'. Again, expenditure on the state bureaucracy was a continually shrinking part of the total budgetary outlay, for unlike other professional groups government employees could not expect their incomes to be raised to meet the steadily rising level of prices.

Expenditure arising out of financial assistance to the unemployed was at first no less onerous than interest and amortization payments. Some 500 million crowns had to be spent on the unemployed from the middle of November 1918 to the beginning of May 1920 – a period of roughly a year and a half. However, a similar amount was required to meet the food subsidies over the comparatively short period from July to December 1919.[10] So it became evident rather early on that food subsidies constituted by far the heaviest fiscal burden. To preserve or abolish this expensive method of subsidizing the standard of living of the masses became one of the most explosive policy issues.

The provisional government which ruled Austria after the collapse of the Monarchy was hopeful at first that it could cope with the financial crisis by traditional fiscal measures, especially with regard to expenditures such as food subsidies and unemployment insurance which were considered as in the nature of an emergency. As for the public debt, which had assumed astronomic proportions towards the end of the war,[11] unorthodox methods of redemption were increasingly put forward. During the war years proposals had been made by both conservative and progressive economists for the most drastic encroachment on existing property relationships. On the Right, two Finance Ministers, Dr Alexander Spitzmüller and his successor, Dr Wimmer, advocated the imposition of a broadly conceived levy on property. On the Left, Dr Rudolf Goldscheid, sometimes referred to as the first sociologist in the fields of financial administration and policy-making, urged that the public debt, the greatest liability of the nation, be transformed into its greatest asset by using it as a means to socialization. By making a considerable part of the productive capital public property, the state could become the largest share-owner in the nation, thereby achieving two objectives: the consolidation of the financial position of the state, and the extension of political control by its democratic organs into economic control. An important step in extending democracy would thus be taken. Goldscheid was the only leading financial theorist who favoured using the great, once-and-for-all levy on property for ambitious objectives of social engineering.[12]

Schumpeter, too, had published in the last year of the war a widely-read paper in which he advocated a rigorous capital levy. By contrast with Goldscheid, however, he did not aim at any change in existing property relations. What he wanted to accomplish through such a radical measure was somewhat less ambitious, but still vitally important: the balancing of the budget by eliminating the greater part of the public debt. After analysing the merits of a capital levy Schumpeter added, somewhat wistfully, that no matter how desirable such a course might be, it would nevertheless prove futile unless pursued by a government popular enough to overcome the predictably strong resistance. In conclusion, Schumpeter set out the characteristics of the political leader who might conceive and put into operation a programme of such scope: 'A man who is to cope with such a task requires genuine political as well as financial talent – and that glamour of word and action which commands the trust of the people' (*Die Krise*, 45). It must be assumed that among the candidates for the post of Finance Minister in the first post-war cabinet he included a person – himself – who exhibited some of the characteristics described in the paper.

The State Secretary of Finance in the first Renner cabinet was, however, Herr Steinwender, a member of the Pan-German Party, who had little professional training and less experience, and consequently attempted to resolve the unprecedented financial crisis by traditional fiscal means. Schumpeter became a member of the second Renner cabinet, which was formed in March 1919 after the impressive victory of the Social Democratic Party in the national election the preceding month. His main sponsor was Otto Bauer, the prominent socialist politician and theorist, whom he had met when a student at Vienna University, and who had regarded him since then as a competent, creative economist, thoroughly conversant with the ideas of socialism. Moreover, Schumpeter's public advocacy of a capital levy had undoubtedly won him the sympathy of Bauer and other prominent socialist leaders.

Soon after assuming his new duties, Schumpeter informed the public of the main features of his reform programme, whose principal points were: first, the great capital levy, which was mainly designed to eliminate the war debt; second, the stabilization of the exchange rate of the Austrian crown (Schumpeter, however, took pains to emphasize in this context that he had no intention of re-establishing the old parity of the crown); third, the founding of a new central bank which was to pursue a lending policy independent of the state; fourth, a stronger reliance on indirect taxation, so that large strata of the population would be given the opportunity to make an adequate contribution towards balancing the budget; fifth, though by no means last, the re-establishment of conditions under which Austrian industry could once again become credit-worthy.[13] In a speech before a select audience at the University of Vienna the new Minister pointed out that 'the provision of foreign credits for Austrian industry was a task that the state must assume in the most resolute fashion'.[14]

The problem of procuring credits, especially abroad, made it necessary, for obvious reasons, to take a clear decision about the extent of the socialization measures which had been debated with increasing intensity since the beginning of the year. On the issue of socialization, Schumpeter underwent an amazingly rapid change of mind. On 20 March 1919 – shortly after assuming office, that is – the Minister made a statement to the press which largely reflected the point of view adopted by the Social Democratic Party:

> We shall have to intervene on a massive scale in the private economy. Socialization is the decisive issue of our time. It is quite hopeless to believe that this idea is a passing fad. We shall have to make efforts to realize it, and we shall have to travel sufficiently far in this direction so that there remains little to the left of us to be socialized. Whatever remains outside the scope of socialization should be administered freely by the private economy.[15]

But on 26 April, five weeks after his peremptory statement on socialization, Schumpeter told his audience at the University of Vienna, in the speech referred to above, that it might prove necessary in the interests of opening up avenues of capital import to steer a more moderate course in matters of socialization:

> We are confronted [he said] with the task of reconstruction. It would be possible, if only at a considerable cost in terms of social friction and unrest, to socialize the whole economy. I have to admit that from a professional point of view I regard such a step with a good deal of sympathy. The other option open to us is a radical, decisive, but *limited* socialization measure affecting certain industries and enterprises but permitting the rest of the economy to operate in its usual manner. For the latter alternative a number of arguments can be marshalled which, one is inclined to believe, must be considered compelling, especially the necessity of importing capital from abroad, which would not be available – to a socialized economy.[16]

With his plea for 'limited socialization measures' Schumpeter made it clear that his views on socialization were not to be identified with those of Otto Bauer – and his audience, it is known, was quick to recognize the defiant undertone in his plea.[17]

While the principle of the capital levy for the purpose of amortizing the public debt was generally accepted, the question of its extent and its social significance remained highly controversial. Another factor which delayed the formulation of a definite measure was the total lack of information concerning the economic clauses of the peace treaty, which was still being hotly debated in a Paris suburb. There was also much internal opposition to the capital levy, especially among the representatives of the peasantry, who were determined to defend their followers against any and all encroachment on their property.

In the meantime the major part of current expenditures had to be covered by short-term treasury bonds which were placed with the commercial banks, but eventually discounted by the Central Bank. The funding of this rapidly mounting debt according to well-established wartime practice proved impossible, in view of the unsettled political situation. But the Austro-Hungarian Bank, which had survived the collapse of the Monarchy, encountered growing resistance in pursuing its inflationary course. It had been forced – under pressure from the new national states – to broaden the composition of its governing body with members from all parts of the defunct Monarchy. The representatives of the new states demanded that the Bank follow a rigorously anti-inflationary course, above all that it cease to make payments on imperial war bonds as had been the practice during the war years.[18]

It may appear strange that the Austro-Hungarian Bank insisted on honouring its obligations vis-à-vis the owners of war bonds. On the whole this was not a time when public authorities put particular emphasis on redeeming the promises of their predecessors. The policy of the Bank becomes more intelligible, however, if one considers the special interests of the new Austria. As was generally known, the German-speaking peoples of the Monarchy held a disproportionately high proportion of the Austro-Hungarian war bonds, whereas most of the other ethnic groups held only small amounts of the bonds, and had preferred to accumulate banknotes instead. By insisting that the Bank continue to make payments on the war debt, whose amount seemed increasingly more dubious with each passing day, the Governor of the Bank of course was protecting the interests of his Austrian compatriots. On the other hand, when the representatives of the new national states attempted to prevent the Bank from following an inflationary policy by generously lending money against Austro-

Hungarian bonds, they had the interests of their fellow-citizens at heart.[19]

The inflationary policy of the Austro-Hungarian Bank left the national states little choice but to move towards the early separation of their currency from the Austrian crown. There can be little doubt, however, that they would have done this in any event, since not one of the new states could consider itself independent of the financial domination of Vienna as long as the former capital of the Monarchy remained responsible for the monetary policy of the Danube basin. The first state which turned its back on the Austro-Hungarian Bank was Yugoslavia. Between 8 and 20 January 1919 the banknotes of the Bank circulating in Yugoslav territory were officially counted and stamped. Czechoslovakia followed suit between 3 and 7 March 1919. With the Czechs and Yugoslavs seceding from the Austro-Hungarian Bank, economic co-operation among the Danubian peoples within the framework of a currency union came to a definite close. Austria, which had shown a genuine interest in the preservation of the union, now had no option other than to follow the example of Yugoslavia and Czechoslovakia. The separation of the Austrian currency was effected between 12 and 24 March 1919.[20]

Otto Bauer, who held the post of State Secretary for Foreign Affairs, was the principal exponent of 'Anschluss' both within the cabinet and in the top echelons of the Socialist Party. He considered the break-up of the currency union, the last economic link between the one-time Danubian partners, a suitable occasion for taking the first step towards Anschluss. In March 1919, when Austria severed its links with the currency union, Bauer visited Berlin, and proposed to the German government that the two countries establish a common currency at the earliest possible moment. The Reichsbank, so Bauer suggested, should grant a loan to a new central bank in Austria which would enable it to exchange German marks for Austrian crowns at a fixed rate. The German government declined Bauer's proposal, pointing out that it was not advisable to saddle the Reichsbank with a burden of unknown proportions before the conditions of the peace treaty became known.[21] It is likely, however, that the reasons why the German negotiators took a negative attitude towards plans aiming at Anschluss at this critical moment were primarily political.[22]

The idea of a currency union between Germany and Austria was, however, not entirely dropped, but received further attention at meetings of a bilateral financial committee which, on 19 April 1919, took the solemn decision that Austria was to introduce the German mark as its sole standard of value on 1 January of next year.[23] The plan, kept secret at first but soon leaked to the press, revealed a state of mind on the part of its sponsors strangely remote from the world of '*Realpolitik*'. Schumpeter, who during the war years had viewed with scepticism (as Professor Verosta has shown) all efforts to form a closely knit economic union between Germany and the Habsburg Monarchy,[24] showed little sympathy for similar plans, even though circumstances had drastically changed since then. Soon after taking office as Minister of Finance he argued, if only indirectly, against Anschluss by pleading for the preservation of Vienna as financial centre of the Danube basin and for close economic co-operation among the successor states. In a speech before the Austrian press, Schumpeter addressed himself particularly to the Czechs:

> Austria and especially Vienna will have to remain financial centres for a considerable period of time. . . . To make a national economy self-sufficient is only feasible within rather narrow limits; it is far easier to accomplish this politically than economically. We shall have eventually to find a *modus vivendi*. The frontiers of future development can be recognized even today with great clarity. In the new organism Vienna will continue to function as the financial centre, and political separation will only marginally affect the purely economic relations.[25]

Ignaz Seipel, a leading conservative politician, who, as the evidence indicates, used the pro-Anschluss agitation as a ploy through which the Allied Powers could be manoeuvred into granting concessions at the peace conference, had established close contacts with the Finance Minister in the spring of 1919, as Professor Verosta reports Seipel made the following revealing comment in a letter to Heinrich Lammasch, the one-time Prime Minister of Austria-Hungary, who is likely to have introduced his young admirer Schumpeter to Seipel: 'I am in close contact with Schumpeter, who is very brave. . . . The policies of Otto Bauer have been shown to be absurd. In the whole of Austria there is an undercurrent of opinion that Anschluss will come to naught.'[26]

Seipel's letter is dated 1 May 1919. His moral support must have encouraged Schumpeter to question ever more openly the wisdom of Bauer's Anschluss strategy. On 8 May Schumpeter gave an interview to an evening paper, the *Neues 8-Uhr-Blatt*, in which he conceded that Anschluss could not be prevented indefinitely; at the same time, he warned that Anschluss, if carried out, would require great sacrifices, and that as a consequence one would have to demand from Germany 'far-reaching concessions'. The main point of the interview came, however, in the statement: 'Our safety lies in our peaceful intercourse with all states, and especially with our immediate neighbours.'[27]

Bauer's reaction to the interview with Schumpeter was a long letter (reprinted in its entirety in the article by Verosta), in which he reproached his colleague for having expressed opinions bound to weaken the bargaining position of the Austrian delegation at the peace conference. He then added, no doubt with some justification, that it had not been customary hitherto for statements on foreign policy to emanate from sources other than the Ministry concerned, unless prior consultation had taken place between the Foreign Minister and his otherwise unauthorized colleague: 'If you believe my policy to be incorrect', Bauer said, 'the proper procedure would be to bring the controversial question before the cabinet for discussion.' Concluding, Bauer held out an olive branch to Schumpeter, emphasizing his readiness to resolve their differences through informal discussions.[28]

It is not known whether such a discussion took place. At any rate, Schumpeter did not seem greatly impressed by Bauer's warnings. Around the middle of May he established contact with the British financial expert, Sir Francis Oppenheimer, who visited Vienna at the request of his government. According to Oppenheimer, Schumpeter acquainted him with a plan of economic reform which provided for long-term credits from the West and gave the Allied nations sweeping powers of control over the Austrian economy. Above all, the management of the central bank, to be established in the near future, was to be entrusted to the Western Powers with the proviso that the sensibilities of the Austrian people be duly considered.[29]

Three weeks after his sensational statement to the *Neues 8-Uhr-Blatt* Schumpeter delivered a major speech before the Viennese Association of Commerce and Industry (Wiener Handels- und Industrieverein) in which he gave a detailed account of the economic policy to be followed in the coming years. There are some indications that he had consulted beforehand with leading financial experts, since his speech reflected to a high degree the opinion of the banking community. To begin with Schumpeter emphasized, once again, that the states of the Danube basin were dependent on close economic co-operation, whether they wanted it or not. He therefore advocated trade and currency agreements among them of one form or another. On the hotly debated question of the viability of the Austrian state, he stressed that national independence, even though imposed from outside, did not mean economic catastrophe. 'One must not think', he said, 'that a country in order to survive economically must possess all the essential raw materials within its own frontiers. True, we must have coal, but even if coal were available in Austrian territory, our industry would still have to purchase it, and this is all it has to do when importing it from Ostrava [the great Czech coal basin].'

The key passage of the speech is in his reference to Vienna as a financial centre:

> Again, the neighbouring countries cannot exist without us or without our financial mediation. It will continue to be the function of Vienna to finance the commerce of the countries, formerly belonging to the Monarchy, with the rest of the world. . . . Only the Viennese banks can act as reliable depositories of foreign capital imports.

At the end, he reiterated that socialization measures should be taken quickly and be limited in scope. Nationalization rather than socialization should be aimed at, for this sort of restructuring of the economy could be assimilated by the capitalist system, and would not noticeably impede the rebuilding of the Austrian economy.[30]

Schumpeter's speech must be seen as an open challenge to Otto Bauer, whose conciliatory gesture had been almost flippantly ignored. His defiant attitude no doubt resulted from the strong, and still growing, support which Schumpeter had found among his conservative cabinet colleagues and some representatives of Western financial interests. Bauer, on the other hand, was now determined to bring about Schumpeter's political downfall on the first possible occasion. In a letter to Karl Renner dated 31 May, Bauer commented on some prominent members of the government: 'Fink is loyal, as far as I can judge; Eldersch develops quite satisfactorily. Schumpeter, however, carries on with his intrigues. I shall do nothing for the time being, but after the conclusion of the peace treaty it will be inevitable to force his resignation.'[31] Bauer was to realize quite soon that his conflict with the Finance Minister had not yet reached its climax.

In the meantime the 'Socialization Commission' under the chairmanship of Otto Bauer continued its deliberations without making much visible progress. On 22 May the government announced, under the prodding of Bauer, that it had decided to nationalize at an opportune moment the iron and steel works, the power stations, the mining

industry, the great forests and certain sectors of the timber industry.[32]
This programme of *partial* nationalization corresponded to the 'first
step' of Bauer's long-term socialization strategy as outlined in his
pamphlet *The Road to Socialism*. Moreover, it did not conflict with
Schumpeter's repeatedly pronounced, more limited nationalization
scheme.

Jodok Fink and other conservative members of the government
could hardly dare to openly oppose the socialist nationalization plan
at a moment when the Austrian working class was deeply agitated by
the seizure of power by the Hungarian Communist Party led by Bela
Kun. In this predicament they had to resort to delaying tactics, which
were considerably facilitated by the resistance put up by the pro-
vincial diets and other government bodies to all initiatives and direc-
tives emanating from Vienna. But the final blow was dealt to the
nationalization scheme of 22 May when the Alpine Montangesellschaft, the largest Austrian enterprise and the sole owner of the
country's considerable iron ore reserves, was taken over by Italian industrial and banking interests.

There was a natural tendency towards the sale of industrial and
other assets abroad at a time when the Austrian economy was def-
icient in foodstuffs and other vital necessities.[33] The influx of foreign
capital was further enhanced as Austrian industrialists made great
efforts to attract foreign partners, in the certain knowledge that their
government would not venture to nationalize enterprises which were
partially backed by Western capital. Italy took a special interest in the
Austrian iron industry, for it seemed to provide the material basis for
the iron-starved heavy industry of the Po region. In the spring and
summer of 1919 the shares of the Alpine Montangesellschaft could be
acquired very cheaply as a result of special circumstances, in addition
to the low exchange rate of the Austrian crown and the depressed
atmosphere on the Vienna stock exchange: the Prager Eisenindustrie-
gesellschaft, the leading steel manufacturer of Czechoslovakia, which
had held a substantial number of shares in Alpine, now disposed of its
entire holdings and thereby contributed to the further decline of these
formerly highly valued industrial assets.

The purchase of Alpine shares by Italian interests was negotiated
by the Vienna banking firm of Richard Kola & Co. Kola, who specialized in dealings on the foreign exchange, had been commissioned by
the Ministry of Finance to procure Western currency on behalf of the
Austrian state. In the spring and summer of 1919 he was instrumental
in the sale of 200,000 shares of the Alpine Montangesellschaft to a

Milanese banking house which was backed by the well-known Fiat works. The foreign currency resulting from the transaction was put at the disposal of the Ministry of Finance, which required such currency for the purchase of foodstuffs and raw materials.[34] The repeated purchasing of Alpine shares on the Vienna stock exchange did not go unnoticed and resulted in a speculative boom which spread to other industrial shares as well.

In its issue of 20 August 1919 the *Arbeiter-Zeitung*, the chief organ of the Social Democratic Party, accused the Minister of Finance of having indirectly supported the transactions of Herr Kola through an attitude of passive acceptance: 'The Ministry of Finance would have been in a position to stop this speculative orgy. And indeed, a circumspect and active financial administration would have found the means of preventing it.' In another passage the author of the article (probably the editor of the paper) implied that the transfer of Alpine shares to foreign interests might have been motivated by anti-socialist designs: 'We admit', the article continued,

> that the sale of Austrian securities to foreigners may be inevitable under certain conditions. As long as we are incapable of paying for foodstuffs and raw materials from abroad with the products of our own labour, we shall have no choice but to trade our industrial assets and natural resources for them. But even if one concedes that much, one remains doubtful whether Alpine shares had to be sold to foreigners, since the Alpine Montangesellschaft figures among the first enterprises to be socialized.

Otto Bauer underscored this charge some years later in his book *Die österreichische Revolution* (1923):

> Schumpeter supported this operation [of Richard Kola] although he knew that we had decided to socialize the Alpine Montangesellschaft. He supported it without consulting the other members of the cabinet. . . . This action on the part of Schumpeter provoked a violent conflict inside the coalition government during which Schumpeter solicited and obtained the support of the Viennese Christian Social Party members.[35]

Schumpeter's reply to this charge came many years later in two letters addressed to Professor Gulick, in which he declared categorically that he had neither authorized nor sanctioned the sale of the Alpine shares. He made it clear, however, that socialization measures under the circumstances prevailing would only have increased the difficulties of a difficult situation, and that the prevention of such measures would have been a service to the country, the government and, above all, to the Social Democratic Party.[36]

Bauer's accusation that Schumpeter had supported Kola's transactions, in the restricted sense of having passively submitted to them, is, however, borne out by a letter from the Finance Minister addressed to the State Chancellor, Dr Renner, shortly after the publication of the denunciatory article in the *Arbeiter-Zeitung*, referred to above:

> At the end of June 1919 I received the surprising letter . . . from the banker Richard Kola saying that he could put at my disposal the amount of 15 million lire, which he had obtained from an Italian party for the purchase of Alpine stock. Although I was pleased at the repletion of our exchange reserves by this unexpected influx of capital, I expressed the wish that the purchases would not alter the majority position of our native shareholders. At the beginning of August Herr Kola provided me on two occasions with the sum of 5 million lire for similar transactions. Again, I prevailed on Herr Kola not to persist in the purchases. . . . I wish to point out in this context that I consider it advantageous if there is some interest abroad in our securities, and if foreigners participate in our security trading. If our securities were to meet with no interest abroad, and were to cease to be an object of foreign transactions, the Austrian crown would be helplessly exposed to every attack from abroad.

Schumpeter concluded his long letter with a reference to his conservative programme of financial reform and with an appeal for loyalty from the Chancellor:

> I know my conservative programme of financial reform and of the smooth and steady reconstruction of our economy without disrupting the social order is being subjected to formidable and, I am ready to admit, deeply felt objections. I hold the opinion that our country can be led out of its impasse without the violent disturbance of its financial and economic foundations. If others do not deem that possible, the resulting conflict should be fought out in a realistic and political manner . . .[37]

A careful reading of Schumpeter's letter to Renner leaves one with the impression that his repeated pleas to Kola to discontinue the sale of Alpine shares to Italian interests were made with little conviction, for it seems hardly possible that the foreign exchange dealer, who acted on the authority of the Finance Ministry, would have ignored an explicit order. Schumpeter may even have intimated in his occasional meetings with Kola that the nationalization of the Alpine Montangesellschaft would be likely to increase the difficulties of a difficult situation, as he expressed it in the letter to Gulick, and that the prevention of such an outcome might be considered a patriotic act. It is only fair to add that in tolerating the transactions of Herr Kola, Schumpeter may have been acting in conformity with the intentions of the moderate wing of the Social Democratic Party which, as Renner once stated, did not aspire to the 'socialization of debts'. Considering this alignment of political forces, the nationalization of key industries, as advocated by Otto Bauer and his left-wing adherents, seems to have been a rather unrealistic programme even in the turbulent spring days of 1919. Schumpeter two years later composed the epitaph for this historical episode: 'Full socialization as an immediate programme has been no more than political phraseology in both Germany and Austria.'[38]

The conservative programme of financial reform which Schumpeter mentioned in the letter to Renner had been submitted to the public, in its rough outlines, soon after the new Finance Minister took office. In the following months he repeatedly announced the preparation of a definite version without actually publishing it, making it appear as if he were slow in making up his mind about the details of the plan. But even his opponents had to admit that 'before the conclusion of the peace treaty the activities of the financial administration were narrowly circumscribed'.[39] An article in the *Arbeiter-Zeitung* of 10 October 1919 criticized Schumpeter especially for having failed to prepare a financial plan ready to put forward immediately after publication of the peace treaty. This criticism proved erroneous, however, for on 16 October, one day before resigning his office, the Finance Minister did present the public with a comprehensive programme of financial reform.[40]

The plan, a rather lengthy document, does not differ essentially from the provisional programme Schumpeter had announced more than six months before. Again, its focal point is the great capital levy, the technical complexities of which are dealt with in detail. Schumpeter is aware of the grave burden which the levy would impose on the Austrian economy, and is prepared to make exempt, at least temporarily, all those enterprises which continue to employ as many people as before or during the war. More importantly, the plan provides for the temporary exemption from the levy of all those persons and enterprises capable of putting substantial foreign credits at the disposition of the government. By utilizing the international reputation of its citizens and enterprises, the Austrian state, so Schumpeter believed, would be able to obtain sufficient foreign credit to meet its budget deficit and to stabilize its currency. It is highly questionable, however, whether this method of procuring foreign credit would have yielded positive results in 1919 and following years. As late as 1925, Walther Federn, the leading Viennese financial writer and editor of the respected *Volkswirt*, observed that 'only very few industrial enterprises in Austria, and those internationally well known, have direct access to foreign credit. All others can obtain it only through the services, and with the guarantee, of one of the Vienna banks. . . .'[41]

Schumpeter's reform programme contains two further important points: the establishment of a central bank, which must not be allowed to make advances to the government under any form or pretext whatever; and the imposition of an indirect tax on the poorer strata of the population, which, according to Schumpeter, 'means nothing other than the extension of the income tax in the downward direction'. The capital levy should be borne by the 'rentier-class'. It would be deceiving themselves, so he concludes, 'if we did not face frankly the force of this overwhelming fact'.

A few passages in Schumpeter's report are devoted to the question of socialization. Even one who considers himself in favour of socialization, he argues, must admit that at the present moment, when the state needs foreign credit, socialization is likely to deter foreign creditors, rather than attract them. On the other hand, he does not dismiss the possibility that socialized capital will attain credit-worthiness in future years through systematic positive work and through achieving real success.

Schumpeter ends his report on the following solemn note:

> . . . the financial programme is based on the conviction that we are able to help ourselves. The well-to-do citizens will have to put at the disposal of the state not only the major part of their wealth, but their credit and good name, so that the preservation of our economic order can be assured. The poorer classes must take upon themselves the full sacrifice of indirect taxation, which will enable the state to put its finances into permanent order without resorting to the issuing of paper money. To foreign powers we shall have to prove that we are prepared to help ourselves; only then will they be ready to extend their help to us.

Schumpeter's appeal fell on deaf ears. It soon became known through a report in the Viennese daily *Neue Freie Presse* that he had lost support in the ranks of the Christian Social Party, which was no longer united behind his financial plan.[42] His resignation was the logical outcome of his total political isolation. Today, we can only speculate as to why a considerable proportion of the conservative party so suddenly deserted him. It is likely that his rigorous conception of the capital levy provoked resistance, especially among the rural membership of the party. This can be inferred from a passage in the article cited above.[43] Moreover, his occasional flirtation with the ideas of socialism may have cost him the sympathy of some influential conservative politicians.

It is hardly surprising that the *Neue Freie Presse* singled out Otto Bauer as the main adversary of Schumpeter's financial plan. Certainly Bauer seized on the programme as a means of getting rid of a cabinet colleague with whom he had crossed swords on several vital issues. But, we may ask today, was Bauer well advised to deprive himself of the co-operation of a man who was the only one among his 'bourgeois' colleagues to have taken up the problem of the capital levy with a great deal of expertise and unequivocally positive intentions? In 1919, it appears, Bauer did not, unlike Schumpeter, consider the capital levy a *conditio sine qua non* for the balancing of the budget and the stabilization of the currency. In *The Road to Socialism* he advocated this measure solely as a means of compensating the former owners of socialized enterprises. Perhaps the proverbial straw that broke the camel's back was Schumpeter's sober warning, tacked on to his financial programme, that socialization must be foregone at a moment when the Austrian state most urgently needed foreign capital.

In conclusion we may say that the early withdrawal of the great economist from Austrian politics must be attributed to the fact that one of the dominant political parties considered his ideas too radical, while the other viewed them as too pragmatic, too wilful, and too hostile towards 'Anschluss'.

1982/1983

Chapter 10

Schumpeter as University Teacher

If I remember rightly, I met Schumpeter for the first time at the Harvard Economics Club in the spring of 1941. The man whose name was to me almost legendary had promised to lecture on the Vienna school of psychoanalysis; the small group of economics students was joined on this occasion by a large number of students from other university departments. At long last the great Schumpeter stood before me: of medium height, corpulent, strong shoulders supporting a massive head whose features remotely reminded me of Napoleon's. His way of lecturing, to which I took exception also on later occasions, was casual and unsystematic. It was obvious that the speaker had not prepared any notes, let alone a written text, on his difficult subject.

I had become fairly well acquainted with Sigmund Freud's main works while a student in Vienna. So I was able during the discussion to point out a number of errors committed by Schumpeter, and in doing so I was barely able to control my irritation, which had increased as the lecture went on. Schumpeter took note of my arguments with condescending politeness, and finally put an end to the discussion by inviting me to visit him at his University office to discuss some of the points at issue without the restraints imposed on us now by time. From then on I visited him regularly in his office in the Littauer Building on Harvard Square.

In presenting the main tenets of psychoanalysis, Schumpeter had relied on his incredible memory, and for once it had failed him. By contrast, in his lectures on economics – I attended classes he gave on theory, money and banking, and socialism – it was only rarely that a student could show that he had forgotten something or made a mistake. These lectures too he delivered without written notes. But in his pockets he had blank strips of paper on which he jotted down in short-hand any new ideas that crossed his mind. This gave rise to the joke that, while his colleagues brought along notes they had prepared at home for their lectures, Schumpeter returned home with notes taken during his. He would greet comments of this kind with a nod of satisfaction.

I attended Schumpeter's lectures (along with others given by Gottfried Haberler, Edward Chamberlain, Abbot Usher and Alvin Hansen) for a full year, then interrupted my studies to join the US Navy. After the war I resumed my studies, mainly at long last to finish my dissertation, the first draft of which I had put aside for three years. Schumpeter took a great interest in the progress of that dissertation, not least because it dealt with a wide-ranging topic of economic history – the economic consequences of the collapse of the Danubian Monarchy. But he was strangely uncommunicative and short with me when I submitted to him a long chapter dealing with the economic developments of 1918-19, a fateful year for Austria. During that year he himself had played an important role as Minister of Finance under the young republic. Only many years later, when I was working on a study of Schumpeter's financial policy in that year,[1] did I realize why he had appeared so uneasy when discussing the matter, an impression which had seemed strange to me at the time.

Other subjects, too, were taboo as far as Schumpeter was concerned. For example, he repeatedly refused his students' requests that he give a special seminar on his own theory of economic development. Since it could hardly be denied that the great Harvard professor bore a considerable load of vanity, as he himself readily admitted in conversation, this reserve seemed unnatural and puzzling. Finally there was a small scandal. During a public discussion on the current significance of socialism, Paul M. Sweezy, then the youngest member of the Harvard economics faculty, discussed the main points of the Schumpeterian theory and asked his eminent colleague to give an opinion on some of the controversial questions *expressis verbis*. Schumpeter ignored Sweezy's challenge and began a long-winded panegyric on the US economic system, paying no attention to provocative remarks from the students.

Schumpeter had written his famous work *The Theory of Economic Development* before he was thirty. Later, in nostalgic moments, he would speak of this period of life as 'the sacred age of fertility'. In later years he repeatedly tried to support his earlier theses empirically and theoretically, especially in his large work *Business Cycles*, which he regarded as his crowning achievement. But only a few years before this *tour de force*, the *General Theory of Employment, Interest and Money* by John Maynard Keynes had appeared, and the Harvard economics faculty, as well as economists outside Harvard, were discussing hardly anything but the Keynesian 'revolution'.

Schumpeter would scarcely have been human if he had not reacted with disappointment and bitterness to the wall of indifference greeting his *magnum opus*. The bitterness manifested itself in, among other things, his stigmatizing the *General Theory* as 'depression economics' (an expression said to have been coined by the British economist Sir John Hicks). The 'stagnation' theory of Schumpeter's colleague Alvin Hansen, in which he tried to demonstrate that there was, as was then widely believed, a permanent 'gap' between savings and investment, was uncompromisingly rejected by Schumpeter, and the intellectual atmosphere among the Harvard faculty was sometimes very strained. Moreover, Schumpeter held political views that were found shocking by a large part of the Harvard community.

One would be less than just to Schumpeter, however, if his criticism of Keynesian theory were seen as no more than a product of hurt vanity and professional jealousy. He was very sceptical about the whole system of 'comparative statics'. To him the mechanisms that lead – or are supposed to lead – from one state of equilibrium to another, and that were described by Keynes and his followers with some deceptively elegant formulae, were the very crux of the process of cyclical growth. Only a genuinely 'dynamic' theory could reasonably deal with all its aspects. However, Schumpeter did sometimes admit that the system of 'comparative statics' contained elements of a more dynamic approach.

It was striking how often Schumpeter, when lecturing on Keynes and Keynesianism, referred to the theories of Karl Marx. With the exception of Paul Sweezy, who was then writing his brilliant early work *The Theory of Capitalist Development*, Schumpeter was the only one among the Harvard faculty to deal in any depth with Marx's economic theories. In my notes taken at the time I recorded a remark made by Schumpeter in passing, that a system like that of Marx 'which changes under its own steam will forever attract more attention than the Keynesian system of comparative statics'.

Schumpeter may have been thinking in this connection of his own work, which ascribed the dynamics of the capitalist mode of production to the innovative activity of the entrepreneur. Elsewhere in this book I have more to say about the Schumpeterian view of the trade cycle and the process of growth. Here I will say only that during my last year at Harvard I came to feel that Schumpeter's striking reserve with regard to his own theory may ultimately have been caused by a feeling of its inadequacy. In Vienna, soon after the appearance of his impressive early work, he had had to endure a negative and very harsh critique from his deeply respected teacher and mentor Böhm-Bawerk. And later on he seems to have had increasing doubts as to whether the phenomenon of interest should be seen as resulting from a purely dynamic process. But in his Harvard years, too, he rejected the notion of linking the agio theory with his dynamic theory. Frustrating reflections of this kind sometimes induced him to remark that the ground of economics was not firm; and once during a lecture he said resignedly that one had the feeling of crossing a swamp.

Schumpeter held the Swiss economist Léon Walras in great esteem, as being the actual founder of the quantitative school of economics. And again and again he talked about the need to dynamize the Walrasian system. But I know of no work by Schumpeter in which he attempted this, unless one views his monumental *Business Cycles* as such an endeavour. Schumpeter also took a favourable view of the new school of econometrics, of which Walras was one of the founding fathers. Although in his lectures Schumpeter discussed the work of Tinbergen, Frisch, Tintner, Hotelling, Samuelson and others, and although he had a certain knowledge of mathematics, I believe he wrote nothing directly relating to the school of econometrics. In this respect, too, his behaviour was ambivalent, not to say puzzling.

Schumpeter was one of the founders of the so-called 'Econometric Society' at Harvard, and he headed it from 1937 to 1941. Initially he fulfilled this office with great care and commitment. But it was obvious, after several years of intensive discussion with well-known representatives of the new school, that his original hopes had given way to a certain scepticism. What seemed most to have put him off was that some of his best students concentrated on partial aspects of the discipline, using the tools of econometrics, and completely losing sight of the broader connections between economics, history and sociology which he himself had demonstrated in several of his works. After my return to Harvard in 1946 I attended some discussions at which it seemed to me that Schumpeter's former open-mindedness towards econometrics had occasionally been replaced by a certain irritation. Later I often asked myself how this man, who had devoted one of his earliest essays to the role of mathematics in economics, would have reacted to some of the recent developments in this discipline.

*　*　*

Soon after completing his *Business Cycles*, Schumpeter started work on a new book in which he wanted to comment on several current problems. His notes and rough drafts, at first hastily jotted down, were soon to develop into a work that met with a surprisingly strong and lasting response even in non-academic circles – a response that greets it even today.

As is well known, the book, *Capitalism, Socialism and Democracy*, which first appeared in 1942, opens with a tribute to the theoretical work of Karl Marx. In particular, the Marxian sociological method, 'historical materialism', is celebrated by Schumpeter as one of the greatest intellectual achievements in the field of sociology. This tribute to Marx's genius was undoubtedly intended by the author as a challenge to the conservatism of orthodox economics as taught at Harvard and at the other major American universities; in this way Schumpeter, the eternal *enfant terrible*, demonstrated once again his complete intellectual independence. But this unusual Prologue to an unusual book had a deeper meaning: with this tribute the author settled an old debt. Only Böhm-Bawerk, his great and unforgettable teacher, had had as profound an influence on Schumpeter's life work as had Karl Marx.

After a critical appreciation of Marx's world of ideas, however, Schumpeter subjects America's monopolist economy to an analysis which must be seen as a sharp rejection of the secular theories of stagnation emanating from Marxist/leftist-Keynesian quarters. The author ascribes to capitalism, marked in its new form by the big monopoloid trusts, a dynamic force as distinguishable dramatically from that of the capitalism of free competition as gun-fire from the slamming of a door. In retrospect it may be said that the economic development of the first three decades of the post-war period, 1945-75, has borne out Schumpeter's theory rather than that of his Marxist/leftist-Keynesian antagonists.

After this prophecy of a golden age of capitalism there follows one of those dialectical leaps characteristic of Schumpeter's thinking. Capitalism, he says, will perish, to be replaced by a socialist system, not because of its inadequacies and outright failures, as Marx had assumed, but – on the contrary – because of its impressive historical achievements. Schumpeter describes some aspects of this process of disintegration. The decisive factor in the replacement of one system by another lies, in the last analysis, in the extinction of the entrepreneurial function, which is taken over by a managerial team – the 'technostructure', to use J.K. Galbraith's vivid expression. The passing of the old capitalist entrepreneur signals the end of a period in the history of mankind marked by the creative individual and by the liberal world of ideas.

As I have said, Schumpeter's new book was an instant success with the public. Some of his left-wing students hailed it as evidence of a wilful and belated conversion to their own point of view. They overlooked the fact that Schumpeter had publicly advanced very similar views in the early 1920s.[2] His conservative friends, on the other hand, were critical of him for writing a book that would contribute to the spread of defeatist feelings, because in it he had postulated the inevitability and higher rationality of socialism. Schumpeter countered such reproaches with the dry remark that it was better to recognize certain negative sociological tendencies early on, so as to be able to develop adequate counter-strategies in time.

In reality the arguments from left and from right mattered not at all to Schumpeter. He had a sentimental and nostalgic attitude towards the great figures of the nineteenth century and the intellectual movements initiated by them, and felt closer to the world of yesterday than to the present, which he saw as brutal and pitiless. He often remarked that the character of a social epoch manifested itself in the way that epoch waged war, and that the wars of our time were aimed at total annihilation of the enemy – by contrast with the wars of the past. Capitalism, which Schumpeter saw as the incarnation of the creative entrepreneurial spirit, seemed to him to have vanished from the world stage some time before. What he thought was apparent during recent decades was a gradual convergence of political systems. A new managerial class was getting ready to usurp the commanding heights of politics and business in both East and West. Behind the various political façades he thought he could discern very distinct tendencies towards convergence.

So it is hardly surprising that Schumpeter found himself in political and personal isolation during the war years, especially after it became known that he viewed National Socialism as the regrettable but understandable reaction of the German people to the Versailles peace treaty, which he considered to have been unjust. Moreover, he found himself unable to share the increasing sympathy for the Russian people, so severely affected by the hardships of the war. Among the students and even a part of the American population the opinion – or rather the illusion – prevailed, that after the victory over fascism, which was viewed as inevitable, the Soviet system would evolve in the direction of social democracy. Schumpeter rejected such views with barely disguised contempt. His favourable response to the then much-discussed book *The Managerial Revolution*, by James Burnham, was characteristic of his attitude towards the issue of 'convergence of the systems'. When during a conversation I said I found Burnham's theses superficial, Schumpeter reacted with unaccustomed sharpness. I realized that I had touched a vital nerve.

My impression of Schumpeter during my time at Harvard was not that of a stable, balanced and happy man. I knew that he had met with much personal misfortune and hardship in Austria. As a political economist he had often encountered unfair or even venomous criticism. His appointment as full professor at Graz was forced through only thanks to the intervention of Böhm-Bawerk and with the aid of an imperial decree. He suffered the painful early loss of his young second wife and a new-born child shortly after he moved to Bonn in 1925.

From very early on, Schumpeter had political aspirations, as diary entries by Josef Redlich, personal letters, and, not least, political memoranda written during World War I show very clearly. But he held office as Finance Minister in a coalition cabinet under Karl Renner for less than half a year, and this brief period ended on an embarrassing note. His activity as a banker – he was president of the private Biedermann bank in Vienna for a few years – was not very successful either. After the liquidation of this bank he was left with a considerable financial burden.

During his time at Bonn, Schumpeter twice accepted invitations from his colleague Frank Taussig to act as a visiting professor at Harvard University. He spent the academic year 1927-8 in Cambridge, Massachusetts, and later the winter term of 1930. He accepted these invitations with some hesitation. His stay in Bonn had been overshadowed by the sudden death of his young wife and the need to pay back the large debts he had incurred in Vienna. On the other hand, he had gathered around him in Bonn a circle of loyal colleagues and gifted students to whom he felt attached and morally obligated. His manifold cultural interests, too, made for close ties with prominent individuals in the Central European university town.

Schumpeter had visited the United States in the academic years 1913-14 at the invitation of Columbia University in New York. Neither then nor later had he been much attracted by New York. Harvard

University, on the other hand, where his lectures had been received with interest and approval, was very congenial to him.[3] In spite of that he seems to have declined Frank Taussig's early offer of a permanent appointment at Harvard. I think I am right in assuming that at the time he did not seriously consider emigrating to the still 'uncomfortable country', as he called the US. It was only when his application for a professorship at the University of Berlin was refused that he seems to have changed his mind.

In the United States after 1932, free at last of financial worries, Schumpeter could devote his time to scholarly work. He put so much effort and energy into this activity that his robust health was gradually undermined. Even in the small hours of the morning one could see him walking up and down in the study of his house, pondering some aspect of his work. One could not help feeling that he was driven by the fear of leaving his life work unfinished.

But a *homo politicus* like Schumpeter was not fully absorbed by his studies. In the lecture hall he abstained almost completely from criticizing the economic policy of the Roosevelt administration. Yet it became clear that he viewed the New Deal and many of its leftist-bourgeois representatives with scepticism and occasionally even with contempt. When at the beginning of the Second World War the lecture halls gradually emptied and many of his colleagues were called to Washington to serve in various agencies of the wartime economy, Schumpeter was occasionally unable to keep from expressing his bitterness. During one of his rare discourses on economic policy he would sometimes utter the strange words: 'If I were among the living, I should . . . '. The old *homo politicus* sometimes considered himself as good as dead.

When I returned to Cambridge after the war, I met a strangely altered, almost cheerful Schumpeter who was obviously at peace with the world. At any rate this was the impression he made on me and on some of my colleagues. Possibly he enjoyed working on his last great book, the *History of Economic Analysis*. But a heartfelt sigh – 'thank God for America' – frequently heard at that time lends itself to a different interpretation of the striking change in his behaviour. Schumpeter, along with the American public, had only at this late date become aware of the full extent of the European tragedy. No wonder he reacted with a rapid and fervent prayer when he heard about the concentration camps, large-scale murder, and the expulsion and extinction of whole ethnic groups. At that time he may have had the first slight doubts about the validity of his 'convergence theory'; I had no opportunity to verify this point.

Schumpeter's intellectual attitude towards the United States and to his closer circle at that time is perhaps best documented by an entry in his diary dated 8 February 1945: 'Good morning friend, how does it feel to be sixty-two – and definitely old and definitely to feel old? One thing to be recorded is my humble thanks to the United States. No re-pining, no sterile regrets, no sorrow about the state of things; accep-tance rather and a feeling that it could be worse.'[4]

In his 1946 obituary of John Maynard Keynes, Schumpeter tried to portray the character of the great English economist. Mentioning Keynes's manifold interests, he wrote:

> This combination of interests is not unusual. What makes it unusual and almost a miracle is the fact that he devoted so much energy to each of these fields of interest as if it had been his only one. His appetite and capacity for efficient work appear incredible, and his power of concentration on whatever he was working on was truly Gladstonian; whatever he tackled was pursued with such determination as to displace any other thought. He knew what it means to be tired. But he seems to have hardly known the dead hours of cheerlessness and frustration. . . . Human machines using up their last reserve of strength usually have something inhuman about them. Such people are almost always cold in their human re-lations, unapproachable and turned in on themselves. But Keynes was the exact opposite of all this – the friendliest fellow one can imagine: friendly, warm and cheerful in the way of people who are not encumbered with anything. . . . He was affectionate. He was always ready to listen and respond to the views, problems and sor-rows of other people. He was generous, and not only in financial matters. He was sociable, loved conversation and excelled in it. And in contrast to a widely held view he was able to be polite, polite in the sense of an Old World etiquette which is time-con-suming. . . .[5]

In those few lines Schumpeter left us not only a portrait of his admired and probably envied rival, but also a picture that displays some of his own particular traits.

1983

Notes

JAS = Joseph A. Schumpeter
Works cited below in condensed form are listed in full in the Bibliography at p. 194.

Chapter 1: Schumpeter's Theory in its Relationship to Marxism

1 'By "development", we shall understand therefore only such changes in the circular flow of the economy as are not forced upon it from without but arise by its own initiative, from within.' JAS, *The Theory of Economic Development* (Cambridge, Mass., 1955), 63 (translation slightly amended by the author – E.M.); cited hereafter as *Theory*.

2 Cf. 'Capitalism', *Encyclopaedia Britannica* (1946), 801 ff.

3 'We speak of entrepreneurs not only with regard to those historical epochs in which the entrepreneur exists as a special social phenomenon, we also attach the concept and name to the function and to all individuals who actually perform it in any social formation, be he a member of the executive body of a socialist community, lord of a feudal manor or chief of a primitive tribe.' JAS, *Theorie der wirtschaftlichen Entwicklung*, 2nd edn., (Munich-Leipzig, 1926), 111. (This passage is only to be found in the German version.)

4 For the problem of credit creation by the banks see JAS, *Business Cycles*, 2 vols. (New York, 1939), I.109 ff.).

5 In his *Theory*, JAS distinguishes between five different kinds of 'productive combinations': (1) the introduction of a new type of goods; (2) the introduction of a new method of production; (3) the opening of a new market; (4) the acquisition of a new source of supply of raw materials; (5) the carrying out of a new organization of any industry, such as the creation of a monopoly position. See *Theory*, 66 ff.

6 'These three propositions, that interest as a great social phenomenon is a product of development, that it flows from profit, and that it does not adhere to concrete goods, are the basis of our theory of interest.' Ibid., 175. The latter remark is to be seen in the context of a polemic with Böhm-Bawerk, for whom interest derives from the value premium on present goods.

7 'What is capital then if it consists neither of a definite kind of goods nor of goods in general? By this time the answer is obvious enough: it is a fund of purchasing power. Only as such can it fulfil its essential function. . . .' Ibid., 119-20.

8 'In this sense, therefore, we define the kernel of the credit phenomenon in the following manner: credit is essentially the creation of purchasing power for the purpose of transferring it to the entrepreneur, but not simply the transfer of existing purchasing power. The creation of purchasing power characterises, in principle, the method by which development is carried out in a system with private property and division of labor.' Ibid., 107.

9 Karl Marx and Friedrich Engels, *Manifesto of the Communist Party*, in *Collected Works* (London, 1985), VI. 489.

10 Cf. Fritz Redlich, 'Entrepreneurship in the Initial Stages of Industrialization', *Weltwirtschaftliches Archiv*, vol. 75 (1955), 62.
11 Cf. Karl Marx, *Capital*, tr. Samuel Moore and Edward Aveling (London, 1970), I. 318-19; cited hereafter in the text.
12 Marx and Engels, *Manifesto*, loc. cit. The four new combinations which we think are to be found in the cited passage are the following: new goods, new methods of production, new markets and new resources.
13 A state of full employment resulting from today's 'active' labour market policy (following the Swedish example) could not have been foreseen by Marx, for obvious reasons. He probably viewed some residual unemployment as normal even in periods of prosperity. Thus a passage in vol. I of *Capital* runs: 'On the basis of capitalism, a system in which ... the law by which a constantly increasing quantity of means of production may be set in motion by a progressively diminishing expenditure of human power, thanks to the advance in the productivity of social labour, ... is expressed thus: the higher the productivity of labour, the greater is the pressure of the workers on the means of employment, the more precarious therefore becomes the condition for their existence ... The fact that the means of production and the productivity of labour increase more rapidly than the productive population expresses itself, therefore, under capitalism, in the inverse form that the working population always increases more rapidly than the valorization requirements of capital.' (I.798, tr. Ben Fowkes)
14 Marx and Engels, *Value, Price and Profit*, in *Collected Works*, XX. 146.
15 Cf. Rudolf Hilferding, *Das Finanzkapital* (Vienna, 1927), 283.
16 Werner Sombart, *Der moderne Kapitalismus* (Munich-Leipzig, 1927), III.pt.1. 14.
17 Hilferding, *Finanzkapital*, 138. The first edition of *Das Finanzkapital* appeared in 1910.
18 JAS, *Capitalism, Socialism and Democracy* (New York, 1947), 134; cited hereafter in the text, as *Capitalism*.
19 'One of the most important features of the later stages of capitalist civilization is the vigorous expansion of the educational apparatus and particularly of the facilities for higher education. This development was and is no less inevitable than the development of the largest-scale industrial unit, but, unlike the latter, it has been and is being fostered by public opinion and public authority so as to go much further than it would have done under its own steam. ... inasmuch as higher education thus increases the supply of services in professional, quasi-professional and in the end all "white-collar" lines beyond the point determined by cost-return considerations, it may create a particularly important case of sectional unemployment.' JAS, *Capitalism*, 152
20 Vilfredo Pareto, *Allgemeine Soziologie* (Tübingen, 1955), 242.

Chapter 2: The Schumpeterian Entrepreneur

1 JAS, 'Die sozialen Klassen im ethnisch-homogenen Milieu', in Schumpeter, *Aufsätze zur Soziologie* (Tübingen, 1953), 210. [References throughout are to the German text of this essay; it was published in English, in a translation by Heinz Norden, in *Imperialism and Social Classes*, ed. Paul M. Sweezy (Oxford, 1951), 137-221.]
2 See JAS, *Business Cycles*, I. 225.
3 Marx, *Capital*, tr. Ben Fowkes, I. 436.
4 JAS, 'Die sozialen Klassen', op. cit., 163; cited hereafter in the text.
5 Cf. JAS, *Ten Great Economists, From Marx to Keynes*, ed. E.B. Schumpeter (London, 1952), 137 ff.
6 Cf. JAS, *History of Economic Analysis*, ed. E.B. Schumpeter (New York, 1954), 790.
7 Fritz Redlich, 'Entrepreneurship in the Initial Stages of Industrialization', *Weltwirtschaftliches Archiv*, vol. 75 (1955), 62.
8 Ibid., 63.
9 Ibid., 64.
10 E.A. Carlin, 'Schumpeter's Constructed Type: The Entrepreneur', *Kyklos* 9 (1956), 27 ff.
11 Yale Brozen, 'Business Leadership and Technological Change', *American Journal of Economy and Sociology* (1954), 19, quoted in Felix Rexhausen, *Der Unternehmer und die wirtschaftliche Entwicklung* (Berlin, 1960), 32.
12 Edward S. Mason, 'The Apologetics of Managerialism', *Journal of Business of the University of Chicago*, 1 (1958).

Chapter 3: On the Genesis of Schumpeter's Theory of Economic Development

1 Cf. JAS, 'Die neue Wirtschaftstheorie in den Vereinigten Staaten', in *Schmollers Jahrbuch*, 1910, 961 ff. See also id., 'Professor Clarks Verteilungstheorie', *Zeitschrift für Volkswirtschaft, Sozialpolitik und Verwaltung*, 1910, 225 ff.

2 To mention only a few of the more comprehensive discussions: Ray V. Clemence and Francis S. Doody, *The Schumpeterian System* (Cambridge, Mass., 1950); Felix Rexhausen, *Der Unternehmer und die volkswirtschaftliche Entwicklung* (Berlin, 1960); Felix Lehnis, *Der Beitrag des späten Schumpeter zur Konjunkturforschung* (Stuttgart, 1960); Erich Schneider, *Joseph A. Schumpeter, Leben und Werk eines großen Sozialökonomen* (Tübingen, 1970).

3 Cf. JAS, *Theory*, 74-5.

4 Ibid., 66 ff. With reference to the odd character of the businessman who clings to the traditional mode of production and at best adapts to outside influences, François Perroux once wittily remarked that 'Schumpeter has not discovered the static producer in history, but in the works of Walras . . . ' Cf. his 'Les trois analyses de l'évolution et la recherche d'une dynamique totale chez Joseph Schumpeter', *Economie Appliquée*, IV (1951), 282.

5 JAS, *Theory*, 93 ff.

6 Cf. JAS, 'Eine dynamische Theorie des Kapitalzinses', *Zeitschrift für Volkswirtschaft und Verwaltung*, reprinted in JAS, *Aufsätze zur ökonomischen Theorie* (Tübingen, 1953), 415.

7 Thus JAS writes in 'Capitalism' (*Encyclopaedia Britannica*, 1946): 'Most of the features that define the capitalist order may be found in the ancient world, and particularly in its Graeco-Roman sector.'

8 JAS considers the technique of credit creation to be so important that he views its introduction as the very birth of modern capitalism. Cf. *Business Cycles*, I. 224.

9 Thus JAS in the article 'Unternehmer': '. . . more and more the social whole gets used to continuous innovation in the economic process; more and more it becomes natural that every new idea, as soon as it is born, is translated into practice. The area of what is strictly calculable . . . becomes larger and larger – technically as well as commercially. But circumstances not only facilitate and democratize the function of leadership in general, and the entrepreneurial function in particular, they also reduce their importance.' In *Handwörterbuch der Staatswissenschaften*, ed. Elster Ludwig *et al.*, vol. VIII, 4th edn. (Jena, 1928).

10 Thus in his polemic with Böhm-Bawerk JAS talks about the 'close relationship of our views'. Cf. 'Eine dynamische Theorie des Kapitalzinses' (n.6), 418. In his first published work, 'Das Wesen und der Hauptinhalt der theoretischen Nationalökonomie' (Leipzig 1908), he mentions his particularly close affinity to the views of Walras and Wieser.

11 Oskar Lange comments on this point: 'The Schumpeterian theory stems from the Austrian variety of the marginal utility school. But Schumpeter deliberately inserts in his theory numerous elements from Marx's works.' Oskar Lange, *Wstep do teorii rozwoju gospodarczego* (Warsaw, 1961), 220 ff.

12 Quoted in Gottfried Haberler, 'Joseph A. Schumpeter', in *Schumpeter, Social Scientist*, ed. Seymour E. Harris (Cambridge, Mass., 1951), 41 n.

13 Cf. Arnošt Klima, 'Industrial Growth and Entrepreneurship in the Early Stages of Industrialization', *Journal of European Economic History* no. 6 (1977), 549-74.

14 Austrian economic history records a large number of 'prophets' who deplored the backwardness of the domestic economy and offered economic recipes for overcoming it. The 'old' mercantilists, Johann J. Becher, Wilhelm Schröder and Philipp W. Hörnigk, raised their warning voices at the end of the seventeenth century. In the eighteenth century they were followed by the neo-mercantilists Justi and Sonnenfels. A very impressive witness to the ineffectiveness of economic policy is Karl Freiherr von Bruck, who around the middle of the nineteenth century, first as Minister of Trade and later as Minister of Finance, carried on a heroic struggle to overcome the backwardness of the Austrian economy and finally, having been forced by the Emperor to resign, committed suicide. Towards the end of the nineteenth century the Minister of Finance, Steinbach, alarmed at the backwardness of Austrian industry *vis-à-vis* that of Germany, reproached the representatives of the large

Vienna banks for 'concerning themselves so little with industrial enterprises'. 'An Interview with the New Minister of Finance'. *Neue Freie Presse*, 13 Feb 1891.

15 The Austrian historian Ferdinand Tremel thinks that Maria Theresa's reforms initiated Austria's industrialization: 'At the end of Maria Theresa's reign Austria was still far from being an industrialized country, but the foundations for industrialization had been laid . . .'. F. Tremel, *Wirtschafts-und Sozialgeschichte Österrreichs. Von den Anfängen bis 1955* (Vienna, 1969), 267.

16 The most important items in the programme of mercantilism – increasing the export of finished products, monopolizing trade with the colonies, forestalling industrial activity in the colonies, promoting the construction of sea-going vessels, the expansion of the money supply or the stock of precious metals (and thereby reducing the 'price' of money), etc. – reflect the needs of the increasingly powerful English merchant class, owners of manufactories, outputters, shipowners, etc. as well as of the commercialized gentry. Cf. Eduard März, *Einführung in die Marxsche Theorie der wirtschaftlichen Entwicklung* (Vienna, 1976), 70.

17 Professor Gross is of the opinion that the Austrian version of enlightened absolutism, also known as 'Josephinismus', may well have survived under the imperial bureaucracy until the 1860s, Cf. Nachum Th. Gross, 'The Industrial Revolution in the Habsburg Monarchy, 1750-1914', in *The Fontana Economic History of Europe: The Emergence of Industrial Societies*, 4 (1), ed. Carlo M. Cipolla (Glasgow, 1976), 239.

18 On 24 June 1833 Metternich wrote 'his famous memorandum explaining that the customs union is a state within the state, that of the 12 votes of the Frankfurt federation only 7 remained independent of Prussia, and that under the circumstances the separation of trade would sooner or later lead to political and moral separation.' Ludwig Lang, *Hundert Jahre Zollpolitik* (Vienna and Leipzig, 1906), 143.

19 In a newspaper article published in the year 1848, Marx called Vienna the 'largest and most active focus of the German revolution'. The complete text of the passage in question runs as follows: 'Finally, the work that was begun on the day of Custozza was completed on November 1 – just as

Radetzky had marched into Milan so did Windischgrätz ad Jellachich march into Vienna. Cavaignac's method was employed, and employed successfully, against the largest and most active focus of German revolution. The revolution in Vienna, like that in Paris, was smothered in blood and smoking ruins.' Karl Marx/ Friedrich Engels, 'The Revolutionary Movement in Italy', *Collected Works* (London, 1985), VIII. 103, 104.

20 Cf. Günther Chaloupek, *Struktur und Dynamik der Wiener Wirtschaft im frühindustriellen Zeitalter* (unpub. MS., Vienna).

21 Information here on the spread of the steam-engine at the beginning and around the middle of the nineteenth century is intended to give the reader an impression of the technological backwardness of the Austrian economy. But it does not accord with statistical data collected by the Central Statistical Commission, published in *Die Presse* (Vienna), 10 June 1864. According to the *Patriotisches Tagblatt* (Brno), 11 May 1805, no. 50, 199 ff., the first steam engine may have been installed as early as 1805; it was part of a water-pumping system in the park of Count Esterhazy's palace at Eisenstadt. Katzer, 'Wenzel Günther 1812-1870', in *Unser Neustadt, Blätter des Wiener Neustädter Denkmalschutzvereines*, 1976.

22 Klima, 'Industrial Growth and Entrepreneurship' (n.13), 569.

23 Johann Slokar, *Geschichte der österreichischen Industrie und ihrer Förderung unter Kaiser Franz I* (Vienna, 1914), 447, 465.

24 Herbert Matis and Karl Bachinger, 'Österreichs industrielle Entwicklung', in *Die wirtschaftliche Entwicklung*, ed. Alois Brusatti (see Adam Wandruszka and Peter Urbanitsch, *Die Habsburgermonarchie 1848-1918* (Vienna, 1973), I. 132.

25 I have summarized elsewhere the achievements of the '*Gründerzeit*' period (1867-73) in the field of railway construction as follows: 'It was to this outbreak of railwaymania – a disease which had appeared earlier in Western Europe – that the Monarchy owed the completion of its communications network and the overcoming of a state of serious backwardness.' Eduard März, *Österreichische Industrie- und Bankpolitik in der Zeit Franz Josephs I* (Vienna, 1968), 143.

26 The periodizing of nineteenth-century Austrian economic history has recently

been the subject of important contributions by N.T. Gross, R. Rudolph, H. Matis, D. Good and others. As I have done in earlier essays I would emphasize here, too, that the year 1848 must be seen as a real turning-point in the realm of economic policy.

27 Heinrich Waentig, *Gewerbliche mittelstandspolitik* (Leipzig, 1898), 53.

28 Carl Freiherr von Czoernig, *Österreichs Neugestaltung, 1848 1858* (Stuttgart and Augsburg, 1858), iv.

29 Hrothgar J. Habakkuk, *American and British Technology in the Nineteenth Century* (Cambridge, 1962), 190 ff.

30 Klima, 'Industrial Growth and Entrepreneurship' (n.13), 573.

31 After a thorough statistical comparison of the German and Austrian economic potentials on the eve of World War I, Professor Gross arrives at a similar result: 'The data confirm our general impression that Austrian industry was not able to catch up with the German development in the second half of the nineteenth century.' Gross, 'Industrial Revolution' (n.17), 275.

32 When the neo absolutist regime collapsed after the battle of Solferino it left behind a national debt of no·less than 3,000 million gulden. This enormous sum contrasts with revenues resulting from taxes and other duties of 300 million gulden in each of the years 1861, 1862 and 1863. Since the annual expenditure on interest payments was about 140 million gulden and the financing required for the army and the navy as a rule even higher, the budget regularly and inevitably showed a deficit. Under the circumstances it was hardly surprising that the Minister of Finance made available only small amounts of money for public projects. Cf. Adolf Beer, *Die Finanzen Österreichs im 19. Jahrhundert* (Prague, 1877); and Joseph Wysocki, *Infrastruktur und wachsende Staatsausgaben. Das Fallbeispiel Österreich 1868-1913* (Stuttgart, 1975).

33 A brief survey of the crisis of the 1860s is given in my book, *Österreichische Industrie- und Bankpolitik*.

34 'The first visible consequences of the new European situation in Austria were the abandonment of the centralist concept of empire prevailing until then . . .'. Hugo Hantsch, *Die Geschichte Österreichs* (Vienna-Graz-Cologne, 1962), 378.

35 An article in the *Neue Freie Presse*, organ of

bourgeois-liberal circles, may be regarded as characteristic of the mood of the Austrian bourgeoisie, enthusiastically welcoming the installation of the so-called '*Bürgerministerium*' (bourgeois government) in the Austrian part of the Monarchy: 'It is now up to us to extract from this constitution which guarantees freedom to the full extent, the elixir for the revival and rejuvenation of Austria. It is up to us! for what are the men who today form our Ministry but our own flesh and blood?' *Neue Freie Presse*, 1 Jan 1868.

36 There are a number of works dealing with the constitutional problems of the Austro-Hungarian '*Ausgleich*' of 1867, and a smaller number on its economic aspects. For a brief yet informative economic analysis see Krisztina Maria Fink, *Die österreichische Monarchie als Wirtschaftsgemeinschaft* (Munich, 1968).

37 'The real damage of the "*Ausgleich*" lies in the economic arrangements, above all in the fact that they were concluded for a short period, ten years, and were subject to notice of termination. The formula "Austria-Hungary – a monarchy subject to notice" exaggerates the fragility of this organization in so far as the basic law, section 12 of the "*Ausgleich*", is permanently valid and can be amended only with the consent of the monarch. But the financial arrangements and, what has had an even nastier effect, also the customs alliance may be terminated. And this thoroughly ill-conceived provision was the source of infinite strife, the cause of the decline in the monarchy's reputation abroad.' Heinrich Friedjung, 'Der österreichisch-ungarische Ausgleich von 1867', in Friedjung, *Historische Aufsätze* (Stuttgart and Berlin, 1919), 156.

38 Robert A. Kann, *Werden und Zerfall des Habsburgerreiches* (Gräz-Vienna-Cologne, 1962), 53.

39 In the Hungarian part of the Monarchy the rate of expansion was greater than in the Austrian. While the railway network in Cisleithania grew by about 135.5 per cent from 1866 to 1873, that in Transleithania grew by about 189.5 per cent. At the end of 1873 the extent of the railway network in Austria was 9,344 km and in Hungary 6,253 km. *Statistische Nachrichten über die Eisenbahnen der österreichisch-ungarischen Monarchie* (Vienna and Budapest, 1899).

40 Matis and Bachinger, 'Österreichs indus-

trielle Entwicklung' (n.24), 160.

41 A study of the Austrian banks in 1883 states that 'the creations of the years 1868 to 1873 proved to have so little viability that of the 70 banks founded in Vienna during this period, and the 65 in the provinces, only 8 and 21, respectively, were still in operation at the end of 1883'. Heinrich Rauchberg, 'Österreichs Bank- und Creditinstitute in den Jahren 1872-1883', *Statistische Monatsschrift* 11 (1885), 108.

42 'Der große Krach in Wien' (The big crash in Vienna), *Politik* (Prague), 10 May 1873.

43 A central tenet of the Neudörfl Social Democratic party congress, held in Hungary close to the Austrian border in the spring of 1874, was: 'The Austrian labour party aims at associating itself with the workers of all countries in order to liberate the working people from wage slavery and from class rule by abolishing the modern mode of private capitalist production. The party strives to replace this mode by the collective production of goods organized by the state.' Herbert Steiner, *Die Arbeiterbewegung Österreichs 1867-1889* (Vienna, 1964), 99.

44 'The trade regulations of 1883 and 1885 with their "individual protection against any economic competiton" were intended to solve two problems at one go; designed on the one hand to improve the position of the industrial worker in small and medium-sized enterprises with more than 20 employees, on the other hand they clearly favoured the small businessmen, who were politically advantaged since the 1882 reform of the electoral law. . . . The speedily formed movement of small traders succeeded in abolishing the freedom of trade and industry and of free competition, as well as the free employment contract, by the re-establishment of the guild system and the certificate of qualification together with a revision of Austrian commercial law in the year 1885.' Herbert Matis, *Österreichs Wirtschaft 1848-1913* (Berlin, 1972), 355.

45 The orientation towards a liberal trade policy took place in Austria under the Minister of Finance Karl von Bruck. According to Alexander von Matlekovits, the trend reached its climax with the conclusion of the customs and trade agreement with Germany of 9 Mar 1868, and the English treaty of accession of 30 Dec 1869. Cf. A. von Matlekovits, *Die Zollpolitik der österreichisch-ungarischen Monarchie* (Leipzig, 1891), 3.

After the crash of 1873 and the economic crisis caused by it, protectionist ideas became stronger in Austria. But only the autonomous customs tariff of 1 Jan 1879, which provided for moderate increases in customs duties on a number of industrial products, can be seen as a break with the liberal trade policy. In this context Lang notes: 'But the change in customs policy only increased the long-existing propensity among the Austrian industrialists to demand protective tariffs, the consequence of which soon was another increase in tariffs; this development neither improved the competitiveness of Austrian industry nor strengthened the entrepreneurial spirit of the Austrian industrialists.' Lang, *Hundert Jahre Zollpolitik*, 261.

46 'On the average, in the last five years of peace about 104,600,000 quintals of wheat and rye were available every year to Austria-Hungary's population of roughly 50 million from its own production. From this 14.5 to 15 million quintals per year had to be set aside as seed corn for the following year's crop . . . about 90 million quintals of the national harvest remained for consumption. In the five years mentioned above, grain imports exceeded rye exports by about 2.7 million quintals on the average.' Gustav Grats and Richard Schüller, *Der wirtschaftliche Zusammenbruch Osterreich-Ungarns* (Vienna, 1930), 40.

47 Matis, *Österreichs Wirtschaft*, 369.

48 There are numerous works on cartels in Austria before World War I, but they deal with legal and statistical aspects rather than with economic issues. See esp. Max von Allmayer-Beck, *Materialien zum österreichischen Kartellwesen* (Vienna, 1910).

49 'The cartels made secure the joint customs territory. By virtue of the prosperity they brought to the economy, the international cartels, of which Austria and Hungary offer a typical example . . . contradict the alleged advantages of the anti-trust laws that originated in the United States.' Heinrich Benedikt, *Die wirtschaftliche Entwicklung in der Franz-Joseph-Zeit* (Vienna, 1958), 159.

50 Theodore Pütz, 'Die Bedeutung der Wirtschaftsverbände für die Gestaltung der österreichischen Wirtschaftspolitik', in *Verbände und Wirtschaftspolitik in Österreich*, ed. Theodor Pütz (Berlin, 1962).

51 Waentig, *Gewerbliche Mittelstandspolitik*, 135.

52 Gustav Stolper, 'Politisches Resumé', *Der österreichische Volkswirt*, 15 Nov 1913.

53 There are a great number of constitutional-law studies on the nationalities problem, including those by Adolf Fischhof, Karl Renner and Otto Bauer.

54 Cf. Iván T. Berend and György Ránki, 'Ungarns wirtschaftliche Entwicklung 1849-1918', in Brusatti, ed., *Wirtschaftliche Entwicklung* (n.24); and see also Juriy Križek, *Beitrag zur Geschichte der Entstehung und des Einflusses des Finanzkapitals in der Habsburgermonarchie in den Jahren 1900-1914. Die Frage des Finanzkapitals in der österreichisch-ungarischen Monarchie, 1900-1918* (Bucharest, 1965).

55 For the period 1901-3 to 1911-13 Friedrich Hertz indicates an increase in the Austrian national income of a nominal 86 per cent, and 49 per cent in real terms. The average annual growth rate in real national income amounted to 4.1 per cent. In per capita terms it was slightly less, or 3.1 per cent, because during the same period the population also increased considerably. F. Hertz, 'Kapitalbedarf, Kapitalbildung und Volkseinkommen', *Schriften des Vereins für Sozialpolitik* (Leipzig, 1929), 39. See also Anton Kausel, 'Nandor Nemctz and Hans Seidel, Österreichs Volkseinkommen 1913 bis 1963', *Monatsbericht des Österreichischen Instituts für Wirtschaftsforschung*, special issue 14 (1965), 8.

56 As early as the beginning of the 1880s the newspapers can be found criticizing the banks' lack of willingness to lend to industrial concerns. In 1882, for example, in a well-known economic journal we read: 'For years this paper has from time to time pointed out the fact that the banks here completely neglect a very important facet of their great task by failing to support and encourage trade, industry and crafts, actually the productive activity of the population as a whole, in ways similar to those of other countries . . .' Cf. *Der Österreichische Ökonomist* (Vienna), 13 Aug 1882.

Almost a decade later the Austrian Minister of Finance, Emil Steinbach, voiced the same reproach in conversation, telling the representatives of the large Vienna banks that he was 'amazed that the banks are so little concerned with the promotion of industrial enterprises'. Cf. 'A Conversation with the Minister of

Finance', *Neue Freie Presse*, 13 Feb 1891.

57 Looking back on those times, a reputable Austrian weekly wrote: 'But this very period marks a turning point in our banking system. Influenced by the new direction of the government, presumably also at the direct urging of individual ministers, the banks suddenly showed an active interest in founding industrial concerns. Even the most reputable banks began to compete with one another in founding new enterprises. To be sure, they did this not just to please the Minister. Business had been slack and the banks' involvement with the state, which previously had helped them to make huge profits, had by that time become so unprofitable that it was taken on only as it were for the sake of honour.' *Volkswirtschaftliche Wochenschrift von Alexander Dorn* (Vienna), 14 Nov 1901.

58 See the essay by Alfred Lansburg, 'Zur Charakterisierung des österreichischen Bankwesens', *Die Bank, Monatshefte für Finanz und Bankwesen*, Mar 1911, 226.

59 This account of the changes in Austrian banking policy is taken almost verbatim from my essay, 'Besonderheiten in der Entwicklung des österreichischen Bankwesens', *Schmollers Jahrbuch*, vol. 77, pp. 67 ff.

60 Eugen Lopuszanski, 'Einige Streiflichter auf das österreichische Bankwesen', *Volkswirtschaftliche Wochenschrift von Alexander Dorn*, 31 Dec 1908.

61 This is clear from the following table:

Average annual increase in bank and state notes as well as commercial bank deposits (in %)

	bank/ state notes	commercial bank deposits
1880-1890	2.2	4.4
1890-1900	5.3	6.9
1900-1913	4.4	9.2

Cf. my study, *Österreichische Bankpolitik in der Zeit der großen Wende 1913-1923* (Vienna, 1981), 64. See also Eduard März, *Austrian Banking and Financial Policy* (London and New York, 1983), 46.

62 Cf. the extremely interesting study, 'Die Teuerung', by Otto Bauer, published in Vienna in 1910, in *Werkausgabe* (Vienna, 1975), I. 641-759.

63 A 1911 report of the Niederösterreichische

Handelskammer contains the following: 'The most important obstacle to a thorough improvement is of course the permanent and spreading increase in the cost of living. . . . It has become axiomatic for the entire urban population and for all tradesmen that the increase in food prices in Austria was directly caused by the excessive tariff protection for agricultural products and by the absurd protectionist policy. . . .'

64 An Austrian economist characterizes the overall economic situation at that time in these words: 'Future economic historians will see as the most notable event in the development of the Austro-Hungarian economy in the first decade of this century the Monarchy's first extensive participation in a worldwide business trend the results of which have left a permanent mark on the economy. Together with the other industrial countries of the world, we have seen an unprecedented and solidly founded prosperity.' Gustav Stolper, 'Die Lösung des Handelsbilanzproblems', *Der Österreichische Volkswirt*, 6 Apr 1915, 544.

65 Cf. Colin Clark, *The Conditions of Economic Progress* (London, 1951), 63, 101, 153.

66 In his essay, 'Der Nationale Besitzstand in Böhmen', Klaus P. Heiss reports that almost all the leading branches of Bohemian industry were located in areas inhabited mainly by Germans. See *Schmollers Jahrbuch*, vol. 30 (1906), 380.

67 Cf. Hermann Hallwich's study of early attempts at industrializing Austria, still one of the best: *Anfänge der Großindustrie in Österreich* (Vienna, 1898). Maria Szecsi has pointed out the importance of several commercial enterprises – for example Fries, Schwarzleitner, Tschoffen, Etzelt and Klinisch – for the process of industrialization in the eighteenth century: *Die Anfänge der Niederösterreichischen Metallindustrie im 18. Jahrhundert* (Univ. of Vienna diss., 1958).

68 Cf. Klima, 'Industrial Growth and Entrepreneurship' (n.13), in *Economic Development in the Habsburg Monarchy*, ed. John Komlos, 98 ff.

69 Cf. Erich Dittrich, 'Sudetendeutsches Unternehmertum', *Deutsche Zeitschrift für Wirtschaftskunde*, vol. IV (1939), 225 ff.

70 The following description of French banking in the first half of the nineteenth century by and large also applied to Austria: 'The banker of that time had not yet established any association with private

industry, that is to say, with manufacturing in so far as it is not part of the public-sector economy. The loans of the good old days to private individuals are consumptive loans. . . .' Fritz Steiner, 'Saint-Simonistische Ursprünge des modernen Bankwesens', *Bank-Archiv*, vol. 30, no. 15 (1 May 1931), 3.

71 Perhaps the best source on industrial enterprises founded at the beginning of the nineteenth century is Johan Slokar, *Geschichte der österreichischen Industrie und ihrer Förderung unter Kaiser Franz I* (Vienna, 1914).

72 On the conceptual as well as the chronological-sociological typology of the entrepreneur, cf. the essay by Wolfgang Zorn, 'Typen und Entwicklungskräfte deutschen Unternehmertums', *Vierteljahresschrift für Sozial-und Wirtschaftsgeschichte*, vol. 44, Mar 1957, 57 ff.

73 Cf. Arnošt Klima, 'The Beginning of the Machine Building Industry in the Czech Lands in the First Half of the 19th Century', *Journal of European Economic History*, vol. 4, no. 1 (spring 1975), 49-78.

74 'The Influence of German Businessmen on Industrial Development' is described in an essay so titled by Friedrich Hertz, *Die Industrie* (Vienna), 13 Nov 1913; cf. also Matis, *Österreichs Wirtschaft 1848-1913*.

75 *Neue Freie Presse*, 1 Jan 1899. The same article points out the 'national relationship' of the Germans in Austria with those beyond its borders, and adds that the German nation 'is made of the stuff which has produced not only Germany's great strategists and statesmen but also the industrial talents, the courageous entrepreneurs'.

76 Max Wirth, *Österreichs Wiedergeburt* (Vienna, 1876), 24.

77 Cf. the essay by Zorn, 'Typen und Entwicklungskräfte' (n.72).

78 A similar development can be observed at that time in England and America. 'In England, but still more in America, this praise of individual effort towards the end of the nineteenth century led to a glaring apotheosis of the struggle for existence. The relations between entrepreneurs and workers were expressed in the militant language of an ethics of the jungle: wealth and poverty are seen only as manifestations of differing abilities and achievements; the success of the factory owner constitutes conclusive evidence of his ability to survive. . . .' Reinhard Bendix, *Herrschaft und*

Industriearbeit (Frankfurt, 1960), 580.

79 Werner Sombart, 'Der kapitalistische Unternehmer', *Archiv für Sozialwissenschaften und Sozialpolitik*, 1909, 689 ff.

80 The most concise formulation by Friedrich Wieser dates, however, from the year 1927: 'The essential achievement of a leader is that of taking the lead; his success induces the masses to follow. . . .' See F. Wieser, 'Führung', in *Handwörterbuch der Staatswissenschaften*, ed. Elster Ludwig *et al.*, 4th edn. (Jena, 1927), IV. 531.

   For a thorough account of Wieser's élitist position, see Erich Streissler, '*Arma virumque cano*, Friederich von Wieser, the Bard as Economist', in *Die Wiener Schule der Nationalökonomie*, ed. Norber Leser (Vienna, 1986), 83-106.

81 I quote a characteristic passage from Gabriel Tarde's *Les Lois de l'Imitation* (Paris, 1907): 'Generally a man endowed with natural prestige gives an impulse: soon thousands will follow him, imitating him in every way and taking prestige from him, with which they themselves influence millions of humble people.' (The quotation is from Paul Reiwald, *Vom Geist der Massen* [Zurich, 1948], 137.)

   Pace Professor Lange, Schumpeter's posthumous work, *History of Economic Analysis*, makes it clear that he knew Gabriel Tarde's theories well.

82 Cf. Fritz Redlich, 'Unternehmerforschung und Weltanschauung', *Kyklos*, vol VIII (1955), 290, 291.

83 This becomes especially clear from his essay, 'Die sozialen Klassen im ethnisch homogenen Milieu'. The class structure of a society is described there as a grouping of individuals according to their qualities of leadership: 'In the same way as the amount of aptitude for leadership (or of qualities on which it is based) inherent in a people is decisive in determining its fate, so individual families within a people arrange themselves in a social hierarchy corresponding to their own degree of that aptitude or those qualities. . . . This hierarchy according to degree of aptitude for leadership, which directly reflects the physical qualities of individuals and can show internal consistency only thanks to the inheritable nature of such qualities, leads to an objective position for that family and in due course to such families having roughly equal rank, according to our criteria, within their class; and as a re-

sult, their position becomes firmly established.' JAS, *Aufsätze zur Soziologie* (Tübingen, 1953), 210 ff.

84 In his essay, 'Joseph A. Schumpeter' (n.12), Gottfried Haberler reports that Schumpeter took part in a seminar held by Böhm-Bawerk in the years 1905-6, which was also attended by Otto Bauer, Rudolf Hilferding and Emil Lederer, and where discussions took place which grew heated from time to time. See *Schumpeter, Social Scientist*, ed. Harris, 26.

85 Karl Marx, 'Wage Labour and Capital', *Collected Works*, IX. 223-4.

86 Perhaps the best summary of this discussion can be found in Paul M. Sweezy, *The Theory of Capitalist Development* (New York, 1942). See esp. the chapters, 'The Breakdown Controversy', and 'Imperialism', 190 ff.

87 Cf. Maurice Dobb, *Studies in the Development of Capitalism* (New York, 1947); *The Transition from Feudalism to Capitalism*, with contributions by Sweezy, Dobb, Hill, Hilton and Takahashi (New York, 1967); E.J. Hobsbawm, 'The Seventeenth Century in the Development of Capitalism', *Science & Society*, vol. XXIV, no. 2 (1960).

88 Fritz Karl Mann explains in an interesting essay Schumpeter's minimal influence on American economics mainly by 'the aversion to a philosophical approach and the tendency towards specialization'. The real reason for the 'popularity' of Keynes's theory and the insignificance of Schumpeter's influence on the formation of systems is, in my view, to be seen in the 'ideology-forming' social currents of our time. Cf. Fritz Karl Mann, 'Bemerkungen über Schumpeter's Einfluß auf die amerikanische Wirtschaftstheorie', *Weltwirtschaftliches Archiv*, vol. 81 (1958), 149 ff. [Since this note was written (1964) Schumpeter's influence on economics in the USA and beyond has undoubtedly increased. – E.M.]

Chapter 4: The Modern Theory of Imperialism

1 Vladimir I. Lenin, *Imperialism, the Highest Stage of Capitalism*, in *Collected Works* (Moscow, 1950); *Selected Works*, vol. I, cited hereafter in the text.

2 John A. Hobson, *Imperialism*, 3rd edn. (London, 1954). Besides Hobson, Lenin is said to have studied 148 books and 232

shorter essays before writing his 1916 study of imperialism. Cf. György Ránki, 'A Few Comments on Lenin's Work *Imperialism*', *Acta Academiae Scientiarum Hungaricae* 22 (1976).

3 Hilferding correctly characterized finance capital as a symbiosis between industry and bank capital. More recently Paul M. Sweezy, following the views of Henryk Grossmann, has called the predominance of finance capital a temporary phase in the development of capitalism. Sweezy refers to the position of the industrial giants in the United States, which meet the major part of their financial requirements out of their internal capital resources, and are thus practically independent of the large banks. It is assumed that a similar development can be expected in Western Europe. But in the post-war period, for reasons not to be gone into here, the situation on the European side of the Atlantic has not developed in the way forecast by Sweezy. Cf. Paul M. Sweezy, *The Theory of Capitalist Development* (New York, 1942), 266 ff.

4 The school of Social Darwinism has recently received strong support from the fashionable movement of 'social biology', whose best-known representatives are Edward O. Wilson and his Harvard colleague Robert L. Trivers. Both believe they have discovered parallels between the behaviour of animals and human beings. Cf. E.O. Wilson, *Sozialbiologie: die neue Synthese* (1975).

5 JAS, 'Zur Soziologie der Imperialismen', in his *Aufsätze zur Soziologie* (1953).Two essays in the collection deal with imperialism, the first with the great empires of antiquity and with feudalism, the second with modern imperialism.

6 Schumpeter points out the 'peaceful' character of the bourgeoisie in another context as well: 'But we may point . . . to the fact that Sir R. Peel . . . and Gladstone . . . fully developed that consistent policy of *détente* which in England has never been seriously challenged since . . . and which could be shown to be the most perfect expression of the economic and cultural structure of capitalist society' (*Business Cycles*, I. 311-12).

7 JAS, 'Zur Soziologie', 131.

8 Ibid., 142.

9 Hobson, *Imperialism*, 59.

10 See William H.B. Court, Appendix I, in *Survey of British Commonwealth Affairs*, Vol. II: *Problems of Economic Policy 1918-1939*, part I, by W.K. Hancock (Oxford, 1940), 298-304; cited in *The Theory of Capitalist Imperialism*, ed. David K. Fieldhouse (London, 1977), 132 ff. Echoing Court, Fieldhouse writes: 'Again, as a theory of historical development, which makes the expansion seem to be a unique phenomenon, capable of being understood only in terms of the special methodology used by Hobson and Lenin, it ignores both the continuity of nineteenth-century developments, and also its similarity to earlier periods of European imperialism.' D.K. Fieldhouse, 'Imperialism, A Historiographical Revision', *Economic History Review*, 2nd ser., vol. XIV, no. 2 (1961), 187 ff.

11 Michael Barratt Brown, 'A Critique of Marxist Theories of Imperialism', in *Studies in the Theory of Imperialism*, ed. Roger Owen and Bob Sutcliffe (London, 1977), 54.

12 'By 1913, the annual investment overseas exceeded investment at home and the total of British capital held abroad may have equalled a third, and was certainly more than a quarter, of all the holdings of British investors.' Michael B. Brown, *After Imperialism* (London, 1963), 93.

13 Barratt Brown calls the expansion of the British Empire after 1880 'truly amazing'. In a period of less than 20 years, 4 million square miles were annexed, a territory twice as large as the Indian possessions. Cf. ibid., 86.

14 Cf. Rudolf Hilferding, *Das Finanzkapital* (Vienna, 1910), most recent edn. 1968.

15 See Hans-Ullrich Wehler, 'Industrial Growth and Early German Imperialism', in Owen and Sutcliffe, eds., *Studies in the Theory of Imperialism* (n. 11), 84. On the fruitfulness of the Marxist approach to the interpretation of the phenomenon of imperialism, Peter-Christian Witt notes in a recent article: 'Obviously, the most fruitful impulses have come from those theoretical models which were influenced by Marxism in one way or another; for they have focused attention on the problems of uneven growth in the industrial economies, the political and social consequences of the process of industrialization, and on the function of imperialism as a strategy of diversion of the traditional power élites. In this connection it is completely irrelevant

if Lenin's or Hilferding or Hobson's theory of imperialism taken individually offers a sufficient model of explanation.' P.-C. Witt, 'Der Imperialismus als Problem liberaler Parteien in Deutschland 1890-1914', in *Liberalismus und imperialistischer Staat*, ed. Karl Holl and Günther List (Göttingen, 1980), 26, n. 7.

16 Leroy-Beaulieu, cited William L. Langer, *European Alliances and Alignments 1871-1890*, 2nd edn. (New York, 1950). 260. In his speech of 11 Oct 1883, Jules Ferry called the existential conditions of a modern nation 'the question of markets', and he added that 'one industrial nation after the other devoted itself to a colonial policy'. Ibid., 86 ff.

17 Brown, *After Imperialism*, 87.

18 See Richard C.K. Ensor, *England 1870-1914* (Oxford, 1936), 191 ff.

19 Hilferding, *Finanzkapital*, 422.

20 'Nor does it make any difference whether the "costs" of imperialism (in terms of military outlays, losses in wars, aid to client states, and the like) are greater or less than the 'returns', for the simple reason that the costs are borne by the public at large while the returns accrue to that small, but usually dominant, section of the capitalist class which has extensive international interests.' Paul A. Baran and Paul M. Sweezy, 'Notes on the Theory of Imperialism', *Monthly Review*, vol. 17, 10 Mar 1966.

21 Cf. Mark Blaug, 'Economic Imperialism, Revisited', *Yale Review*, vol. L (1961), 355 ff.

22 A concise summary of the crisis theory can be found in Sweezy, *Theory of Capitalist Development*, 156 ff. In a certain sense the crises, resulting from the disproportionate development of the various branches of production, must be traced back to the phenomenon of 'underconsumption', because the periodic gap between capital goods and consumer goods industries can ultimately be explained by the 'restricted consumption of the masses'.

23 In their best-known early essay, *The Communist Manifesto*, Marx and Engels wrote: 'For many a decade past the history of industry and commerce is but the history of the revolt of modern productive forces against modern conditions of production, against the property relations that are the conditions for the existence of the bourgeoisie and of its rule. It is enough to men-

tion the commercial crises that by their periodic return put on trial, each time more threateningly, the existence of the entire bourgeois society.' Marx and Engels, *Collected Works* (London, 1985), VI. 489.

24 Note that the Depression of the 1870s is referred to as 'setting off' a development. As Harry Magdoff puts it: 'The depression of the 1870s and 1880s, the agrarian disruptions as well as the industrial crises of those years, probably speeded up the birth of the new imperialism. But they themselves were not the cause of imperialism. If anything, both the severity of the economic disruptions and the imperialist policies are rooted in the same rapid transformation of the late nineteenth century.' Harry Magdoff, 'Imperialism without Colonies', in Owen and Sutcliffe, eds., *Studies in the Theory of Imperialism* (n. 11), 160.

25 Joseph Steindl's *Maturity and Stagnation in American Capitalism* (Oxford, 1952) was reprinted by the Monthly Review Press, New York, in 1982. Paul A. Baran and Paul M. Sweezy have summarized Steindl's thesis of the tendency of monopoly capital towards over-capacity and high profits as follows: Under monopoly capital 'innovations are typically introduced (or soon taken over) by giant corporations which act not under the compulsion of competitive pressures but in accordance with careful calculations of the profit-maximizing course. Whereas in the competitive case no one, not even the innovating firms themselves, can control the rate at which new technologies are generally adopted, this ceases to be true in the monopolistic case. It is clear that the giant corporation will be guided not by the profitability of the new method considered in isolation, but by the net effect of the new method on the overall profitability of the firm. And this means that in general there will be a slower rate of introduction of innovations than under competitive criteria.' P.A. Baran and P.M. Sweezy, *Monopoly Capital* (New York, 1966), 93-4.

26 Ibid., 105.

27 Alec Cairncross, *Home and Foreign Investment, 1870-1913* (Cambridge, 1935), 180.

28 Magdoff, 'Imperialism without Colonies' (n. 24), 147.

29 While Hilferding does not see any serious problems of sale or realization under the

capitalist mode of production, Rosa Luxemburg believes that this problem cannot be solved at all under 'pure' capitalism. The existence of non-capitalist areas is of vital importance not only for early, but also for mature capitalism. It is only able to overcome the limitations of the domestic market by the violent conquest and economic penetration of the 'former hinterlands'. Thus Luxemburg arrives at her often-cited definition of imperialism, which Lenin would presumably have called too narrow: 'Imperialism is the political expression of the process of capital accumulation in its competitive struggle for the rest of the undivided non-capitalist world.' Rosa Luxemburg, *Die Akkumulation des Kapitals. Ein Beitrag zur ökonomischen Erklärung des Imperialismus* (Berlin, 1913), 423.

30 Magdoff, 'Imperialism without Colonies' (n. 24), 155.

31 Cf. n. 10.

32 In 1947 Kurt Rothschild pointed to the complex character of the price strategies of monopoly (or oligopoly): 'Not only is military terminology increasingly used in price theory (e.g. economic warfare, price strategy, aggressive and peaceful price policy); a number of economic theorists and empirical economists have pointed out that oligopolistic pricing behaviour shows similarities to this branch of human activity.' K.W. Rothschild, 'Price Theory and Oligopoly', *Economic Journal*, vol. 57 (1947); see also Rothschild's *Marktform, Löhne, Außenhandel* (Vienna, 1966), 47. His observations also apply, of course, to the business strategy, in the wider sense of the term, of large corporations.

33 By contrast with Lenin, Rosa Luxemburg was clearly aware of the economic function of militarism. As Michael Kalecki shows, she realized that military spending was a suitable means of mitigating, if not eliminating, the tendency of capitalism towards under-consumption (or 'demand deficiency', as Keynes called it). But since her analysis does not go beyond Marx's reproduction schemes, which proceed on the assumption of full employment, she was unable to solve the problem in a logically satisfying way. Cf. M. Kalecki, 'The Problem of Effective Demand with Tugan-Baranovsky and Rosa Luxemburg', in Kalecki, *Selected Essays on the Dynamics of the Capitalist Economy* (Cambridge, 1971), 153

ff.

34 At the beginning of the 1970s military spending probably amounted to 8-9 per cent of the gross world product and 50 per cent of total gross capital formation, as well as 70-100 per cent of the national income of all developing countries. Cf. Kurt W. Rothschild, 'Militärausgaben und Wirtschaftswachstum', in *Festschrift für Eduard März, Sozialismus, Geschichte und Wirtschaft* (Vienna, 1973), 160.

35 This attitude on the part of the population gave impetus to a school of social scientists who held the naïve view, Rothschild writes, 'that a "reasonable" presentation of the enormous costs of armament and the working out of practicable plans for disarmament would suffice to bring about a change in the arms society.' Ibid., 162.

36 Cf. Friedrich Pollock, *Automation; Materialien zur Beurteilung ihrer ökonomischen und sozialen Folgen* (Frankfurt, 1966).

37 United Nations, *Economic and Social Consequences of Disarmament* (New York, 1962).

38 Blaug, 'Economic Imperialism' (n. 21), 146.

39 Baran and Sweezy, *Monopoly Capital*, 143 ff. The reader will be aware that the phenomenon described is the 'Haavelmo Theorem', well known in economics.

40 'Krupp in Germany, Schneider in France, Armstrong in Britain are instances of firms which have close connections with powerful banks and goverments and which cannot easily be "ignored" when a loan is being arranged.' Lenin, *Imperialism*, 244.

41 C. Wright Mills, *The Power Elite* (New York, 1957), 215, 224.

42 Barratt Brown thinks that Lenin's thesis contains three different elements: 'The falling rate of profit at home, the outward drive of monopoly, and colonial exploitation and the investment income.' *After Imperialism*, 97.

43 Marx and Engels, 'The Future Results of the British Rule in India', *Collected Works*, XII. 220 ff.

44 Cf. Marx, *Capital*, vol. I, ch. 15, 'Machinery and Modern Industry'.

45 Maurice Dobb ascribes great historical significance to this phase of development: 'The historic mission of capitalism mainly consisted in this expansion of production without a corresponding expansion of consumption.' M. Dobb, 'Rosa Luxemburg's *The Accumulation of Capital*', *Modern Quarterly* (London), 1952, 100 (tr. I.H.).

46 Marx, *Theorien über den Mehrwert*, Part 3, in *MEW*, vol. 26, p. 358.

47 Cf. Joseph M. Gillman, *The Falling Rate of Profit* (London, 1957), esp. 58 ff.; also Paul M. Sweezy, 'Some Problems in the Theory of Capital Accumulation', *Sozialismus, Geschichte und Wirtschaft* (Vienna, 1973); cf. also Eduard März, *Einführung in die Marxsche Theorie der wirtschaftlichen Entwicklung* (Vienna, 1976), 292 ff.

48 Maria Szecsi in a well-researched study has shown the constant level also maintained over the long term by the share of wages in the national income of Austria. Cf. 'Der Lohnanteil am österreichischen Volkseinkommen 1913 bis 1967', *Beiträge zur Wirtschaftspolitik und Wirtschaftswissenschaft* (= *Schriftenreihe der Wiener Kammer für Arbeiter und Angestellte*, no. III) (Vienna, 1970).

49 See Kazimierz Laski, 'Zur Marxschen Theorie des tendenziellen Falls der Profitrate', *Wirtschaft und Gesellschaft*, 3 (1976), 29, 31.

50 Cited in Lenin, *Imperialism*, 545.

51 Frederick Engels, *The Condition of the Working Class in England*, tr. and ed. W.O. Henderson and W.H. Chaloner (Oxford, 1971); Preface to the English edition of 1892, 368, 370 [italics mine]. First pub. *Commonwealth* (London), 1 Mar 1885, under the title 'England 1845 and 1885'.

52 We cannot examine here whether, apart from its material betterment under the capitalist system, the thorough disillusionment of the working class about the social order resulting from the October Revolution has contributed to the strengthening of 'opportunist' trends.

53 Brown, *After Imperialism*, 149.

54 At the 6th Special Session of the United Nations (spring 1974) the '77 non-aligned nations' proclaimed their objective of establishing a 'new international economic order'. At the 7th Special Session of the United Nations (autumn 1975) representatives of the 'First' and Third Worlds agreed on several principles which were to serve as a basis for discussion in future negotiations. It must be added [1983] that the '77 non-aligned nations' do not yet form a consolidated power bloc with a uniform political will. It is in the light of this that the much-discussed concept of the 'New Economic Order' has to be seen.

55 According to figures made public by the US Department of Commerce, the American direct investment abroad in 1970 amounted to US$ 75.5 billion and increased in 1977 to US$ 149 billion, i.e., it almost doubled. In 1985 it stood at $232.6 billion; thus it has roughly trebled since the base year. Foreign direct investment in the USA, on the other hand, amounted to only US$ 13.3 billion in 1970, but increased in the same period of time to more than US$ 34 billion, i.e. to more than two and a half times the 1970 figure. In 1985 it stood at $164.5 billion; thus it has increased roughly twelvefold since the base year. (These figures are from various issues of the *Survey of Current Business*, US Department of Commerce.)

56 A characteristic example is the attempt of the United States to forestall the German and French export of nuclear reactors to South America and Pakistan. Another example is the current monetary war between the big Western powers, led with particular aggressiveness in the past two years [1983] especially by the USA.

57 *Die Neue Zeit*, 30 Apr 1915, p. 144, cited in Lenin, *Imperialism*, 556.

58 See Harry Johnson, *Money, Trade and Growth* (London, 1962), 153.

59 Cf. A.R. Khan and Keith B. Griffin, *Growth and Inequality in Pakistan* (London, 1972), 204.

60 My comments on Pakistan are mainly based on the article by Naved Hamid, 'Alternative Development Strategies', *Monthly Review*, Oct 1974.

Chapter 5: The Crisis of the Tax State

1 JAS, *Die Krise des Steuerstaates* (Graz-Leipzig, 1918), repr. in *Rudolf Goldscheid, Joseph Schumpeter, Die Finanzkrise des Steuerstaates*, ed. Rudolf Hickel (Frankfurt/Main, 1976); cited hereafter in the text as *Die Krise*.

2 R. Goldscheid, *Staatssozialismus oder Staatskapitalismus, ein finanzsoziologischer Beitrag zur Lösung des Staatsschuldenproblems* (Graz-Leipzig, 1917).

3 This undated letter contains the following passage: 'I know that my programme for a conservative solution to the current financial difficulties – a programme which would ensure smooth and undisturbed reconstruction according to a financial plan, without upsetting the existing social order – has incurred important and, as I readily admit, convinced opposition. I believe it is

possible to lead the country out of its difficulties without violently disturbing the foundations of the national economy and of the credit system.' JAS to State Chancellor Renner, AVA, Bundeskanzleramt, Präsidium (Korrespondenz Renner, Karton 65a).

4 JAS, 'Finanzpolitik', *Aufsätze zur Wirtschaftspolitik*, ed. W.F. Stolper and Christian Seidl (Tübingen, 1985), 63; cited hereafter in the text.

5 'It is with good reason that a magic aura still surrounds Gladstone's Budget speeches of the years 1853 and 1860. This policy expressed a social system, not only the one prevailing at the time, but also the one still to come, which was to dominate the next fifty years: the social system in which the industrial, commercial and financial bourgeoisie was a decisive factor. . . .' Cf. JAS, 'Finanzpolitik', 66.

6 Eugen von Böhm-Bawerk, 'Unsere passive Handelsbilanz', *Neue Freie Presse*, 6, 8, 9 Jan 1914: 9 Jan 1914.

7 Ibid.

8 Without doubt the enormous expenditure on defence since the annexation crisis of 1908 contributed considerably to the deterioration in the budgetary situation. Cf. Eduard März, *Österreichische Bankpolitik in der Zeit der großen Wende 1913-1923* (Vienna, 1981), 45.

9 Christian Seidl, 'The Tax State in Crisis: Can Schumpeterian Public Finance Claim Modern Relevance?', *Lectures on Schumpeterian Economics*, ed. C. Seidl (Berlin–Heidelberg–Tokyo, 1984), 91.

10 JAS, 'Ökonomie und Soziologie der Einkommenssteuer', *Aufsätze zur Wirtschaftspolitik*, 130.

11 Ewald Nowotny, 'Staatsquote und Staatsfunktion', *Wirtschaft und Gesellschaft* (Vienna), vol. 8, no. 2 (1982), 342.

12 In practically every OECD country social spending has proved to be the fastest-growing part of government expenditure during the 1960s and '70s. Thus Manfred Prisching writes: 'While between 1960 and 1975 the gross national product was growing at about 4.5 per cent, the annual increment of social spending reached the highly gratifying level of about 8.55 per cent in real terms; for the years from 1975 to 1981 economic growth in the OECD countries was only 2.6 per cent, social spending increased by 4.8 per cent. As expected, pension payments and health benefits account for the largest part of these sums: on the average in the industrial countries, one third of social spending goes for pensions, while health and education each have close to one fourth.' M. Prisching, 'Wohlfahrtsstaat und Marktwirtschaft', in *Nachdenken über Politik. Jenseits des Alltags und diesseits der Utopie*, ed. Josef Krainer, Wolfgang Mantl and Manfred Prisching (Graz-Vienna-Cologne, 1985), 96.

13 JAS, 'The March into Socialism', *American Economic Review*, vol. 40 (1950), 446 ff. See also Joachim Starbatty, 'Die Staatskonzeption bei Keynes und Schumpeter', *Schriften des Vereins für Sozialpolitik*, Neue Folge 115/IV (1985), 104-5.

14 D. Bös, 'Krise des Steuerstaates', *Möglichkeiten und Grenzen der Staatstätigkeit, Schriftenreihe des wirtschaftswissenschaftlichen Seminars Ottobeuren*, ed. G. Bombach, B. Gahlen, A.E. Ott (Tübingen), vol. II, 354-93, esp. 369.

15 Here we follow the observations of Gerhard Lehner in 'Perspektiven 90', *Sozialdemokratische Wirtschaftspolitik*, ed. Ewald Nowotny and Herbert Tieber (Vienna, 1985), 256 ff.

16 P. Mooslechner and E. Nowotny, *Gesamtwirtschaftliche Finanzierung und öffentliche Verschuldung*, Österreichisches Forschungsinstitut für Sparkassenwesen (Vienna, 1980); also P. Mooslechner, 'Der Staat als Bankier', *Das öffentliche Haushaltswesen in Österreich*, I (1982). And see Nowotny, 'Staatsquote und Staatsfunktion' (n. 11), 350.

17 JAS, 'Ökonomie und Soziologie der Einkommenssteuer (n. 10), 130.

18 This probably applies as well to the two large Anglo-Saxon countries, where the campaign against the welfare state has assumed the most damaging dimensions.

19 The figure corresponds to an average annual income of roughly $24,000 [£14,000], at the 1987 rate of exchange. See Günther Chaloupek, 'Verteilungspolitik,' *Perspektiven 90*, 190.

20 Beirat für Wirtschafts- und Sozialfragen, *Arbeitszeitentwicklung und Arbeitszeitpolitik* (Vienna, 1984).

Chapter 6: Schumpeter's Vienna

1 Among the many recent studies by non-Viennese, see Carl E. Schorske, *Fin-de-siècle Vienna* (New York, 1980). Another noteworthy foreign study is Allan Janik

and Stephen Toulmin, *Wittgenstein's Vienna* (New York, 1973).

2 An awareness of the growing danger of internal disintegration and of the threat from outside is perhaps most clearly visible in the many Social Democratic publications on the conflict over nationality, of which the best known are: 'Das Nationalitätenproblem der österreichischen Sozialdemokratie, Brünner Parteitag 1899', in Ludwig Brügel, *Geschichte der österreichischen Sozialdemokratie* (Vienna), vol. 4 (1923), 335; Rudolf Springer (Karl Renner), *Der Kampf der österreichischen Nationen um den Staat* (Vienna, 1902); Otto Bauer, 'Die Nationalitätenfrage und die Sozialdemokratie', in *Werkausgabe* (Vienna, 1975) I. 49 ff.

3 The gap between the two systems is nowhere illustrated so clearly as in the well-known polemical study by Böhm-Bawerk, *Zum Abschluß des Marxschen Systems* (Vienna, 1896), and in Rudolf Hilferding's answer, *Böhm-Bawerks Marx-Kritik* (Vienna, 1904).

4 The best-known work of the Viennese school is probably Eugen von Böhm-Bawerk's *Kapital und Kapitalzins*, 3 vols.; vol. III, rev. and enlarged (Innsbruck, 1914). The two most important economic studies of the Austro-Marxist school are Otto Bauer's 'Die Nationalitätenfrage und die Sozialdemokratie' (n. 2) and Rudolf Hilferding's *Das Finanzkapital*, 1st edn. (Vienna, 1910).

5 Besides his main work referred to above, Schumpeter's first book must also be mentioned: *Das Wesen und der Hauptinhalt der theoretischen Nationalökonomie* (Leipzig, 1908).

6 Ludwig von Mises's main work published before World War I was *Theorie des Geldes und der Umlaufsmittel* (Munich and Leipzig, 1912).

7 Otto Bauer, 'Zwischen zwei Weltkriegen?', in *Werkausgabe* (Vienna, 1976), IV. 49 ff.

8 The most important work by Karl Polanyi is his book written during World War II, *The Great Transformation* (London, 1944); cf. the essay by Maria Szecsi, 'Rückblick auf die *Great Transformation*', *Wirtschaft und Gesellschaft*, vols. III and IV (1977).

9 The most passionately discussed topic was the 'viability' of the new Austria; most of the authors took a decidedly negative view.

10. A 'detailed draft for an emergency law on socialization' was published by the renowned economist R. Wilbrandt in the German *Vorwärts* as early as 24 Nov 1918. Cf. Erwin Weissel, *Die Ohnmacht des Sieges* (Vienna, 1976), 139.

11 Otto Bauer (Karl Mann), 'Das Selbstbestimmungsrecht der Nationen', *Der Kampf* (Vienna), Apr 1918, p. 205.

12 Bauer, 'Zwischen zwei Weltkriegen?' (n. 7), 247.

13 At the comparatively early date of 1912 Karl Korsch had pointed out the 'emptiness of the socialist formula for the construction of the economy'. Cf. Karl Korsch, 'Die sozialistische Formel für die Organisation der Volkswirtschaft', in *Kommentare zur deutschen Revolution und ihrer Niederlage. Neunzehn unbekannte Texte zur politischen Ökonomie, Politik und Geschichtstheorie* (s'Gravenhage, 1972), 4.

14 Karl Kautsky, *Sozialdemokratische Bemerkungen zur Übergangswirtschaft* (Leipzig, 1918).

15 Max Adler, 'Sozialismus und Kommunismus', *Der Kampf*, May 1919, p. 254.

16 See Rudolf Gerlich, *Die gescheiterte Alternative. Sozialisierung in Österreich nach dem 1. Weltkrieg* (Vienna, 1980), 68.

17 Cf. Otto Bauer, 'Der Weg zum Sozialismus', in *Werkausgabe*, II. 89 ff.

18 Bauer, 'Die österreichische Revolution', in ibid., 711.

19 Bauer, 'Bolschewismus oder Sozialdemokratie', in ibid., 292, 301.

20 Otto Bauer: ibid.; at the 1926 party congress, cited in Otto Leichter, *Otto Bauer. Tragödie oder Triumph* (Vienna, 1970), 175; also Bauer, 'Einführung in die Volkswirtschaftslehre', in *Werkausgabe*, IV. 852; in a lecture, cited in Gerlich, *Die gescheiterte Alternative* (n. 16), 32.

21 Walter Schiff, *Die Planwirtschaft und ihre ökonomischen Hauptprobleme* (Berlin, 1932), 48.

22 Ludwig von Mises: 'Die Wirtschaftsrechnung im sozialistischen Gemeinwesen', *Archiv für Sozialwissenschaft und Sozialpolitik*, vol. XLVII (1920/21); *Die Gemeinwirtschaft. Untersuchungen über den Sozialismus* (Jena, 1922).

23 Cf. Otto Neurath: *Wesen und Weg der Sozialisierung* (Munich, 1919); *Durch die Kriegswirtschaft zur Naturalwirtschaft* (Munich, 1919); *Gildensozialismus, Klassenkampf, Vollsozialisierung* (Dresden, 1922).

24 Mises, *Die Gemeinwirtschaft*, 338.

25 Ibid., 202.

26 Cf. Enrico Barone, 'The Ministry of Production in the Collectivist State', in *Collectivist Economic Planning*, ed. F. Hayek (London, 1935).

27 Frederick Engels, *Herr Eugen Dühring's Revolution in Science* (London, n.d.), 345 ff.

28 An excellent presentation of this discussion can be found in the book by Wlodzimierz Brus, *Funktionsprobleme der sozialistischen Wirtschaft* (Frankfurt, 1971), 50 ff.

29 Oskar Lange, *On the Economic Theory of Socialism* (Minneapolis, 1938).

30 Hayek, quoted in Brus, *Funktionsprobleme*, 53 f.

31 Mises, *Die Gemeinwirtschaft*, 65.

32 Joseph A. Schumpeter, 'Sozialistische Möglichkeiten von heute', *Archiv für Sozialwissenschaft und Sozialpolitik*, vol. 48 (1921), 309.

33 Ibid., 312, 314.

34 Ibid., 317.

35 I refer to the passage in *Capital* on the 'transformation of the actually functioning capitalist into a mere manager, an administrator of other people's capital, and of the owners of capital into mere owners, mere money-capitalists. Even if the dividends, which they receive, include the interest and profits of enterprise, that is, the total profit . . . , this total profit is henceforth received only in the form of interest, that is in the form of a mere compensation of the ownership of capital, which is now separated from its function in the actual process of reproduction in the same way in which this function, in the person of the manager, is separated from the ownership of capital.' Marx, *Capital*, III. 516-17.

36 Schumpeter, 'Sozialistische Möglichkeiten', op. cit., p. 319.

37 The dangers which arise under socialism with regard to the efficient performance of the entrepreneurial function were very clearly perceived by Otto Bauer many years before Schumpeter:

> Only the top management of a business enterprise and of its individual operating units has to do work that cannot be standardized, has to make decisions that cannot be calculated. The top management has to organize the managerial teamwork, its task is to put the right man in the right place, it is supposed to decide whether new methods of production should be tried out, where new businesses are to be established – these

are tasks which, in spite of making every conceivable preparation for each decision, still require intuition, imagination, a knowledge of human nature, initiative and the courage to take responsibility. One of the major organizational problems of socialism is to organize the social management of production in such a way that the leading men of the industrial bureaucracy enjoy the intellectual freedom necessary to perform such creative work, and still remain under the social control without which they would develop from the executive body of the socialist community into its masters.

Otto Bauer, 'Rationalisierung – Fehlrationalisierung', in *Werkausgabe*, III. 901.

Chapter 7: The Periodization of the Austrian and German Economies

1 Cf. Eduard März, 'Die wirtschaftliche Entwicklung der Donaumonarchie im 19. Jahrhundert; Gedanken zu einem neuen Buch von David F. Good', *Wirtschaft und Gesellschaft* (Vienna), vol. II, no. 3 (Mar 1985), 367-92.

2 Further recessionary tendencies emerge from the saturation of certain markets, from the repayment of loans out of profits, leading to a gradual shrinking of the volume of credit, from the elimination from the production process of newly founded but non-viable enterprises, and from increasing insecurity within the entrepreneurial class. Cf. Günther Tichy, 'Schumpeter's Business Cycle Theory, Its Importance for Our Time', in *Lectures on Schumpeterian Economics*, ed. Christian Seidl (Berlin - Heidelberg - New York - Tokyo, 1984), 79.

3 Professor Streissler in particular has dealt with the inflationary aspect of Schumpeter's business cycle. Cf. Erich Streissler, 'Schumpeter's Vienna and the Role of Credit in Innovation', in *Schumpeterian Economics*, ed. Helmut Frisch (Vienna, 1981), 60-83.

4 Cf. JAS, *Business Cycles*, I. 175.

5 Th. Gross, 'Die Stellung der Habsburgermonarchie in der Weltwirtschaft', in *Die wirtschaftliche Entwicklung*, ed. Alois Brusatti (= A. Wandruszka and P. Urbanek, *Die Habsburgermonarchie 1848-1919*, vol. I)

(Vienna, 1973), 5. According to Paul Bairoch the average income in Austria around 1840 reached 80 per cent of the German level. P. Bairoch, 'Europe's Gross National Product 1800-1975', *Journal of European History* 5 (1976).

6 Karl Bachinger, 'Das Verkehrswesen', *Die wirtschaftlich Entwicklung*, ed. Brusatti, 280. Thomas F. Huertas, *Economic Growth and Economic Policy in a Multinational Setting. The Habsburg Monarchy: 1848-1865*, (Univ. Of Chicago Ph.D. diss., 1977), 6.

7 Birgit Bolognese-Leuchtenmüller, *Bevölkerungsentwicklung und Berufsstruktur, Gesundheits- und Fürsorgewesen in Österreich 1750-1918* (Vienna, 1978), table 54, p. 152. Walter G. Hoffmann *et al.*, *Das Wachstum der deutschen Wirtschaft seit der Mitte des 19. Jahrhunderts* (Berlin, 1965), 35.

8 *Die wirtschaftliche Situation in Deutschland und Österreich um die Wende vom 18. zum 19. Jahrhundert*, ed. Friedrich Lütge (Stuttgart, 1964).

9 Herbert Matis and Karl Bachinger, 'Österreichs industrielle Entwicklung', in *Die wirtschaftliche Entwicklung*, ed. Brusatti, 110.

10 Kurt W, Rothschild, 'Wurzeln und Triebkräfte der Entwicklung der österreichischen Wirtschaftsstruktur', in *Österreichs Wirtschaftsstruktur gestern-heute-morgen*, ed. Wilhelm Weber (Berlin, 1961), I. 28 ff.

11 John Komlos, *The Habsburg Monarchy as a Customs Union* (Univ. of Chicago Ph. D. diss., 1978), 54 ff., 59.

12 See Knut Borchardt, 'The Industrial Revolution in Germany 1700-1914', in *The Fontana Economic History of Europe: The Emergence of Industrial Societies*, 4(1), ed. Carlo M. Cipolla (Glasgow, 1976), 76 ff. Alan Milward and S.B. Saul, *The Economic Development of Continental Europe 1780-1870* (London, 1973), 365 ff.

13 Bairoch, 'Europe's Gross National Product' (n. 5).

14 Eduard März, *Österreichische Industrie- und Bankpolitik in der Zeit Franz Josephs I* (Vienna, 1968), 370.

15 Anton Kausel, 'Österreichs Volkseinkommen 1830-1913', *Geschichte und Ergebnisse der zentralen Statistik in Österreich 1829 bis 1979* (Vienna, 1979); Richard L. Rudolph, 'Quantitative Aspekte der Industrialisierung in Cisleithania', in *Die wirtschaftliche Entwicklung*, ed. Brusatti, 233 ff.; Komlos, *Habsburg Monarchy*, 61.

16 Nachum Th. Gross, 'Austrian Industrial Statistics 1880/85 and 1911/13', *Zeitschrift für die Gesamte Staatswissenschaft*, 124 (1968), 67; Huertas, *Economic Growth and Economic Policy*, 5 ff.

17 März, *Österreichische Industrie- und Bankpolitik*, 57 ff.; Herbert Matis, *Österreichs Wirtschaft 1848-1913* (Berlin, 1972), 83 ff.

18 From 1860 to 1864 the circulation of bank and state notes fell by 26 per cent, from 474 to 351 million guldens. Alfred F. Přibram, *Materialien zur Geschichte der Preise und Löhne in Österreich* (Vienna, 1938), I. 58.

19 When the neo-absolutist regime broke down after the battle of Solferino (1859), it left behind a national debt of no less than 3 billion guldens. Considering the annual revenue of 300 million guldens in each of the years 1861, 1862 and 1863, and the expenditure on debt service and on the army and navy of 140 million guldens each, it is hardly surprising that the Minister of Finance made available only small amounts of money for public works. Adolf Beer, *Die Finanzen Österreichs im 19. Jahrhundert* (Prague, 1877), 315; Ernst Mischler and Josef Ulbrich, *Österreichisches Staatswörterbuch*, 1 (Vienna, 1895-7), 99 ff.

20 Ferdinand Tremel, *Wirtschafts- und Sozialgeschichte Österreichs* (Vienna, 1969), 369.

21 Rudolph, 'Quantitative Aspekte' (n. 15), 240 ff.

22 Tremel, *Wirtschafts- und Sozialgeschichte*, 369.

23 Alexander Matlekovits, *Die Zollpolitik der österreichisch-ungarischen Monarchie und des Deutschen Reiches seit 1868 und deren nächste Zukunft* (Leipzig, 1891), 616 ff.

24 Josef Neuwirth, *Bank und Valuta in Österreich*, vol. II: *Die Spekulationskrisis von 1873* (Leipzig, 1874); Albert Schäffle, 'Der "große Börsenkrach" des Jahres 1873', in *Gesammelte Aufsätze* (Tübingen, 1885), 67 ff.; Max Wirth, *Geschichte der Handelskrisen* (Frankfurt, 1883).

25 Kausel, 'Österreichs Volkseinkommen 1830-1913' (n. 15).

26 Rudolph, 'Quantitative Aspekte' (n. 15), 239 ff.

27 Ibid., 238; Kausel, 'Österreichs Volkseinkommen' (n. 15).

28 Rudolph, 'Quantitative Aspekte' (n. 15), 238.

29 Hoffmann *et al.*, *Wachstum*. Arguments in favour of business-cycle research based on the development of the real national product are advanced also by Gerd Hardach, *Deutschland in der Weltwirtschaft 1870-1970*

(Frankfurt, 1977), 37.

30 Reinhard Spree, *Wachstumstrends und Konjunktur in der deutschen Wirtschaft von 1820 bis 1913* (Göttingen, 1978), 100.

31 Ibid., 108.

32 Ibid., 101 ff.

33 Problems of method cannot be dealt with here in detail; for this reason I am presenting both Hoffmann's and Spree's results, but in what follows I rely on my own calculations.

34 The growth rates of net value added and gross domestic product are comparable on the assumption that depreciation and indirect taxes develop proportionately to net value added.

35 The development of per capita income in Austria from 1900 onwards is even more favourable than in Germany because of the smaller increase in the population. Gross also points out that during the 30 to 35 years before the war Austria was linked more closely with the international business cycle than previously. Nachum Th. Gross, 'The Industrial Revolution in the Habsburg Monarchy, 1750-1914,' in *Fontana Economic History*, ed. Cipolla, 4 (1), 273.

36 Rothschild, 'Wurzeln und Triebkräfte . . . der Österreichische Wirtschaftsstruktur' (n.10), 28.

37 Friedrich Hertz, *Die Produktionsgrundlagen der österreichischen Industrie vor und nach dem Krieg* (Vienna, 1917), 149. Compass 1914, II. 55.

38 In 1878 the first cartel of the Austrian iron industry, that of the rail rolling mills, was formed. Ibid., 42 ff.

39 Milward and Saul, *Economic Development* 380.

40 Gross, 'Industrial Revolution' (n. 35), 274.

41 Wilfried Spohn, *Weltmarktkonkurrenz und Industrialisierung Deutschlands 1870-1914* (Berlin, 1977), 187.

42 Rothschild, 'Wurzeln und Triebkräfte . . . der Österreichische Wirtschaftsstruktur' (n. 10), 34 ff.

43 März, *Österreichische Industrie- und Bankpolitik*, 292.

44 W.A. Cole and Phyllis Deane, 'The Growth of National Incomes', *The Cambridge Economic History of Europe*, ed. Hrothgar J. Habakkuk and M. Postan, vol. VI (1) (Cambridge, 1965), 51 ff.

45 The flow of trade between the two parts of the Austro-Hungarian Empire, i.e. within the joint customs area, are, of course, not taken into consideration here.

46 *Statistische Übersichten, betreffend den auswärtigen Handel der wichtigsten Staaten in den Jahren 1907-1911*, ed. by the Handelsstatistischer Dienst of the k.k. Handelsministerium (Vienna, 1914).

47 Kausel, 'Österreichs Volkseinkommen' (n. 15), and the data on foreign trade cited in n. 46.

48 Only if the time sequence were known for all components of the gross domestic product could the influence of exports on the course of the cyclical development be determined.

49 Huertas, *Economic Growth and Economic Policy*, 5 ff.

50 K. Mamroth, *Die Entwicklung der österreichisch-deutschen Handelsbeziehungen (1849-1865)* (Berlin, 1887), 180 ff.

51 Franz Bartsch, 'Statistische Daten über die Zahlungsbilanz Österreich-Ungarns vor Ausbruch des Krieges', in *Mitteilungen des k.k. Finanzministeriums* (Vienna, 1917), 1 ff.

52 Jury Křižek, *Die wirtschaftlichen Grundzüge des österreichisch-ungdrishchen Imperialismus in der Vorkriegszeit (1900-1914)* (Prague, 1963), 56.

53 Cf. Rudolph, 'Quantitative Aspekte' (n. 15); also Komlos, *Habsburg Monarchy*. Profesor Alois Mosser has thoroughly analysed Rudolph's calculations and concludes that the 'source of error implied in this method' is that 'the partial series chosen by Rudolph – mining, metal production and processing, mechanical engineering, the food and textile industries – represent a total of only two-thirds of the gross production value of Austrian industry, and the partial series themselves (above all mechanical engineering and food production) are more or less incomplete'. Moreover, Mosser adds, 'the fact that Rudolph exclusively used typical growth industries and sectors – e.g. leaving the recessionary linen industry out of consideration in calculating the index of textile production – is bound to lead to an upward bias in the overall index. The rapidly rising index figures for the food industry reflect the development of industrial production, while in the early period the small businesses accounted for a large part of output. The calculation of the value of production of mechanical engineering, which is based on the metals processed in the industry, necessarily leads to excessive growth steps because as late as the 1880s

timber was used extensively in the construction of machines. The final result of [Rudolph's] calculations, according to which Austria's industry recorded an average annual growth rate of 3.6 per cent between 1880 and 1913, should therefore be regarded as having only limited validity.' See A. Mosser, *Die Industrieaktiengesellschaft in Österreich 1880-1913* (Vienna, 1980), 172-3.

54 Herbert Matis, *Österreichs Wirtschaft 1848-1913* (Berlin, 1972), 332.

55 *Statistisches Jahrbuch der Stadt Wien, 1913* (vol. XXXI), 44 ff.

56 Cf. Eduard März, *Austrian Banking and Financial Policy, Creditanstalt at a Turning Point, 1913-1923* (London and New York, 1984), esp. 44-7.

Chapter 8: Schumpeter and the Austrian School of Economics

1 The essay, 'Das wissenschaftliche Lebenswerk Eugen von Böhm-Bawerks', was first published in *Zeitschrift für Volkswirtschaft, Sozialpolitik und Verwaltung* (Vienna), vol. XXIII (1914), 454-528. I refer here to the translation by Herbert K. Zassenhaus, included (in a condensed version by Gottfried Haberler) in JAS, *Ten Great Economists, from Marx to Keynes* (1952), 143-90 (cited hereafter in the text as *TGE*).

2 See JAS, 'Epochen der Dogmen- und Methodengeschichte', in *Grundriß der Sozialökonomik*, 2nd enlarged edn. (Tübingen, 1924), 117.

3 Ibid., 118.

4 See JAS, *Capitalism, Socialism and Democracy* (1947), 24, and n.4.

5 Cf. *Ten Great Economists*, 175.

6 JAS, *Theorie der wirtschaftlichen Entwicklung* (Leipzig, 1912), translated as *The Theory of Economic Development* (1934); citations in the text of this chapter are to the German edition.

7 Eugen von Böhm-Bawerk, 'Eine "dynamische" Theorie des Kapitalzinses', in *Zeitschrift für Volkswirtschaft, Sozialpolitik und Verwaltung*, vol. XXII (1913), 1-62 (cited hereafter in the text as Böhm-Bawerk, *Zeitschrift* XXII); Schumpeter's reply appeared in the same volume under the same title, 599-639.

8 Eugen von Böhm-Bawerk, 'Schlußbemerkungen', ibid., 640-56. The sentence quoted is on p. 656.

9 Elsewhere in this work Schumpeter refers to the original static condition as an 'edi-

fice of thought created simply for reasons of methodology' (*Theorie*, 447).

10 Cf. JAS, *Ten Great Economists*, 175.

11 Cf. JAS, *Theorie*, 54.

12 The quotation is from the second revised edition of the *Theorie* (1926), for which Schumpeter completely re-wrote Chapters 2 and 7. But I am obliged to use the first edition wherever I refer to the dispute between Böhm-Bawerk and Schumpeter.

13 Cf. above, Chapter 2, pp. 23-5

14 Cf. Adam Smith, *An Inquiry into the Nature and Causes of the Wealth of Nations*, ed. Edwin Cannan (London, 1950), 421, 16.

15 Fritz Redlich, 'Entrepreneurship in the Initial Stages of Industrialization', *Weltwirtschaftliches Archiv*, vol. 75 (1955), 62.

16 Eugen von Böhm-Bawerk, *Positive Theorie des Kapitales* (Jena, 1921), I. 131.

17 See Eduard März, *Österreichische Bankpolitik in der Zeit der großen Wende, 1913-1923* (Vienna, 1981), 63-4.

18 I quote, as elsewhere, from the 3rd German edition of Marx's *Capital*, tr. Samuel Moore and Edward Aveling (London, 1970).

Chapter 9: Schumpeter as Austrian Minister of Finance

1 Schumpeter's early theoretical works are *Das Wesen und der Hauptinhalt der theoretischen Nationalökonomie* (1908) and *Theorie der wirtschaftlichen Entwicklung* ([1911] 1912, tr. 1934 as *The Theory of Economic Development*).

2 JAS: *Die Krise des Steuerstaates* (1918), and 'Zur Soziologie der Imperialismen', *Archiv für Sozialwissenschaft und Sozialpolitik*, 46 (1919), 1-39.

3 Some relevant works are Otto Bauer, *Die österreichische Revolution*, in *Werkausgabe*, vol. II (Vienna, 1976); C.W. Gulick, *Austria from Habsburg to Hitler*, vol I (Beverly, Mass., 1948); G. Cratz and R. Schüller, *Der wirtschaftliche Zusammenbruch Österrreichs* (Vienna, 1930); F. Kreissler, *Von der Revolution zur Annexion* (Vienna, 1970); D.F. Strong, *Austria, October 1918 – March 1919, Transition from Empire to Republic* (New York, 1939).

4 See Sir William Goode, *Economic Conditions in Central Europe*, Cmd 641, part II (London: HMSO, 1920), 4. The turnover on the black market is not included in this figure. It must at times have been considerable, for in the spring of 1919, Walther Federn estimated that one-quarter of the

meat consumed was from illegal sources; see W. Federn, *Volkswirt*, 1 Mar 1919, 373.

5 Goode, *Economic Conditions*, 6, 7.

6 There were frequent references in the newspapers to these incidents, as when, in its issue of 7 Feb 1919, the *Volkswirt* reported that the province of Oberösterreich had stopped all exports of foodstuffs to other provinces including Vienna.

7 E. Palla, 'Ein Jahr Arbeitslosenfürsorge in Österreich', *Nachrichten des Staatsamtes für soziale Verwaltung* (1920), no. 21/22.

8 The 'Socialization Commission' was created by an act of parliament.

9 Walther Federn, 'Die finanzielle Liquidation der Monarchie in Deutsche-Österreichs Finanzen', *Volkswirt*, 31 May 1919, 631 ff.

10 K. Přibram, 'Die Sozialpolitik im neuen Österreich', *Archiv für Sozialwissenschaft und Sozialpolitik*, 48 (1921), 636.

11 The war debt of the western half of the Monarchy amounted to 58 billion crowns. After allowing for additional obligations of the Austrian government resulting from the purchase of war material and other war-related expenditures, Paul Grünwald arrived at the much higher figure of 65 billion crowns. See P. Grünwald, 'Das Finanzsystem Deutschösterreichs', *Schriften des Vereins für Sozialpolitik* 158 (1919), 70.

12 R. Goldscheid, 'Staatssozialismus oder Staatskapitalismus', in *Beiträge zur politischen Ökonomie der Staatsfinanzen*, ed. R. Hickel (Frankfurt, 1976).

13 *Neue Freie Presse*: 'Das Programm des Staatssekretärs Schumpeter', *Der Economist*, 20 Mar 1919; 'Das Programm des neuen Staatssekretärs für Finanzen' (from an interview), 16 Mar 1919; 19 Mar 1919.

14 Ibid., 27 Apr 1919.

15 'Staatssekretär Schumpeter über die wirtschaftlichen Aufgaben der Zukunft', *Neue Freie Presse, Der Economist*, 21 Mar 1919.

16 Ibid., 27 Apr 1919.

17 See *Das politische Tagebuch Josef Redlichs*, ed. F. Fellner (1954), II. 342.

18 Cf. A. Rasin, *Die Finanz- und Wirtschaftspolitik der Tschechoslowakei* (Munich, 1923), 151 ff.

19 See L. von Mises, 'Der Wiedereintritt Deutsch-Österreichs in das Deutsche Reich und die Währungsfrage', *Schriften des Vereins für Sozialpolitik* 158 (1919), 151 ff.

20 For a brief account of the various phases of the currency separation see R. Kerschagl, *Die Währungstrennung in den National-Staaten* (Vienna, 1920). For a review of the Czech separation measures, see W. Federn, 'Die Währungstrennung und der Wert der Krone', *Volkswirt*, 15 Feb 1919.

21 Bauer, *Österreichische Revolution*, 144.

22 N. Schausberger *Der Griff nach Österreich* (Vienna, 1978), 68.

23 Finanzarchiv Vienna, Zl. 691/Präs. 1919.

24 See S. Verosta, 'Josef Schumpeter gegen das Zollbündnis der Donaumonarchie mit Deutschland und gegen die Anschlußpolitik Otto Bauers (1916-1919)', *Festschrift für Christian Broda* (Vienna, 1976), 373 ff.

25 'Staatssekretär Schumpeter über die wirtschaftlichen Aufgaben der Zukunft', *Neue Freie Presse*, 21 Mar 1919.

26 Verosta, 'Josef Schumpeter', (n. 24), 401.

27 Ibid., 401 f.

28 Ibid., 402 ff. Otto Bauer's letter is dated 11 May 1919.

29 Cable of Oppenheimer to Keynes, 18 May 1919, PRO FO 608229/10960. (Cf. R. Hoffmann, 'Die wirtschaftlichen Grundlagen der britischen Österreichpolitik 1919', *Mitteilungen des österreichischen Staatarchivs*, Sonderdruck 30 (1977), 268 ff.)

30 'Staatssekretär Dr Schumpeter über die industrielle Zukunft Österreichs', *Neue Freie Presse*, 31 May 1919.

31 HHStA Vienna, NPA, Präs. K. 261, Nachlaß Bauer. Renner, too, reacted negatively to the public utterances of the Finance Minister, as is evident from a cable sent to Vienna from the Paris peace conference; cf. HHStA, NPA, K. 349, 8 June 1919.

32 *Volkswirt*, 31 May 1919, Kalendarium, 642.

33 K. Ausch, *Als die Banken fielen* (Vienna, 1968), 12.

34 R. Kola, *Rückblick ins Gestrige* (Vienna, 1922), 247.

35 Bauer, *Österreichische Revolution*, 178 ff.

36 Gulick, *Austria*, 141.

37 Undated letter of the Finance Minister, Schumpeter, to the State Chancellor, Renner, HHStA, AVA, Bundeskanzleramt, Präs., Korrespondenz Renner, Karton 65a.

38 J.A. Schumpeter, 'Sozialistische Möglichkeiten von heute', *Archiv für Sozialwissenschaft und Sozialpolitik*, 48 (1921, pt. 2), 342.

39 'Der Fall Schumpeter', *Arbeiter-Zeitung*, 10 Oct 1919.

40 'Der Finanzplan des Staatssekretärs a. D. Dr Schumpeter', *Neue Freie Presse*, 18 Oct 1919.

41 'W. Federn 'Die Kreditpolitik der Wiener

Banken, Geldwert und Stabilisierung in ihren Einflüssen auf die soziale Entwicklung', *Österreich*, 169 (1925), 69.

42 'Der Personenwechsel im Staatsamt für Finanzen', *Neue Freie Presse*, 9 Oct 1919.

43 In the *Neue Freie Presse* for 9 Oct 1919 there is a reference to the sudden change in attitude towards Schumpeter on the part of Stöckler, the State Secretary for Agriculture.

Chapter 10: Schumpeter as University Teacher

1 See Chapter 9 of the present book.

2 Cf. JAS, 'Sozialistische Möglichkeiten von heute', *Archiv für Sozialwissenschaften*, vol.

48 (1921).

3 In a letter of 29 Oct 1927 to a friend he wrote: '. . . accepted only one invitation to Boston, but I see many young colleagues, there are splendid fellows among them, I have discussions with them in the evenings. There you are: in Vienna political economy is taught by 3 full professors and 4 other people, and here by 8 full professors and 32 other people. This doesn't bear comparison! I'd stay here if Bonn were not Bonn. . . .'

4 Cited by Arthur Smithies, 'Memorial: Joseph Alois Schumpeter, 1883-1950', in *Schumpeter Social Scientist*, ed. Seymour E. Harris (Cambridge, Mass., 1951), 15.

5 *American Economic Review*, vol. 36, no. 4 (Sept 1946).

Select Bibliography

Following is a list of principal primary sources, including books and articles by J.A. Schumpeter, quoted or referred to in the text; secondary and latter-day sources, published and unpublished, are cited in full in the chapter Notes at p. 173.

Max Adler, 'Sozialismus und Kommunismus', *Der Kampf* (Vienna), May 1919

Max von Allmayer-Beck, *Materialien zum österreichischen Kartellwesen* (Vienna, 1910)

Arbeiter-Zeitung (Vienna): 20 Aug 1919; 'Der Fall Schumpeter', 10 Oct 1919

Franz Bartsch, 'Statistische Daten über die Zahlungsbilanz Österreich-Ungarns vor Ausbruch des Krieges', *Mitteilungen des k.k. Finanzministeriums* (Vienna, 1917)

Otto Bauer: (Karl Mann), 'Das Selbstbestimmungsrecht der Nationen', *Der Kampf* (Vienna), Apr 1918

   Tragödie oder Triumph (Vienna, 1970)

   Werkausgabe, vols. I-IV (Vienna, 1975-6); individual works as cited in Notes *passim*

Adolf Beer, *Die Finanzen Österreichs im 19. Jahrhundert* (Prague, 1877)

Eugen von Böhm-Bawerk: 'Eine dynamische Theorie des Kapitalzinses', *Zeitschrift für Volkswirtschaft, Sozialpolitik und Verwaltung* (Vienna), vol. XXII (1913)

   Positive Theorie des Kapitals, vol. I (Jena, 1921)

   'Unsere passive Handelsbilanz', *Neue Freie Presse* (Vienna), 6, 8, 9 Jan 1919

Carl Freiherr von Czoernig, *Österreichs Neugestaltung 1848-1858* (Stuttgart – Augsburg, 1858)

Frederick Engels: *The Condition of the Working Class in England*, tr. W.O. Henderson and W.H. Chaloner: Preface to 1892 edn. (Oxford, 1971)

   Herr Eugen Dühring's Revolution in Science (London, n.d.)

Walther Federn: 'Die finanzielle Liquidation der Monarchie in Deutsch-Österreichs Finanzen', *Der österreichische Volkswirt* (Vienna),

31 May 1919
'Die Kreditpolitik der Wiener Banken', *Schriften des Vereins für Sozialpolitik* (Leipzig), vol. 169

Heinrich Friedjung, 'Der österreichisch-ungarische Ausgleich von 1867', in id., *Historische Aufsätze* (Stuttgart – Berlin, 1919)

Paul Grünwald, 'Das Finanzsystem Deutsch-Österreichs', *Schriften des Vereins für Sozialpolitik* (Leipzig), vol. 158.

Hermann Hallwich, *Anfänge der Grossindustrie in Österreich* (Vienna, 1898)

Klaus P. Heiss, 'Der nationale Besitzstand in Böhmen', *Schmöllers Jahrbuch* (Leipzig), 1906

Friedrich Hertz: 'Der Einfluss reichsdeutscher Unternehmer', *Die Industrie* (Vienna), 13 Nov 1913

'Kapitalbedarf, Kapitalbildung und Volkseinkommen', *Schriften des Vereins für Sozialpolitik* (Leipzig), 1919

Die Produktionsgrundlagen der österreichischen Industrie vor und nach dem Krieg (Vienna, 1917)

Rudolf Hilferding, *Das Finanzkapital* (Vienna, 1927)

Karl Kautsky, *Sozialdemokratische Bemerkungen zur Übergangswirtschaft* (Leipzig, 1918)

Felix Klezl, 'Die Lebenskosten', *Schriften des Vereins für Sozialpolitik* (Leipzig), vol. 169

Richard Kola, *Rückblick ins Gestrige* (Vienna, 1922)

Ludwig Lang, *Hundert Jahre Zollpolitik* (Vienna – Leipzig, 1906)

Alfred Lansburg, 'Zur Characterisierung des österreichischen Bankwesens', *Die Bank, Monatsheft für Finanz- und Bankwesen* (Vienna), Mar 1911

Vladimir I. Lenin, *Imperialism as the Highest Stage of Capitalism*, in id., *Selected Works*, vol. I (Moscow, 1950)

Rosa Luxemburg, *Die Akkumulation des Kapitals. Ein Beitrag zur Ökonomischen Erklärung des Imperialismus* (Berlin, 1913)

K. Mamroth, *Die Entwicklung der österreichisch-deutschen Handelsbeziehungen (1849-1865)* (Berlin, 1887)

Karl Marx, *Capital. A Critique of Political Economy*: vol. I, tr. Ben Fowkes (London, 1979); vol. III, ed. F. Engels (New York, 1967)

— —and Frederick Engels, *Collected Works*, vols. 6, 8, 9, 12, 20 (London, 1985); individual works as cited in Notes *passim*

Alexander Matlekovits, *Die Zollpolitik der österreichisch-ungarischen Monarchie und des Deutschen Reiches seit 1868 und deren nächste Zukunft* (Leipzig, 1891)

Ludwig von Mises: *Die Gemeinwirtschaft. Untersuchungen über den Sozialismus* (Jena, 1922)

'Der Wiedereintritt Deutsch-Österreichs in das Deutsche Reich und die Währungsfrage', *Schriften des Vereins für Sozialpolitik* (Leipzig), vol. 158

'Die Wirtschaftsrechnung im sozialistischen Gemeinwesen', *Archiv für Sozialwissenschaft und Sozialpolitik* (Tübingen), vol. 47 (1920-1)

Neue Freie Presse (Vienna): 13 Nov 1891; 16, 20, 21, 29 Mar, 27 Apr, 31 May, 26 June, 9, 18 Oct 1919

Die Neue Zeit (Vienna), 30 Apr 1915

Der österreichische Ökonomist (Vienna), 3 Aug 1882

Der österreichische Volkswirt (Vienna), 1, 15 Mar, 31 May 1919

Edmund Palla, 'Ein Jahr Arbeitslosenfürsorge in Österreich', *Nachrichten des Staatsamtes für soziale Verwaltung* (Vienna), no. 21/22 (1920)

Vilfredo Pareto, *Allgemeine Soziologie* (Tübingen, 1955)

Patriotisches Tagblatt (Brno), 11 May 1805

Politik (Prague), 10 May 1873: 'Der grosse Krach in Wien'

Alfred Přibram, *Materialien zur Geschichte der Preise und Löhne in Österreich*, vol. I (Vienna, 1938)

Karl Přibram, 'Die Sozialpolitik im neuen Österreich', *Archiv für Sozialwissenschaft und Sozialpolitik* (Tübingen), vol. 48 (1921)

Alois Rašin, *Die Finanz- und Wirtschaftspolitik der Tschechoslowakei* (Munich – Leipzig, 1923)

Heinrich Rauchberg, 'Österreichs Bank- und Creditinstitute in den Jahren 1872-1883', *Statistische Monatsschrift* (Vienna), vol. 11 (1885)

Josef Redlich, *Schicksalsjahre 1908-1919*, ed. Fritz Fellner, vol. II (Graz – Cologne, 1957)

Albert Schäffle, 'Der "grosse Börsenkrach" des Jahres 1873', in id., *Gesammelte Aufsätze* (Tübingen, 1885)

Walter Schiff, *Die Planwirtschaft und ihre ökonomischen Hauptprobleme* (Berlin, 1932)

Joseph A. Schumpeter: *Aufsätze zur ökonomischen Theorie* (Tübingen, 1953)

Aufsätze zur Soziologie (Tübingen, 1953)

Aufsätze zur Wirtschaftspolitik, ed. W.F. Stolper and Christian Seidl (Tübingen, 1985)

Business Cycles. A Theoretical, Historical, and Statistical Analysis of the Capitalist Process, 2 vols. (New York and London, 1939)

Capitalism, Socialism and Democracy (New York, 1942; 2nd edn. rev., 1947; enlarged 3rd edn., 1950)

'Eine dynamische Theorie des Kapitalzinses', *Zeitschrift für Volkswirtschaft, Sozialpolitik und Verwaltung* (Vienna), vol. XXII (1913) (repr) in id., *Aufsätze zur ökonomischen Theorie*, 1953)

'Epochen der Dogmen- und Methodengeschichte', *Grundriss der Sozialökonomik* (Tübingen), 1924

'Finanzpolitik', in id., *Aufsätze zur Wirtschaftspolitik*. 1985 (q.v.)

History of Economic Analysis, ed. E.B. Schumpeter (New York, 1954)

Die Krise des Steuerstaates, in *Zeitfragen aus dem Gebiete der Soziologie*, and sep. in book form (Graz – Leipzig, 1918) (repr. in Rudolf Goldscheid, Joseph Schumpeter: *Die Finanzkrise des Steuerstaates*, ed. Rudolf Hickel [Frankfurt, 1976])

'The March into Socialism', *American Economic Review*, vol. 40 (1950)

'Die neue Wirtschaftstheorie in den Vereinigten Staaten', *Schmollers Jahrbuch* (Leipzig), 1910

'Ökonomie und Soziologie der Einkommenssteuer', in id., *Aufsätze zur Wirtschaftspolitik*, 1985 (q.v.)

'Professor Clarks Verteilungstheorie', *Zeitschrift für Volkswirtschaft, Sozialpolitik und Verwaltung* (Vienna), vol. XVIII (1910)

'Die sozialen Klassen im ethnisch homogenen Milieu', *Archiv für Sozialwissenschaft und Sozialpolitik* (Tübingen), vol. 57 (1927) (repr. in id., *Aufsätze zur Soziologie*, 1953; tr. as 'Social Classes in an Ethnically Homogeneous Environment' in id., *Imperialism and Social Classes*, ed. Paul M. Sweezy [Oxford, 1951])

'Sozialistische Möglichkeiten von heute', *Archiv für Sozialwissenschaft und Sozialpolitik* (Tübingen), vol. 48 (1921)

'Zur Sociologie der Imperialismen', *Archiv für Sozialwissenschaft und Sozialpolitik* (Tübingen), vol. 46 (1919) (repr. in id., *Aufsätze zur Soziologie*, 1953; tr. as 'The Sociology of Imperialisms' in id., *Imperialism and Social Classes*, ed. Paul M. Sweezy [Oxford, 1951])

Ten Great Economists: From Marx to Keynes, ed. E.B. Schumpeter (New York and London, 1952)

Theorie der Wirtschaftlichen Entwicklung. Eine Untersuchung über Unternehmungen, Kapital, Kredit, Zins und den Konjunkturzyklus (Leipzig, 1911 [1912]; 2nd edn. rev., Munich – Leipzig, 1926) (tr. as *The Theory of Economic Development. An Inquiry into Profits, Capital, Credit, Interest, and the Business Cycle*, Harvard Economic Studies, vol. XLVI [Cambridge, Mass., 1961; repr. Galaxy Books, New York, 1961])

'Unternehmer', *Handwörterbuch der Staatswissenschaften*, ed. Elster Ludwig et al. (Jena), vol. 8 (4) (1928)

Das Wesen und der Hauptinhalt der theoretischen Nationalökonomie (Munich – Leipzig, 1908)

'Das wissenschaftliche Lebenswerk Eugen von Böhm-Bawerks', *Zeitschrift für Volkswirtschaft, Sozialpolitik und Verwaltung* (Vienna), vol. XXIII (1914)

Johann Slokar, *Geschichte der österreichischen Industrie und ihrer Förderung unter Kaiser Franz I* (Vienna, 1914)

Werner Sombart: 'Der kapitalistische Unternehmer', *Archiv für Sozialwissenschaft und Sozialpolitik* (Tübingen), vol. 24 (1909)

Der moderne Kapitalismus, vol. III (Munich – Leipzig, 1927)

Adam Smith, *An Inquiry into the Nature and Causes of the Wealth of Nations*, ed. Edwin Cannon (London, 1950)

Statistische Nachrichten über die Eisenbahnen der österreichisch-ungarischen Monarchie (Vienna – Budapest, 1899)

Statistische Übersichten, betreffend den auswärtigen Handel der wichtigsten Staaten in den Jahren 1907-1911, ed. Handelsstatistischer Dienst des k.k. Handelsministériums (Vienna, 1914)

Gustav Stolper: 'Die Lösung des Handelsbilanzproblems', *Der Österreichische Volkswirt* (Vienna), 6 Apr 1915

'Politisches Resume', *Der Österreichische Volkswirt* (Vienna), 15 Nov 1913

Gabriel Tarde, *Les Lois de l'imitation* (Paris, 1907)

Volkswirtschaftliche Wochenschrift, by Alexander Dorn (Vienna), 14 Nov 1901

Heinrich Waentig, *Gewerbliche Mittelstandspolitik* (Leipzig, 1898)

Friedrich von Wieser, 'Führung', *Handwörterbuch der Staatswissenschaften*, ed.
    Elster Ludwig *et al.* (Jena), vol. IV (4) (1927)
Max Wirth: *Geschichte der Handelskrisen* (Frankfurt, 1883)
    Österreichs Wiedergeburt (Vienna, 1876)

Index